Financial Statement Analysis
and Business Valuation
for the Practical Lawyer

Financial Statement Analysis
and Business Valuation
for the Practical Lawyer

Robert B. Dickie

Section of Business Law
American Bar Association

The materials contained herein represent the opinions of the authors and editors and should not be construed to be the action of the American Bar Association or the Section of Business Law unless adopted pursuant to the bylaws of the Association.

Nothing contained in this book is to be considered as the rendering of legal advice for specific cases, and readers are responsible for obtaining such advice from their own legal counsel. This book is intended for educational and informational purposes only.

Library of Congress Cataloging-in-Publication Data

Dickie, Robert B.
  Financial statement analysis and business valuation for the
practical lawyer / Robert B. Dickie.
    p.   cm.
  Includes index.
  ISBN 1-57073-499-2
  1. Lawyers—United States—Accounting.   I. Title.
HF5686.L35D53 1998
657′.024344—dc21

98–8104
CIP

Cover design by Catherine Zaccarine

Discounts are available for books ordered in bulk. Special consideration is given to state and local bars, CLE programs, and other bar-related organizations. Inquire at Book Publishing, American Bar Association, 750 North Lake Shore Drive, Chicago, Illinois 60611.

02 01 00 99   5 4 3 2

To my advisors, friends, and children:

Amy, John, and Tommy

Contents

Sidebars

Preface

Most of the legal work done by law firms and house counsel involves representing businesses. The language of business is finance. Yet few lawyers have been trained in either accounting or finance, and the training that does occur tends to be either too pedestrian or too esoteric to be useful in practice.

This has three major adverse consequences. First, in the practice of business law (a loose term that includes corporate law, securities, corporate tax, commercial litigation, employment law, and other areas involved in providing counsel to businesses), the emphasis is usually on only half the term ("law") rather than on both words. Lawyers thus tend to focus on what the law says, without being as effective as they could by linking their advice and counsel to the particulars of the businesses they are advising.

Second, business development frequently suffers. The lawyer with the best book of clients is often the one who not only has strong technical legal skills, but also knows enough about business and finance to give clients confidence that their lawyer understands their circumstances and interests. From a client's perspective, the law is but one of several disciplines to be considered and woven into an integrated strategy, and the lawyer who can fit his or her legal advice into that corporate strategy has achieved a competitive advantage.

That competitive advantage is all the more important because over the past two decades, American companies have been under unrelenting pressure from foreign competition and, more recently, domestic competition to innovate and cut costs. That pressure has been unmistakably passed on to law firms, as reflected in the emergence of new billing arrangements. To have a competitive advantage in this era, lawyers must offer more than new billing practices and commodity lawyering—they must offer a higher value added, which often requires connecting advice and services to the client's financial interests.

Third, at the macro level, the top high school students typically go to the top colleges, and many of the top college students go on to the top law schools and then into law practice. No lesser light than Derek Bok, the former president of Harvard University, has expressed concern that so many of the brightest minds have gone into a profession that is essentially non-value adding, rather than into disciplines such as engineering, medicine, and other sciences, which more clearly enhance our national standard of living and quality of life. He has a point. In assessing our contribution to society, credit should be given to lawyers who help our capital markets work efficiently. Because our capital markets do the best job in the world of allocating capital to its highest and best use, at least our securities bar plays a key role in our economy. A response to Dr. Bok might also give credit to those lawyers whose counsel results in better formation and enforcement of contracts, the cornerstones of economic activity. My hope is that by better understanding the business and financial interests of their clients, lawyers will make a contribution—to both the performance of our companies individually and our economy generally—that is more commensurate with their intelligence and abilities.

In short, I hope this book will not only reward the reader by helping him or her be a more effective lawyer, but also enhance lawyers' abilities generally so they may proactively help companies chart and implement strategies that serve the interests of their shareholders, employees, and customers, thereby enriching our standard of living and quality of life.

Acknowledgments

I have two trepidations in writing these acknowledgments. The first is that I will fail to thank one or more individuals to whom for good reason I sincerely feel very appreciative. The second is that I will bore the reader before he or she even gets started by reeling off a seemingly endless list of names, many of which any particular reader would not recognize. I will try to thread that needle.

I am certainly grateful to a great many clients, colleagues, and friends. Although naming each would be a hopeless task, there are two individuals who enriched my interest in and conversance with finance so immeasurably that they must be named. One is David Ross, formerly of The Sterling Group in Houston, who has been generous in sharing with me so much of his extraordinary working knowledge of the practice and theory of corporate finance. The other is Jules Schwartz, the former Dean of Boston University's School of Management, who, like David, brings to life the practiced application of sophisticated techniques of financial analysis.

I am also grateful for the work that thinkers and researchers have done in the fields of finance and accounting to improve our body of knowledge. Among them is Diana Harrington, Professor of Finance at Babson College, who made valuable suggestions for this book. I am also thankful to Philip Saunders of Weston, Massachusetts, for his analysis of minority discounts, control premiums, and liquidity discounts, which is included in chapter 5. In addition, the editors of this book, namely Michael Schmeer, of the Portland, Oregon, office of Davis, Wright & Tremaine; Dan Goldwasser, of the New York office of Vedder, Price, Kaufman & Kammholz and head of the American Bar Association Business Law Section's Committee on Law & Accounting; and Matthew Barrett, Associate Professor at the University of Notre Dame Law School, were generous with their time and certainly merit my sincere thanks. I am also very grateful to Bob Taggart, Chair of the Finance Department at Boston College, who provided helpful comments and to Jackie McGlamery of the American Bar Association, who made a pleasure out of a chore as we edited the book in its final preparation for publication. Finally, my assistant Maria Blanck must be commended for her ever gracious and effective work in consummating this book.

The Income Statement

Most lawyers represent businesses. Because the language of business is finance, it behooves lawyers to have a good working knowledge of the practical aspects of corporate finance.

There are three major financial documents: the income statement, the balance sheet, and the cash flow statement. Each is important, and chapters 1, 2, and 3, respectively, will explain what to look for in each one of them.[1]

Usually, the best place to begin your analysis of financials for a business is with the income statement, sometimes called the profit and loss statement or statement of operations. The income statement shows the company's revenues and expenses for a specific period of time, which can be a year, a quarter, a month, a week, or other period.

Revenues

A good place to start your analysis of the income statement is with the revenue line. First, check the sheer size of the company. (The term *company* includes not only corporations but also limited liability companies, limited liability partnerships, and limited liability limited partnerships.) Size is usually measured by revenues, except that the size of financial institutions is usually measured by assets. In 1997, the largest American company was General Motors, with revenues of $178 billion, and the largest American financial institution was Fannie Mae, with $392 billion in assets,[2] soon to be dwarfed by the mergers of Citicorp with Travelers Group Inc. and of NationsBank with BankAmerica.

At the other extreme, there are small, privately owned businesses, such as print shops, restaurants, bookstores, limousine services, and the like. Most companies fall between these extremes, and where they fall on the size spectrum provides

---

1. Audited financials must include a statement of changes in owners' equity, which may be in statement form or may be included in the notes to the financials. This is usually not particularly enlightening for interpretive purposes, although in some cases it can be a useful way to pick up the fact that a company has bought a substantial amount of treasury stock. Even this, however, can be noticed elsewhere in the financials, most notably in the cash flow statement.

2. *The Ins and Outs of This Year's Five Hundred*, FORTUNE, Apr. 27, 1998, at F-1.

an indication of the resources that each has at its command. To be sure, size alone is not the whole story, for, as we will see, there are some very big companies that are doing poorly, and some small companies doing extraordinarily well. Yet at the first cut, it is useful to make note of the size of the company. As of 1997, a company with revenues of $13.7 billion or more was in the Fortune 100, which means that it was one of the one hundred largest corporations in the United States. If it had revenues between $2.7 billion and $13.7 billion, then it was in the Fortune 101–500.

The business community sometimes classifies companies by the market value of their outstanding stock. This can be measured by the market value per share times the number of shares outstanding. The total market value of the outstanding stock is often referred to as a company's *market capitalization* or simply as its *market cap*. As of March 18, 1998, the company with the largest market cap in the United States was General Electric, with a market cap of $260 billion, followed by Microsoft, Coca-Cola, and Exxon, with market caps of $199 billion, $185 billion, and $159 billion, respectively.[3] Capitalization categories are defined in different ways but, as a general guideline, large-cap companies have a market value of $3 billion or more, mid-cap companies have a market value of $1 billion to $3 billion, small-cap companies have a market value of $300 million to $1 billion, and micro-cap companies have a market value less than $300 million.

Revenue Recognition

Returning to the revenue line, there are other matters to probe. First, there are some technical accounting matters that merit attention. Lawyers are not trained as accountants and are not expected to function as accountants. Nonetheless, it is worth noting that approximately 50% of all securities fraud cases involve revenue recognition that is, the incorrect and typically premature recording of revenue. Hence, a "head's up" concerning the problems that may be lurking will help a lawyer advise his or her client in many situations, such as negotiating or documenting an acquisition or financing.

Sidebar 1

Compensation Systems

In early 1980, the H.J. Heinz Company, the food giant headquartered in Pittsburgh, reported the results of an investigation conducted by its audit committee with the assistance of outside counsel and independent accountants. The

---

3. *Id.* at F-1–F-4.

investigation had found that its Heinz USA, Starkist Foods, and Ore-Ida divisions had allegedly engaged in improper income transferal practices. Primarily, these companies had recorded advertising and market research expenses in the current fiscal year when in fact the services were performed in a later fiscal year. Recognition of certain sales was also deferred to subsequent fiscal years. As a result, net income was understated in the current fiscal year and overstated in the subsequent fiscal year. If it was going to overshoot the earnings goals, it deferred booking some revenues and accelerated some expenses to just meet the Management Incentive Plan (MIP) goals and not set too high a base for the following year. This conduct was a clear violation of U.S. generally accepted accounting principles (GAAP), but had been systematically taking place for years.[4]

Heinz's management of revenues, expenses, and earnings might never have come to light except that Heinz had brought a suit against the Campbell Soup Company for an alleged attempt to monopolize the canned soup business. Campbell countersued, alleging that Heinz had monopolized the ketchup market. While deposing the president of the Heinz USA division about "off book" accounts, the executive refused to answer, citing the Fifth Amendment.[5] Short of a deposition, a good way to uncover practices involving the improper management of earnings is through the compensation or incentive system, for once the incentives are clear, tracking the conduct becomes a great deal easier. In Heinz's case, division executives had a powerful incentive to meet the profit goals. They also had an incentive not to exceed them by very much because they did not get significant extra credit for doing so. In fact, exceeding the goals set a higher base on which they would have to improve the next year. Thus, if toward year-end division management thought the goal would be significantly exceeded, it would delay invoicing the customer or accelerate payment of expenses (mainly by prepaying ad agencies or media carrying Heinz commercials).

Understanding compensation systems, both in general and as they impact incentives and behavior at particular companies, can also be highly useful to lawyers with responsibility for preparing or reviewing the management discussion and analysis (MD&A) portion of disclosure documents or handling public offerings, as discussed in later chapters.

---

4. Material regarding the H.J. Heinz Company in this context was drawn in part from *H.J. Heinz Company: The Administration of Policy (A), (B) and (C)*, MBS Case Services, Harvard Business School, Boston, Massachusetts, 1981.

5. *Id.* at 4 (H.J. Heinz Company (A)).

The governing principle under generally accepted accounting principles in the United States (GAAP), known as the completed contract method, is that revenues should not be booked until the goods have been shipped (or the services rendered) and cash has been received or the right to cash payment has arisen. More specifically, Statement of Financial Accounting Concept No. 5[6] provides that a business should not recognize revenue until (1) an exchange transaction or its equivalent has taken place and (2) the enterprise has substantially accomplished the earnings process. For example, a publisher may record sales to a bookstore only when the bookstore has ordered the books and the publisher has shipped them. Furthermore, if the bookstore has a contractual right to return the books if it has not sold them in, say, 60 days, then the publisher may not book the sale until the 60 days have lapsed. However, if experience shows that on average only 10% of the books are returned, then the publisher may book the sale for 90% of the books at the time of shipment and for the other 10% after the 60 days have lapsed. This may be easy for a publisher with a long track record, but it can be very difficult for a company built around a new product. The problem can also be complicated if there is a post-delivery service contract or arrangement, raising the question of whether part of the payment for the product was really pre-payment for future services.

There can be a question of fact about whether the seller has a legal obligation to take the goods back. Late in 1994, Bausch & Lomb, a consumer products company, faced a serious revenue recognition problem and an SEC investigation.[7] Seeking to boost revenues, in December 1993 the company's sales force in one of its U.S. divisions allegedly insisted, under threat of termination, that distributors take huge new stocks of the company's contact lenses (up to a two-year supply) but reportedly gave verbal assurances that the distributors would not have to pay for the goods until the lenses were sold. The sales were booked in 1993. By June 1994 the distributors still held a substantial supply of unsold products and some sought to return them to the company, arguing that the sales force had promised to take back the unsold goods. The company contended that the talk about taking back the unsold goods was no more than loose talk by a few salespeople and should not have been understood as a promise. The auditor, a Big Six firm, had the unenviable task of determining whether the words used by the sales force rose to the level of a binding commitment to take back the goods. If there was a legal commitment, then the revenue should not have been booked, except for the percentage of the goods that, based on experience, would not be returned.

The problem was even more serious in Bausch & Lomb's Asian operations. To meet headquarters' goals, one of the company's Asian units is alleged to have booked substantial sales of products to distributors in Southeast Asia. To throw headquarters and the auditors off the track, it recorded the "sales" on bogus invoices. Although the reported sales were rising handsomely, the goods were piling up in the warehouse. To compound the problem, the unit's management began deeply discounting the stockpiled goods into the European and South American gray markets, where they took sales at full price away from other company units. The problem came to light

---

6. CODIFICATION OF ACCOUNTING STANDARDS AND PROCEDURES, Statement of Financial Accounting Concept No. 5, Recognition and Measurement in Financial Statements of Business Enterprises Para. 83 (American Inst. of Certified Pub. Accountants, Financial Accounting Standards Board 1984).

7. *The Numbers Game at Bausch & Lomb?*, BUS. WK., Dec. 19, 1994, at 108–10. *See also* Mark Maremont & Joyce Barnathan, *Blind Ambition*, BUS. WK., Oct. 23, 1995, at 78–92.

because receivables began to rise to 90 days, well above the normal 45 to 60 days, because management could prepare bogus invoices (and hence create receivables, albeit bogus ones) but could not collect on them. Even the tip-off of rising receivables was masked because management factored the receivables, bringing in the cash.

A more dramatic example of improper revenue recognition involved Kurzweil Applied Intelligence, Inc., a small but leading edge computerized speech recognition company based in Waltham, Massachusetts. In December 1996, its former CEO was sentenced by the federal district court in Boston to two years and nine months in federal correctional institutions and fined $2.3 million. Its former vice president of sales was sentenced to one year and six months for fraudulently booking sales of unordered goods for a two-year period from 1992 to 1994.[8] Apparently believing that the company needed to show six consecutive quarters of revenue and earning growth in preparation for an initial public offering, the defendants forged customer signatures on purchase orders. When the auditors, Coopers & Lybrand, probed why the accounts receivable had risen, the company shipped the goods to a warehouse, instead of shipping them to customers. Coopers & Lybrand nearly uncovered the fraud by asking customers for confirmation of the sales. However, Kurzweil salespersons wrangled the auditors' confirmation request forms from the customers, forged the customers' signatures, and returned the forms to the auditors.

The tip-off occurred when a Coopers & Lybrand staffer noticed a charge for nine months of warehouse storage for a product that was supposed to have been shipped a year earlier. The auditors then demanded a list of all goods that had been stored and the board called in an outside law firm to investigate. Their questioning was penetrating enough that the corporate treasurer, a secretarial school graduate, confessed during an interview with the outside counsel. The appropriate press releases were issued, the stock price dropped from a high of $21 per share to $2.50 per share, and the process culminated in the two jail sentences.

Although fabricating sales, as in Kurzweil's case, is unacceptable under GAAP, there is one category of circumstances in which revenue may be recognized before goods are delivered or services are rendered. When contracts are for such large items, or projects, the GAAP rules permit companies to book revenues before the entire project is completed. This progressive or fast-track billing is known as the percentage of completion method and occurs in large construction projects, such as hotels, pipelines, office buildings, and ships, and the design and building of unique, expensive products or systems such as space stations. The applicable GAAP rule is that revenue may be booked based on the percent of the project that has been completed provided (1) the percentage of the work in fact completed can be reasonably estimated, (2) the company is likely to complete the contract, and (3) there is no important uncertainty about the contract. Any expected losses must be recognized immediately under the percentage completion or the completed contract methods.

When the use of the percent completion test is appropriate, the company records that portion of the revenues, expenses, and profit that corresponds to the portion of the contract life that elapsed during the year (or other period). For instance, if a company has a contract with the Department of Defense to deliver armaments in five

---

8. Telephone interview with Amy Rindskopf, director of public information, Office of the U.S. Attorney, Waltham, Massachusetts (July 8, 1998). *See also* Mark Maremont, *Anatomy of a Fraud*, Bus. Wk., Sept. 16, 1996, at 90–94.

Table 1					
Percentage of Completion Accounting/Contract Cancelled					
Contract price	$5 billion				
Estimated costs	$3 billion				
Estimated profit	$2 billion				
Year	**1**	**2**	**3**	**4**	**5**
Percent completed	20%	20%	20%	0	0
Revenues booked	$1B	$1B	($2B)	0	0
Expenses booked	$0.6B	$0.6B	($1.2B)	0	0
Profit booked	$0.4B	$0.4B	($0.8B)	0	0

years for $5 billion, then it might (if the above tests are met) be appropriate to use the percent completion test rather than waiting and booking the full $5 billion when the armaments are delivered. However, what if a new administration changes national defense policy and cancels the contract just before the end of year 3? Unless the contract contains terms that obligate the government to pay for the work completed, the company may have booked revenues and profits it will never receive.

In such an event the company must, in year 3, reverse the revenues, expenses, and profits booked during the earlier years of the contract, as shown in Table 1.

Another problem with the percent completion test is that it necessitates estimates of future expenses and thus lends itself to purposeful distortion of such estimates to manage the timing of the booking of profits. The result can be a front-end loading of revenues and a deferral of expenses.

Another area where there is room for aggressively booking the revenues involves the sale of franchises. One normally thinks of the major revenue producing activity of franchisors being the collection of royalties from franchisees. However, if the franchisor collects a front-end fee (usually bearing a name such as *area development right*), perhaps in return for exclusive rights to a territory, then franchisors may book the fee as revenue. This practice can make the growth rate in the early years look spectacular. However, in return for a high front-end fee the franchisor might accept low royalties for the life of the franchise agreement. Then, once the market penetration has been completed and the rate of signing up new franchisees declines, the franchisor's growth rate in revenues and earnings drops.

Jiffy Lube International, a Baltimore-based franchisor of quick oil changes, illustrates the point. During its growth phase in the mid 1980s, its stock price jumped from $78 per share in 1986 to $250 in 1987. But much of the growth was due to the collection of front-end fees from new franchisees. When the growth from this source tapered off and investors looked at Jiffy Lube's value based only on royalty revenues, the stock price fell to $3.50 a share in 1990 before it was mercifully acquired by Penzoil, its major vendor.[9]

---

9. HOWARD M. SCHILIT, FINANCIAL SHENANIGANS 46–47 (1993).

Interpretation of the Revenue Line

In addition to the GAAP-related questions about revenue recognition, there are qualitative or analytical areas to probe. First, it is useful to check the company's growth rate—that is, how its revenues compare with the previous year or other period. At the risk of overgeneralizing, a baseline for growth rate is that a company should grow annually at the inflation rate plus the population growth rate. If it is growing at that rate, it is holding even. If it is growing faster, it is outperforming the economy, and if it is growing less rapidly, it is underperforming the economy and losing ground. The rate of growth also sets a baseline of expectations concerning the rate at which expenses are growing, as discussed in chapter 2.

Further, one should look back several years—at least through a business cycle. This is particularly important if the company is in a cyclical business, such as steel, housing, or autos, as contrasted with a noncyclical, recession-proof business such as food processing, personal care products, or medical supplies. If the business is cyclical, one ought to determine where the company is in the business cycle and interpret the financials accordingly, as explained more fully in chapter 5.

Sidebar 2

Comparison of Sales and Earnings Patterns
for a Cyclical and a Noncyclical Company

Autos, chemicals, steel, airlines, and some other industries are cyclical because in recessions and periods of high interest rates buyers often defer or forego their purchases. By contrast, some companies' products—notably foods, medical products, and personal care items—are noncyclical, as people buy them despite the state of the economy. Chrysler Corporation provides an example of the former. Johnson & Johnson, a maker of a broad range of health care and hygiene products and toiletries, is an example of the latter, as shown in Table 2. Notice how much more regular Johnson & Johnson's sales and earnings are than Chrysler's. Notice also that the percentage changes in Chrysler's earnings are greater than the percentage changes in its sales. To a large extent, this reflects the impact of operating leverage discussed in chapter 4.

Strategic Context

The revenue line also invites questions about the company's strategy. First, how diversified is it? By and large, the less diversified it is, the more risky it is, although that does not necessarily mean that diversification is good. (Diversification is a very important dimension of corporate strategy and is discussed in chapters 10–12.)

Second, the financials ought to be read in light of the context in which the company operates. First, one might ask how far afield the company competes geographically. This is usually a function of transportation costs, although at times government policies (such as trade barriers), spoilage, or convenience factors, determine the

Table 2
Cyclical vs. Noncyclical Sales

	Year									
	'87	'88	'89	'90	'91	'92	'93	'94	'95	'96
			($ billion except growth rates)							
Cyclical: Chrysler										
Sales	26.3	35.5	35.0	30.6	29.4	36.9	43.6	52.2	53.2	61.4
Sales growth	16%	35%	(1%)	(13%)	(4%)	26%	18%	20%	2%	15%
PAT*	1.3	1.1	.3	.1	.5	.5	2.4	3.7	2.0	3.5
PAT growth	(7%)	(15%)	(73%)	(67%)	400%	0%	380%	54%	(46%)	75%
Noncyclical: Johnson & Johnson										
Sales	8.0	9.0	9.8	11.2	12.4	13.8	14.1	15.7	18.8	21.6
Sales growth	14%	13%	9%	24%	11%	11%	2%	11%	20%	15%
PAT*	.883	.974	1.08	1.14	1.46	1.63	1.79	2.01	2.40	2.89
PAT growth	24%	10%	11%	6%	28%	12%	10%	12%	19%	20%

*Profit after tax

Sources are 1996 annual reports of Johnson & Johnson and Chrysler, respectively.

Table 3
Chrysler vs. J&J Percent Sales Growth

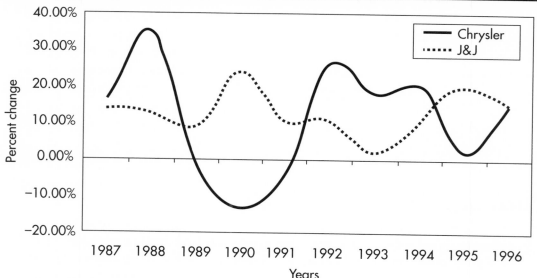

geographic scope of competition. At one extreme, diamonds and computer chips are so light and compact that the costs of transportation are negligible relative to their value, with the result that they have become international businesses. By contrast, the cement and can businesses are generally local due to the high costs of transportation; the weight or bulk of these products is high relative to their value.

Table 4
Chrysler vs. J&J Earnings

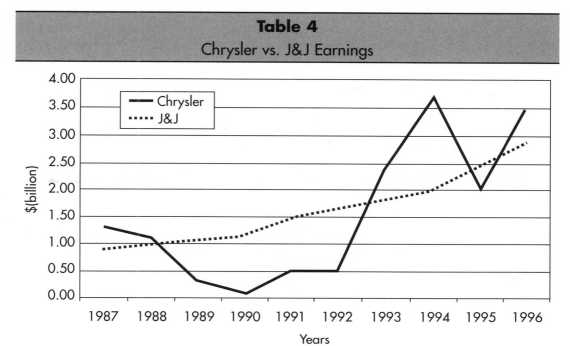

Further, it is often useful to get a read on the company's strength relative to its competitors. This is not evident in the financial statements alone but can be assessed by checking other sources (such as analysts' reports or the trade press), physically comparing the products, asking experts with intimate knowledge of the products, or other ways. In addition to sheer size, it can be useful to assess the comparative financial performance, growth rates, product quality, management reputation, and, if possible, comparative costs of the company and its competitors.

_____ **Sidebar 3** _____

The Cash Flow Cycle

There is a cash flow cycle that is common to most companies. Though the model pertains most explicitly to manufacturing companies, only minor adjustments are normally needed to adapt it to service companies. As you read this, please keep in mind that a company's operations and finances are integrally related although distinct from one another.

To keep it simple, let's suppose a company is new and has raised money from its shareholders. As a next step it uses much of that cash (as well, perhaps, as some cash obtained from a lender or two) to purchase production equipment. Then it uses more cash to buy raw materials and hire some labor. At this point the company has lost flexibility. It has converted cash into comparatively illiquid investments and has taken on the risk that the market for its products will be sufficiently poor that the inventory and equipment will not be worth as much as the cash used to buy them.

Next the company sells the inventory, thereby converting it to cash, which it can use to pay down its debt, pay a dividend, hire more workers, or buy more inventory or productive assets. Alternatively, and more typically, it has sold the goods for a promise and extended credit to the buyer, resulting in an account receivable. In that event, the company receives the cash only when it collects the receivable.

Let's suppose the company believes business is good and uses the cash to buy more inventory. Indeed, let's suppose business is so good that it wants to buy more raw materials and make more inventory than possible with the cash on hand. It may have several alternatives. It can sell more stock, borrow more money, or buy equipment or materials on credit from vendors. In the latter event, the company has used its accounts payable as a source of financing. The following diagram illustrates graphically the flow of cash described above.

Table 5
Cash Flow Cycle

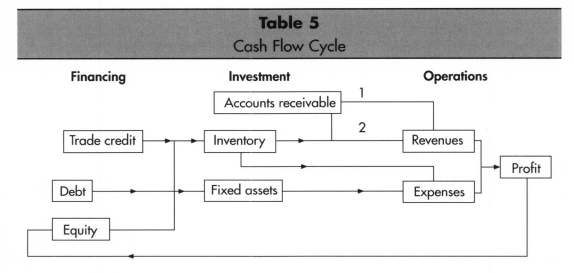

1. Buyer receives the inventory and seller gets an account receivable.
2. Buyer pays for the goods and seller's account receivable is converted into cash.

Sources of cash	*Uses of cash*
Decrease in an asset[10]	Increase in an asset
Increase in a liability[10]	Decrease in a liability
Increase in equity[10]	Decrease in equity
Profits[10]	Losses

The above summarizes the cash flow cycle. It also introduces another point. When the goods are sold or the services are rendered for credit, the company recognizes the sale, which impacts the income statement, but it does not receive the cash until the customer pays. The sale is recognized on the income statement because the latter is kept on an accrual basis rather than on a cash basis; that is, the income statement and balance sheet use accrual accounting. The cash flow statement reconciles the income statement to the actual cash flow of the business.

---

10. If you do not know the meaning of these words, you might want to read chapter 2 at this point.

Cost of Goods Sold

The second line on the income statement is usually the cost of goods (or merchandise) sold (CGS) or, in a service business, the cost of providing services. In the case of retailers, this is the cost of the goods purchased from vendors. At Wal-Mart for example, the CGS reflects the amount paid (or owing) to its vendors such as Russell Athletic for T-shirts, Kimberly-Clark for Kleenex, and so forth.

CGS is calculated as follows: (1) add purchases made during the period to the beginning inventory (the sum is what the company will have in inventory at the end of the period if it does not sell anything); (2) from that sum, deduct the ending inventory; and (3) the net is the cost of goods sold. For example, if a retailer has $200 of inventory at the beginning of the period, purchases $800 of additional inventory, and ends the period with inventory worth $400, then its CGS is $600, as shown in Table 6.

Table 6 Calculation of Cost of Goods Sold for a Retailer	
Beginning inventory	$200
Plus purchases	+800
Subtotal	1,000
Minus ending inventory	−400
Cost of goods sold	600

In the case of manufacturers, the calculation of CGS is more difficult. It includes not only the direct costs of raw materials and labor directly associated with the production of the goods but also indirect costs, including indirect materials; indirect labor; depreciation or rent on factory buildings and machinery; and utilities, insurance, taxes, and maintenance on factory buildings and equipment indirectly associated with the production of the goods.

The Overstatement of Ending Inventory and Resulting Overstatement of Profits

Just as about half of all securities fraud cases involve incorrect booking of revenue, about 25% of such cases involve misrepresenting CGS. When this happens, it usually (but not always) involves companies overstating their earnings by overstating their ending inventory. To illustrate, consider a company with $1,200 in revenues, $500 in CGS, and $700 in gross profit. If it wants to overstate its gross profit to, say, $900, it might understate its CGS, in this case $300 rather than $500. As shown in Table 7, it might do this by overstating its ending inventory as $700 rather than $500. By doing this, the company understates its CGS by $200 (that is, $300 rather than $500), and thereby overstates its gross profit by $200 (that is, $500 rather than $300). Thus, overstating ending inventory is a way to overstate profit.

Table 7		
Manipulation of Cost of Goods Sold		
	Without Fraud	**With Fraud**
1. Revenues	$1,200	$1,200
2. Cost of goods sold*	500	300
3. Gross profit	$700	$900
	Without Fraud	**With Fraud**
4. Beginning inventory	$200	$200
5. Purchases	800	800
	1,000	1,000
6. Ending inventory	−500	−700
7. Cost of goods sold	$500	$300

*From line 7

Comptronix Corporation, an Alabama-based vendor of components for the electronics industry, announced in 1992 that three of its top executives had used this method to defraud investors in the early 1990s. Wanting to bolster its earnings, the executives sought to understate CGS. They knew that inflating ending inventory would understate CGS, and they created fictitious inventory. When their actions came to light, Comptronix's stock price dropped by 78%, and more than a dozen shareholder suits were filed.[11]

Perhaps even more egregious was Attilla Industries (a real company but a fictitious name), a New York manufacturer of copper wire. Knowing that its outside auditors would be at Plant A on day 1 and Plant B on day 2, the company moved inventory overnight between days 1 and 2 and let the auditors watch company personnel count the same inventory at both plants. By understating costs, Attilla converted a large loss into a profit, but soon thereafter it declared bankruptcy and defaulted on its loans, and numerous suits were filed against the company, its top executives, and its hapless auditors.

In the acquisition context this trick can trap the unwary buyer. If the buyer is basing the purchase price on earnings, the seller has an incentive to overstate the ending inventory. However, many sellers, especially privately held companies, have an incentive to understate ending inventory and minimize earnings to minimize their tax payments. Even publicly held companies may have the same incentive, particularly if they want to understate earnings to smooth them out or if they believe the company's value is driven by factors other than current earnings (such as by the buyer wanting access to technology, distribution channels, or future growth). One Fortune 100 company avoided an unexpected tax liability in an acquisition when, during due diligence, it noticed that the seller had been renting a fleet of trucks at the end of every fiscal year. The trucks had been used by the seller to hide inventory,

---

11. *See, e.g.,* Diana B. Henriques, *Behind Comptronix's Sudden Fall,* N.Y. TIMES, Dec. 4, 1992, at D-1; Lee Berton, *Inventory Chicanery Tempts More Firms, Fools More Auditors,* WALL ST. J., Dec. 14, 1992, at A-1; Kurt Eichenwald, *Chairman Dismissed in Scandal,* N.Y. TIMES, Dec. 12, 1992, at 17.

Table 8
Calculating Cost of Goods Sold for a Manufacturer

	Raw Materials		Work in Process ($ million)		Finished Goods
Beginning inventory	50	+	75	+	100
Purchases (additions)	150*	+	175**	+	225***
	200	+	250	+	325
Ending inventory	−75	+	−25	+	−150
Cost of materials used	125				
Cost of goods produced			225		
Cost of goods sold					175

*The additions to raw materials represent merely the cost of buying new raw materials.

**The additions to work in process include the cost of the raw materials used in the work in process plus all incremental direct labor, direct materials, and factory overhead.

***The additions to finished goods inventory include the cost of the raw materials used to produce the finished goods plus the direct labor, any incremental direct materials, and overhead. The number includes the direct labor, any incremental materials, and factory overhead expenses incurred since the raw materials were purchased, not only the incremental expenses beyond the amounts included in the work in process inventory.

thus overstating CGS, understating pretax and after tax profits, and reducing its tax bill. Had the buyer not detected the problem, the buyer would have found itself at the end of its first reporting period with a much larger-than-expected ending inventory, lower-than-expected CGS, and higher-than-expected pretax profit and tax bill.

Engaging in inventory shenanigans is much easier for a manufacturer than for a retailer. Although the accounting principles are the same, their application to manufacturing is more difficult. Because there are three categories of inventory, namely raw materials, work in process (WIP), and finished goods inventory, the calculation described above for the retailer (begin with ending inventory, add purchases, and deduct ending inventory) must be taken through three iterations for the manufacturer, as illustrated in Table 8.

The WIP inventory is often the most difficult number in the financials to know with certainty. Though GAAP allows for other methods, the rule followed by most companies is the percent completion test, which provides that the WIP inventory should include (1) the raw materials used in the WIP and (2) the portion of the direct and indirect expenses that correspond to the percentage of completion of the goods. For example, if the company is producing an order of extra-large Hawaiian shirts and believes that at the end of the accounting period the shirts are two-thirds completed, then it should allocate to that order two-thirds of the average total cost of making such a shirt; that is, two-thirds of all direct labor, direct material costs, and factory overhead (the latter of which includes indirect labor, indirect materials, insurance, depreciation, and utilities).

The problem with the percent completion test is that it can be difficult to determine whether the shirt is two-thirds or only, say, one-half finished. Although there are GAAP guidelines, they can be difficult to apply, and one must keep in mind that the company may have an incentive to overstate the inventory (that is, to deem the shirt to be two-thirds rather than one-half finished) because overstating inventory will understate the cost of goods sold and increase the earnings. Please keep in mind, however, that if the company's incentive is to minimize its taxes (or to minimize its reported earnings for any other reason, such as to shortchange a minority investor), the incentive may be reversed, and it may want to understate its inventory to understate earnings (to reduce its tax expense, for example, or to minimize the value of stock being bought under a mandatory stock redemption at a price based on earnings). Often the easiest way for a company to understate earnings is by tinkering with the WIP inventory. Although lawyers are not auditors, the WIP inventory is often a good place to probe in connection with due diligence, reviewing an MD&A, or litigation involving rights of minority shareholders.

The finished goods inventory can be almost as difficult to pin down. Although there is no need to determine the degree of completion, allocation of overhead is difficult. Overhead allocation, however, is a problem in connection with particular units of a product. For example, how much of General Electric's headquarters' overhead ought to be allocated to a particular refrigerator is a difficult question, the answer to which can be disagreed upon by good accountants. Similarly, the allocation of headquarters' overhead among divisions is difficult. When one is examining the issuer, the overhead allocation problem washes out, because it does not matter where it is allocated. However, if one is representing the buyer of a division, one should be mindful that the seller may have allocated overhead unevenly to enhance the earnings of the division being sold.

Inventory is to be carried at the lower of cost or market value. Although the rule is applied to all categories of inventory, because it is difficult to know the market value of WIP (such as a two-thirds completed extra-large orange Hawaiian shirt), the rule is most often applied to finished goods inventory. The "lower of cost or market" rule means that if goods have become obsolete, then the company must reduce to market value the value at which they are carried on the books. For example, if the company produces software and the software has just been leapfrogged by a competitor's product so that the company will have to discount its software deeply to sell it, then the company must mark down such inventory on its books to market value, which may be negligible. That write-down has a direct and adverse impact on pretax earnings. To elaborate on the example, if the company has on its books $100 in finished goods software, and must write that software down to zero, then its pretax profits will be reduced by $100. Inventory write-downs are less common in many industries such as furniture or clothing (except fashion or seasonal clothing, the market value of which can drop dramatically), but it is not unusual in electronics or software, where technology changes rapidly. Commodore International, for example, caught in the battle of too many companies making PC clones, in 1985 posted a fourth-quarter loss of $124 million, which included a $63 million write-down of inventory, most of it finished goods, resulting from obsolescence of its microcomputers.[12]

One consequence of the foregoing is that executives and analysts are leery of seeing a large amount of finished goods inventory on a company's books if it is in an industry where rapid obsolescence is a problem. If such a company shows inventory, especially finished goods inventory, rising more rapidly than its revenues, the

---

12. THORNTON O'GLOVE, QUALITY OF EARNINGS: THE INVESTOR'S GUIDE TO HOW MUCH MONEY A COMPANY IS REALLY MAKING 111–15 (1987).

sell orders for the company's stock will probably not be far behind. For example, Commodore International's inventory write-down was preceded by a quarter in which its revenues declined but its finished goods inventory rose 82%.

Gross Margin

The net of revenues less cost of goods sold is gross profit. The gross margin is the gross profit divided by revenues, that is, a percentage. By and large it is desirable to see the gross margin rising, for it suggests that the company has the power in the marketplace to increase its prices. Conversely, it is usually a bad sign to see the gross margin declining. To illustrate, I was at a board meeting a few years ago and probed why the gross margin had declined relative to the prior quarter and the comparable quarter of the prior year. The CEO explained that the decline was due to a rise in raw material costs, but that gave me no comfort and my follow-up question was why the company had not passed on the cost increases.

Ninety percent of the time, declining gross margins indicate that the company cannot pass on cost increases, which indicates that its vendors have more power over it than it has over its buyers. That is a bad sign, for it means that the company has strategically positioned itself in the wrong place. For example, for decades the manufacturers of cans (first tin and then aluminum) had inferior returns relative to their vendors (the steel and then the aluminum producers) and their buyers (primarily beer and soft-drink bottlers). The result over time was that one of the two biggest can producers of a generation ago (American Can) has exited the business, seeking greener pastures elsewhere in insurance and financial services. (By 1998, American Can had become Travelers Corp., bought Salomon, Inc. and agreed to merge with Citicorp.)

Because cans are commodity products, the buyers are in a good position to whipsaw the can makers on price. To compound the problem, it makes economic sense to build can plants near the buyers to save on transportation costs, rather than to incur the expense of shipping a lot of air around, in, and between the yet-to-be-filled cans. Yet once a can plant is built next to a brewer or soft-drink bottler, the buyer has enormous bargaining power. Consequently, can makers usually will not build a plant unless they first get a long-term requirements contract from the buyer. A key reason why Continental Can exited the business is that the federal government had brought an antitrust case against it, and part of the settlement precluded Continental from entering such contracts. That made an already mediocre business even worse, so Continental exited the business, as did American Can. Since then the remaining companies have done better. The stock price of Philadelphia's Crown Cork & Seal, one of the nation's two largest can producers, has risen from $3.25 in 1983 to a high of $59.75 in 1997.

In approximately 10% of the cases, declining gross margins are a sign of strength, not trouble. One way this can happen is if the CEO responds to the question about why gross margins have declined by saying, in effect, "We could have raised our prices. However, we have chosen not to for now because we want to penetrate the market and work our way down the cost curve. That is, we are in a new field, and costs are dropping quickly. We are the first ones in the business, and by keeping our prices down we are getting business, and by virtue of the incremental experience we are learning how to drive our costs down. If someone else wants to compete with us, they will start out with higher costs than we have and will have to subsidize losses to catch us. The more we sell, the greater the losses they will have to subsidize, and hence the less likely they are to want to chase us." This can be a clever strategy, but there can be a trap. The company might subsidize the losses and stake out an impenetrable low cost advantage only to find that a competitor has trumped its technology and is ahead of it on the cost curve for a different, more advanced product.

The second purpose for intentionally living with a low and/or declining gross margin is to establish an installed base of customers. Although it can be a sleeper, in many industries companies can earn as much on service and spare parts as they do on original sales. Key among such industries are those producing copiers, medical equipment, elevators, and computer systems. Otis Elevator built a strong business for its Class A elevators (for upscale high-rise buildings) in Europe starting in the late 1960s in large measure by pricing aggressively and developing such dense penetration in cities such as Hamburg that it was able to service elevators profitably in many cities where no other competitor had a sufficient installed base to do so. Its superior service then facilitated sales—a virtuous cycle.

Gross margins are often the best window into pricing policy, which may be the least understood dimension of corporate strategy. Probing gross margins can reveal a great deal about pricing policy and about whether the company is strong in its market, weak in its market, or perhaps pursuing a subtle but potentially powerful drive down the cost curve or installed base strategy.

As a result, lawyers probing for antitrust violations are often best advised to probe a company's gross margin as well as net margin (discussed later). Companies with high gross margins are the most likely (but by no means the only companies) to be accused by the Department of Justice or the Federal Trade Commission of monopolistic practices, as illustrated by the Department of Justice's action against Microsoft, which had 84% gross margins in 1994.[13] The suit settled in early 1995, although in 1997 the Department of Justice brought an action alleging that Microsoft was in violation of the consent decree.[14] High gross margins also connote strength in the marketplace, and companies enjoying high gross margins are those most likely to have high-quality images that they will want to defend. Conversely, gross margins may be low because of competitive pressures, as illustrated by Conner Peripherals (which merged with Seagate Technology in 1995), as discussed in Sidebar 4, or because of pricing aggressiveness.

Sidebar 4

Gross Margins

In 1993, Conner Peripherals, the San Jose-based maker of disk drives, had gross margins of only 11%. That means that for every $1 in revenue the company spent $.89 making the products. The other $.11 had to cover all the overhead (including research and development, marketing and selling expenses,

---

13. MICROSOFT CORPORATION, 1994 ANNUAL REPORT.

14. *See, e.g.,* Steve Hamm, Amy Cortese & Susan B. Garland, *Microsoft's Future,* BUS. WK., Jan. 19, 1998, at 58–68.

	Conner Peripherals*		Lear Corporation**	
(1993 Financials)	($ million except percentages)			
Net sales	$2,152	100%	$1,950	100%
Cost of sales	1,914	89%	1,780	91%
Gross profit	238	11%	170	9%
Operating expenses	684	32%	91	5%
Operating profit	(446)	(21%)	79	4%

Table 9
Gross Margins

*1993 Annual Report, Conner Peripherals.
**1993 Annual Report, Lear Seating Corporation (name later changed to Lear Corporation).

executive compensation and other administrative expenses, legal and audit fees, occupancy costs, and so forth) as well as any interest expenses and taxes. In fact, the company had negative earnings in 1993, which strongly indicates that its thin gross margins were involuntary. They were the result of an inability to raise prices, due to the intensity of competition in the disk drive business.

Table 9 compares Conner with Lear Corporation, the Southfield, Michigan-based designer and manufacturer of car and truck seats, whose 1993 gross margin was a mere 9%—astoundingly low—reflecting the very strong bargaining power of its buyers, the major auto manufacturers. Despite the low prices, Lear keeps its operating expenses so low that it is able to turn a profit, a very rare feat for a company with such a low gross margin.

Companies may have low gross margins because of the nature of the business (for example, groceries) or because they are trying to expand and grow. The companies most likely to be accused of predatory pricing are those with low gross margins—indicating aggressive pricing. A full discussion of the antitrust laws is beyond the scope of this book, but it is worth noting that although margins provide only a soft signal of an antitrust issue, they can be a signal worthy of attention. This is especially true of gross margins, as they reveal the most about pricing policy.

Selling, General, and Administration Expenses

Usually the next item on the income statement is the selling, general, and administration (SG&A) expenses. This includes the cost of maintaining and supporting a sales force, marketing and advertising expenses, executives' salaries, the costs of running the administrative offices (headquarters' computer systems, office staff, rent, utilities for headquarters, insurance expenses), plus corporate, legal and auditing fees, and other overhead expenses.

Often the notes give further details, although none is required under GAAP unless a particular category of expense exceeds 10% of revenues. Until December 1994, the SEC (51211 Rule 12-11) required that for each of the following items that exceeds 1% of sales or expenses the amount charged to costs or expenses be set forth in the notes to the financials: (1) maintenance and repairs, (2) depreciation and amortization of intangible assets, preoperating costs, and similar deferrals, (3) taxes other than payroll and income taxes, (4) royalties, and (5) advertising costs. However, this requirement was dropped in 1994, primarily in the interest of moving toward integrating U.S. disclosure requirements with foreign requirements.[15]

The notes can be revealing, as illustrated by the H.J. Heinz Company. From fiscal 1990 to fiscal 1994, Heinz's revenues rose 23%, from $6.6 billion to $8.1 billion. However, the notes revealed that early in that period the company cut back on advertising and promotions, and its U.S. advertising budget had been cut by 40%.[16] Although the cutback in such expenses caused earnings to rise in the short run, the diminished product support resulted in weakened brands. As the market began to spot this, the stock price fell from a high of $48.62 a share in mid-1991 to a low of $30.75 a share in early 1994, reflecting 1993 operating and net profits that were below 1991 levels.

By and large SG&A expenses are fixed expenses, which means they do not vary as the volume of sales rises or falls. By contrast, costs that do rise or fall as sales rise or fall are variable expenses. If a company is growing, it will have to add to its fixed costs over time, usually by adding to its headquarters staff, adding a new plant (witness Intel's 1995 announcements of its plans to add five new plants and Walt Disney Co.'s plans to launch its first cruise ship in mid-1998), hiring marketing and sales personnel, increasing its advertising budget, and the like.

Some companies put their sales force at least partially on a commission basis. When this occurs it is often done not only to motivate the sales force, but also to minimize fixed costs as a way of protecting the company against downturns. After all, a company does not want to be stuck with high fixed expenses if the revenues are not coming in. Hence, if a company's sales force is heavily compensated on a commission basis, it is often worth finding out whether that is a human resource (incentive oriented) idea, whether the compensating package is financially driven (keep fixed costs down), or whether it is intended to serve both these interests. The financially driven reason is most suitable if the revenue stream is uncertain, for it is under that circumstance that management will usually most want to minimize fixed costs.

In general, one likes to see the SG&A decline as a percent of revenues as the company grows. If the revenues grow 25%, the company should not need 25% more support staff, office space, controllers, and so on. In the case of privately held companies (and the occasional publicly held company), if revenues are growing, the SG&A might not in fact decline as a percent of revenues, even if the economic realities are that it could. In some cases the owner/manager or control party of a private or even public company might be taking some or all the profits out as tax deductible compensation earnings rather than as a taxable dividend. Internal Revenue Service (IRS) regulations limit tax deductible compensation, but many owner-managers push the envelope hard on this (unless they are subchapter S corporations). The

---

15. SEC Release No. FR 44, 59 Fed. Reg. G5632 (Dec. 20, 1994).
16. H.J. HEINZ COMPANY, 1993, 1994 ANNUAL REPORT. *See also* Patricia Sellers, *H.J. Heinz: Has Cost Cutting Gone Too Far?*, FORTUNE, Nov. 2, 1992, at 81–82.

minority shareholders may find themselves with interests identical to the IRS. Indeed, the risk of owner-manager actions along these lines, the difficulty in detecting it, and the expense of doing anything about it are reasons why minority interests sell at a discount, as discussed in chapter 5.

At times the SG&A expense rises as a percentage of revenues. Usually this is an unhealthy sign, indicating that management has not been vigilant in managing costs. However, particularly if the company is small enough to have only one or two main product lines, if there has been a new product launch with intensive advertising or marketing and sales expenses, or if there are costs associated with adding major new capacity, then there may be a good reason for a rise in SG&A expenses before the revenues ramp up. During such a period, it is helpful to know what lag effect to expect from the time the new capacity is put into service, the new product is introduced, and the marketing push begins until the revenues rise. One should begin to see results in the first quarter in the case of the introduction of low-priced impulse items, such as toys, but perhaps not for several years for very high-priced products, especially those that are difficult for customers to switch to. Such delays can occur if other equipment is designed around the new product, the labor force is trained to work with something else, or there are high carrying costs. If a company were to introduce a new braking system for freight trains, for example, it might take several years for the handful of domestic rail freight companies to incorporate the new brakes into their systems.

Research and Development

Neither GAAP nor the SEC require that research and development (R&D) expenses be separately disclosed, although some companies do so voluntarily. Usually this occurs in industries where R&D expenses are a significant percentage of revenues, most notably pharmaceutical and software companies. If a company is just starting up, the R&D expenses may be substantial even before the company has any revenues.

GAAP requires R&D expenses to be expensed as incurred. The only exception is software R&D, which must be expensed until the product's technological feasibility is established.[17]

_____ *Sidebar 5* _____

Orientation Concerning GAAP and SFAS

The term *GAAP* refers to generally accepted accounting principles. This is a generic term and includes what might be thought of as the common law of accounting as well as some accounting rules that might be analogized to statutory law. The generic part pertains to what belongs on a balance sheet and in an income statement, their configuration, and the like.

---

17. CODIFICATION OF ACCOUNTING STANDARDS AND PROCEDURES, Statement of Financial Accounting No. 86 (American Inst. of Certified Pub. Accountants).

The Securities Exchange Act of 1934 granted the Securities and Exchange Commission (SEC) authority regarding the accounting rules. In 1939, the SEC delegated that authority to the Commission on Accounting Procedure (CAP), which consisted exclusively of accountants. In 1959, the CAP was succeeded by the Accounting Principles Board (APB), which included not only professional CPAs but also representatives from industry, academia, and government. Its pronouncements were known as Accounting Principles Bulletins, or APBs. In 1973, the Financial Accounting Standards Board (FASB) replaced the APB. The FASB's pronouncements, of which there have been 125 as of May 1996, are known as Statements of Financial Accounting Standards (SFAS), which apply both to publicly owned and privately owned companies, as did the SFAS's predecessors.

The above is not to be confused with GAAS and the SAS. GAAS is the acronym for generally accepted auditing standards (for example, if you are auditing inventory, you must observe a specified portion being counted, and so on). The Auditing Standards Board, a committee of the American Institute of CPAs, has adopted Statements of Auditing Standards (SAS), which, like the FASB's specific rules, are pronouncements regarding auditing. The SASs thus became part of GAAS.

From that point, the costs must be capitalized until the product is released to customers, at which point costs must be amortized. The periodic amortization prescribed by FASB-86 is the greater of (1) the amount computed by the straight line method over the estimated useful life of the product or (2) the amount computed by using the ratio that current gross revenues bear to total estimated gross revenues. (If capitalizing is a concept with which you are not familiar, please refer to Sidebar 6 for an explanation of capitalization, depreciation, and amortization.)

The concept behind the rule concerning software is that as long as the research is basically pure R&D, too speculative to provide much certainty of commercial feasibility, it must be expensed. Once it becomes technologically feasible, further work is essentially an investment for future gain, and ought to be capitalized because accountants like to match expenses with the revenues that most directly relate to them. Later, when the product is released to customers, further R&D expenses are refinements, the benefit of which can be promptly enjoyed in the marketplace, once again justifying immediate expensing.

Sidebar 6

Capitalization, Depreciation, and Amortization

In ordinary parlance, we tend to equate the terms *costs* and *expenses*. "Today I started out with $40. I spent $10 for lunch and $30 for a shirt. Thus I spent $40." The accountant, however, treats both expenditures as costs, but *expenses* one and *capitalizes* the other. That is, to the accountant, there are two categories of costs—those that are expensed in the period in which the cost is incurred, and those that are capitalized and expensed in a later period. If the accountant were a purist, he or she would not treat the $30 cost of the shirt as an expense of the day it was bought because the benefit of the shirt will be enjoyed over an extended period—let's say two years. Hence the accountant would treat the shirt as an asset and expense the shirt over two years.

There are a number of ways to handle depreciation expenses under GAAP, including the straight line method and various accelerated methods, most notably the sum-of-the-years' digits methods. Similarly, the Internal Revenue Code (IRC) has rules on depreciation,[18] most notably the Modified Accelerated Cost Recovery System (MACRS), which is beyond the scope of this book. Accounting and tax rules differ in a number of areas, including revenue recognition, deduction of contingent losses and expenses, goodwill accounting[19] (even after the Revenue Reconciliation Act of 1993), and depreciation schedules. As for the latter, the tax rules allow more rapid depreciation than companies often use, under GAAP, and the result is a deferred tax liability (which is discussed in chapter 2).

Returning to our lunch and shirt example, under GAAP, if one were to capitalize the shirt and depreciate it under the straight line method over two years (that is, $15 per year), then, without giving effect to tax consequences, the income statement and balance sheet would be as set forth in Table 10. The example assumes that the purchaser is depreciating the shirt against a very meager revenue stream.

As a result of capitalizing the cost, the expense is deferred over more than one reporting period. You might start thinking now about how the fact that we capitalized the shirt will affect the company's cash flow in year 2. We examine cash flow statements in chapter 3.

It is important to consider a company's R&D expenses as a percent of revenues. In general, it is expected that companies will hold their R&D expenses fairly constant as a percent of revenues—usually about 10% of revenues in the pharmaceutical industry, for example.

If the percentage spent on R&D drops, it can be cause for concern. Just as Heinz's cutback in advertising expenses was seen by analysts as too facile and gimmicky a way to increase earnings, a cutback in R&D expenses can prove shortsighted. One has to probe the company and its industry qualitatively to determine the basis for, and ramifications of, a cutback in R&D.

In general, cutbacks in R&D as a percent of revenues are a cause for concern unless one of two phenomena is at work. First, young companies, as they grow, may still be spending as much as before on R&D, but the percentage may decline as their revenues build. Far from being an unhealthy sign, it may be essential for survival. In 1991, Powersoft, a software company in Concord, Massachusetts, had an R&D budget

---

18. I.R.C. §§ 167, 168.
19. This remained even after the Revenue Reconciliation Act of 1993 (Pub. L. No. 103-66).

Table 10
Capitalizing the Cost

Year 1 (beginning):

Balance Sheet

Assets		Liabilities	
Cash	30	Equity	30

Year 1 (end):

Balance Sheet				**Income Statement**	
Assets		Liabilities			
Cash	30			Revenues	40
Shirt	30			Lunch	(10)
Less accumulated depreciation	(15)			Depreciation	(15)
Net investment in shirt	15	Equity	45	Pretax profit	15

Year 2 (end):

Balance Sheet				**Income Statement**	
Assets		Liabilities			
Cash	70			Revenues	45
Shirt	30			Other expenses	(5)
Accumulated depreciation	(30)			Depreciation	(15)
Net investment in shirt	0	Equity	70	Pretax profit	25

of $1.3 million, amounting to 28% of its $4.7 million in revenues.[20] By 1993, its revenues had risen to $50 million, and its R&D expense, although more than triple the 1991 level, had fallen to 8% of revenues.[21] This decline in percentage was a consequence of the dramatic tenfold increase in revenues—not an alarming cutback in R&D. Indeed, in their earlier phases, many companies have R&D expenses and no revenues. Second, a company may in rare instances reach a point where its technology is so much better than that of its competitors (especially if it has obtained a strong and defensible patent) that it can afford to reduce its commitment to R&D to focus more intently on marketing and selling. Polaroid in its early years, for example, had a strong technological position in instant photography and found that it was under more pressure to sell the products than to improve them. In the 1980s, it unfortunately missed the transition to electronic imaging, which left it with some catching up to do. Yet for a brief period in the late 1960s, Polaroid was in a position to rest on its technological oars to free resources for other, then more pressing needs, most notably the challenge of selling the product; but doing so for too long can court serious trouble.

20. POWERSOFT CORPORATION, 1991 ANNUAL REPORT.
21. POWERSOFT CORPORATION, 1993 ANNUAL REPORT.

Operating Profit

The net of revenues less CGS, SG&A, and R&D expenses is the company's operating profit. Although this is often referred to as earnings before interest and taxes (EBIT), there are some differences, as explained in Sidebar 7.

Sidebar 7

Difference between Operating Profit and EBIT

Operating profit and EBIT are nearly, but not always, exactly the same. Whereas operating profit is a creature of GAAP, EBIT has been used in the world of finance for the past several decades and is the result of bankers and their lawyers creating and defining EBIT as a surrogate for operating income and EBITDA as a surrogate for operating cash flow. EBIT therefore is what the parties (or analysts) define it as being. Usually the difference between EBIT and operating profit is that operating profit virtually never includes gains or losses on litigation, other extraordinary or nonrecurring items, affiliate earnings, EPA penalties or remediation charges, restructuring charges, foreign currency gains or losses, interest revenues, the marking of certain investment securities to their fair market value, or asset dispositions. Although lenders may intend to use EBIT to get a closer approximation of cash operating profit, they sometimes do not fully appreciate that EBIT does include non-cash items. EBITDA is sometimes used rather than EBIT to include depreciation and amortization, these being non-cash determinants of income.

EBIT is not the same as cash flow from operations, which appears on a statement of cash flows, because it does not include the cash effects of changes in working capital, such as those resulting from changes in accounts receivable, inventory, or accounts payable.

Some commentators define EBIT as operating profit plus depreciation (the latter being added back because it is a non-cash expense). However, the more common reasoning is that the latter measure is best referred to as earnings before interest, taxes, depreciation, and amortization expense (or EBITDA), which can be readily calculated by adding to EBIT the depreciation and amortization expenses (found in the cash flow statement and discussed in chapter 3).

The operating profit is a very important number for several reasons. Above all, it shows the amount of earnings available to all parties expecting a return on the company's capital. There are three such parties: lenders, the government, and the equity investors. (Hybrid securities are deemed for these purposes to be either debt or equity.) In a going concern, the first category of party to be paid a return is the lender, which is paid interest in accordance with the contractual provisions of the loan agreement. The interest expenses are deductible for federal income tax purposes, with the result that the interest expense is deducted from the operating profit to calculate the pretax income. The next party to be paid is the government, which, as we all know, imposes income taxes. (Remember, taxes accrued for GAAP purposes are often not equal to the taxes due and payable in cash under the IRC, as discussed in chapter 2.) The net, after tax, income (that is, the company's earnings after interest and taxes) is available to the equity holders and may, subject to the corporate law of the state of incorporation, be paid out as a dividend or used to redeem shares of the company's stock. However, across the American economy, well over half the earnings of all publicly held companies are reinvested in the business rather than paid out to the shareholders in the form of dividends or stock redemptions.

Thus, the operating profit tells us, for the period in question, the amount the company earned that is available for payments to the three categories of capital providers (assuming the company is liquid enough to make the payments, as discussed in chapter 2).

The second and very much related reason why the operating profit is important is that it indicates how much is available to support debt service. In the extreme case, all the operating profit could be used to pay interest. Indeed, in some of the more highly leveraged buyouts, this was the case until enough operating profit was generated to reduce debt levels. If the operating profit is not enough to meet interest obligations, the company must find cash from other sources, such as selling off some assets (for example, a division, a line of business, or nonessential assets) and use the proceeds to service the debt.

Corporate predators look at the operating profit to determine whether the company has unused debt capacity. If it does, then they may consider it "underlevered" and borrow funds to use for a hostile takeover, later using the company's own debt capacity to service their debt if the takeover attempt is successful. How much debt is suitable for a company is an intricate and interesting topic that will be treated later in chapters 5 and following. Suffice it here to note that many companies with consistent and solid operating profits that carry little debt have been attractive targets of hostile takeover attempts (often successful).

The third reason why operating profit is important is that in making comparisons between or among different companies, it is often more useful to compare their operating profits than their net profits. This is because different companies may have different degrees of financial leverage, impacting net profits disproportionately. Consider two companies, Company A and Company B, each with revenues of $20 million and assets of $10 million. Company A has after tax profits of $1 million and Company B has after tax profits of $2 million. It appears at first blush that Company B has performed better than Company A. One cannot be sure of that inference, however, without comparing their operating profits.

As illustrated in Table 11, Company A has $4 million operating profit—clearly better than Company B's $3 million operating profit. Yet Company B has a higher profit after tax. The difference lies in the fact that Company A has debt and Company B does not. Though this topic will be discussed at length in subsequent chapters, please note at this stage that different degrees of financial leverage can cause significant differences in the bottom line. Here, were we to consider only the profit after tax (PAT), we would probably conclude that Company B has a higher margin business than Company A because its net margins ($2 million of PAT on $20 million of revenues, or 10%) are higher than Company A's net margins ($1 million of PAT on $20 million of revenues, or only 5%). However, comparing the operating profits

Table 11		
Why to Use Operating Profit When Comparing Companies		
	Company A	**Company B**
	($ thousand)	
Revenues	20,000	20,000
Operating profit	4,000	3,000
Interest	−2,500	0
Pretax profit	1,500	3,000
Tax (@ 33%)	−500	−1,000
Profit after tax	1,000	2,000
Assets	10,000	10,000

Table 12		
Advantage to Company A		
		($ thousand)
Operating profit $1,000 higher than B's:	$1,000 \times (1 - .33)$ =	667
Interest tax shield:	$2,500 \times .33$ =	833
Total advantage to Company A:		1,500

reveals that Company A has operating profits of $4 million on revenues of $20 million (amounting to operating margins of 20%), whereas Company B only has operating profits of $3 million on revenues of $20 million (amounting to operating margins of only 15%). Assuming that the year under scrutiny was typical, this indicates that Company A is a stronger operating company than Company B, which in turn indicates that Company A is stronger in the marketplace. It merely has substituted some debt for some equity.

Although this topic is examined in greater detail in later chapters, you might want to make a mental note now that Company A is able to pay $3.5 million out to its investors, including both debt and equity holders ($2.5 million in interest, plus a $1 million dividend if it wanted to). By contrast, Company B is only able to pay $2 million out to its nongovernment providers of capital (no interest—only the $2 million dividend if it chooses to do so). Loosely speaking, Company A could pay a total of $1.5 million more to investors, ostensibly $1 million more because of its higher operating profit and $0.5 million more because it has a lower tax bill. More precisely, it is because (1) its $1 million higher operating profit when adjusted for taxes was $667,000 higher than B's and (2) the tax shield on $2,500,000 in interest was $833,000. Table 12 shows the advantage to Company A.

Hence operating profit is important as a measure of how well a company is managing its operations, quite apart from how it is financed. Whereas profit after tax is a function not only of how well the company runs its operations but also of how it is financed (that is, how much interest and tax it has to pay), operating profit is purely a function of the effectiveness of the company's operations and thus provides a better measure for comparing companies' operating performance.

Minority Interests

Under GAAP, if a company owns more than 50% of the outstanding stock of another company, then the latter is considered a subsidiary, and the numbers are consolidated. Consider the case, then, where Company A owns 51% of the stock of Subsidiary A. The numbers are consolidated, and 100% of Subsidiary A's revenues and expenses are included in Company A's income statement. However, 49% of those earnings essentially belong, as a matter of economic reality, to someone else. To reflect this reality, the portion of the earnings equal to the minority interest is deducted as though it were an expense. For example, if 49% of the shares of Subsidiary A is held by another party, then all of Subsidiary A's revenues and expenses are included in the consolidated income statement, but a minority interest expense equal to 49% of Subsidiary A's earnings is subtracted from the combined earnings to calculate the consolidated profit after tax. (For federal income tax purposes Company A and Subsidiary A are consolidated if the ownership interest exceeds 80%. Thus, when the financials are consolidated under GAAP but not for tax purposes, the minority interest expense reflects the after tax earnings of Subsidiary A.) Company A's balance sheet will show all of Subsidiary A's assets, liabilities, and equity, as though Company A directly owned them all. Company A's balance sheet will, however, on the equities side, show an amount reflecting the minority ownership interest a third party has in Subsidiary A, and the equity of Company A's stockholders will be decreased by a like amount.

If Company A owns between 20% and 50% of Company B, then the "equity method" of accounting for the investment applies. This means that the two companies' financials are not consolidated under GAAP rules (or for tax purposes). In that event, Company A's financials will reflect its share of Company B's earnings, whether or not Subsidiary A pays a dividend. For example, if Company B earns $1 million and Company A owns 30% of its stock, then Company A will report as income $300,000, whether or not it receives any dividend from Company B. Company A's balance sheet will display as an asset (1) the cost of its investment in Company B plus (2) its equity in Company B's undistributed net earnings.

If Company A owns less than 20% of the stock of Company B, a nonpublic company, then the "cost method" applies to the investment. This means that Company A's income statement reflects the ownership interest only to the extent of any dividends received. Company A's balance sheet reflects the interest as though it were a passive outside investment; that is, as a distinct long-term asset other than property and equipment, assuming the intent is to hold the stock for more than a year.

Under FASB 115, adopted in 1994, if Company A holds a public company's debt securities or less than 20% interest in its equity securities issued by another entity, then how these are carried on the balance sheet depends upon management's intent regarding the securities: (1) if they are held for trading, they are classified as current assets (trading securities), or (2) if they are "available-for-sale" securities, their classification depends upon management's intent regarding liquidation—(a) if the intent is to liquidate them within a year, they are classified as current assets; (b) if the intent is to hold them for a year or more, they are classified as noncurrent assets.

Both trading securities and available-for-sale securities are carried at their market values, and cash dividends received are income. Any unrealized changes in market value are treated as income only in the case of trading securities. Any unrealized changes in market value are recognized on the balance sheet in owners' equity in the case of available-for-sale securities. An investment in debt securities that management expects to hold until maturity is carried at cost, not market value.

Extraordinary Items

Sometimes the extraordinary happens, whether for good or bad, and the accountants have a way of dealing with that. The underlying rationale is that if an event or occurrence is really out of the ordinary, then it ought to be treated separately so it does not confuse the reader of the financials by leading him or her to think that the upside or downside performance was part of the normal business of the company. Accordingly, accountants create a separate entry, reported as "extraordinary," for any event that is both unusual and nonrecurring.

To illustrate, suppose an earthquake occurs and causes uninsured damage to a company. If the earthquake took place in Florida, where earthquakes are virtually unknown, it would be both unusual and nonrecurring and hence the financial loss resulting from the earthquake would be treated by the accountants as extraordinary. However, if the earthquake occurred in southern California, where earthquakes are unusual but not nonrecurring, the damage would not be deemed extraordinary but rather an ordinary part of doing business.

Conversely, what if the uninsured damage had been caused by a hurricane (which is unusual)? Whether this is extraordinary depends upon whether hurricanes are nonrecurring. If the damage occurred in southern California, where hurricanes are very rare, then it would be deemed nonrecurring. However, if the damage occurred in Florida, where hurricanes occur all too often, then it would not be nonrecurring and hence would be an ordinary part of the business. Table 13 depicts the method of determining whether an item is extraordinary.

The distinction between extraordinary and ordinary makes little difference in terms of the bottom line. However, the difference is worth noting because in valuing a business (discussed in greater length in chapters 9 through 11), it is often useful to know whether a source of revenue can be counted on and whether an expense must be factored in as a normal part of the business. If they are not, that is if they are extraordinary, then they are displayed separately on the income statement and treated differently in valuing the company.

Corporate Income Taxes

The above elements of the income statement bring one down to the profit before tax, or taxable income. The next item is the accrual for income taxes.

As noted earlier, the income tax accrual entry reflects the tax accrued for GAAP purposes, which often does not equate with the taxes due and payable in cash in accordance with the Internal Revenue Code (IRC) and its regulations. The issuer is required to explain any such differences in the notes to the financial statements. Any

Table 13
Determination of Extraordinary Items

| | **Frequency of Occurrence** | |
	Recurring	**Nonrecurring**
Usual	I None*	II None**
Unusual	III California earthquakes Florida hurricanes	IV California hurricanes*** Florida earthquakes

Nature of event (row group label between Usual and Unusual)

*For instance, if a trucking company has a fleet of twenty trucks and replaces four of its trucks annually, then any gain or loss on the sale of trucks is usual and recurring and thus part of the ordinary course of business even though the company is not in the business of buying and selling trucks.

**Litigation gains or losses virtually always fit in quadrant II.

***Only events in quadrant IV are deemed to be extraordinary. Events in each of the other quadrants are deemed to be part of the ordinary course of business.

difference between tax accrued and tax payable creates a deferred tax asset or a deferred tax liability and is discussed more fully in chapter 2.

Profit after Tax

Finally, one arrives at the profit after tax (PAT). I once heard two litigators arguing about whether the PAT was the same as the net income. The answer is that it is, and it is sometimes referred to as net earnings. The terms are interchangeable. PAT is the item on the income statement that matters most to the equity owners because it represents the amount to which they can lay sole claim, and when the sun sets, this is what they care most about. There is, however, a refinement on this that we will address in chapters 5 and following. This term is literally the bottom line, and it is the source of the term *bottom line* that one hears in common parlance in other contexts.

The reader should appreciate, however, that what happens above the bottom line is highly important—some would say more important even than the bottom line.

Most people, even many highly sophisticated people, read financials believing that they were prepared in a clinically sound and purely scientific context and that the reported financials are not only right, but the only right way that the company's performance could have been reported.

For better or worse, in practice that is not the way it usually works, even at very fine companies. What happens in fact is more akin to the following. Sometime between Thanksgiving and Christmas (assuming the company is on a calendar year), the CEO calls the CFO into his or her office for a one-on-one, and the conversation might go like this:

CEO: "Well, how do earnings for the year look?"

CFO: "It's hard to be sure, but it looks like we'll come in at about $2.10 a share."

CEO: "Drat. That's only 7% above last year. I'm looking for 9%. What can we do to get 4 cents a share more to the bottom line?"

CFO (who has anticipated the question): "We still have some old layers of LIFO inventory around. We could liquidate some of that." (LIFO liquidations are discussed in chapter 2.)

CEO: "Great. Tell the folks in the plant to slow it down a little bit until after New Year's. Work out the numbers. I don't want them to liquidate too much of the old LIFO inventory because if we go over 9% that will just establish a higher base to improve upon next year. Besides I want to leave as much old LIFO inventory around for future years as we can but still hit 9% this year."

Please keep in mind that the numbers are not the auditors' numbers. They are the company's numbers, prepared by management under the direction of the board of directors and its audit committee. The auditors confine their report, even in the best of times, to saying that they believe that the financials were prepared in accordance with GAAP and fairly present the company's financial performance and condition.

Finally, the profit after tax as a percentage of revenues constitutes the net margin. For example, if the company earns $1 million on revenues of $20 million, then its net margin is 5%. This is an important percentage, and a high net margin is better than a low net margin. However, in understanding a company we need to know the size of the asset base on which the company earned the $1 million and how much capital it was using. That takes us to the balance sheet, the topic of chapter 2.

The Balance Sheet

Chapter **2**

The balance sheet provides a snapshot of a company at a given point in time, usually at the end of the company's fiscal year or at the end of a quarter. The left-hand side lists the assets in descending order of liquidity. The right-hand side lists the company's liabilities, in the descending order in which they will come due. If the assets exceed the liabilities, the excess is the company's net worth, often referred to as the book value or equity. The equity, like the liabilities, is shown on the right side of the balance sheet. Indeed, the reason why the balance sheet balances is via the net worth, or equity, account. To the extent that management has run the business so the assets exceed the liabilities plus the original investment in the business, the company has added to its net worth.

One should keep in mind that the balance sheet does not purport to give the market value of assets or liabilities. Rather, the assets and liabilities are displayed at their historic values (that is, their exchange prices) because accountants like to put numbers on transactions and shy away from, indeed assiduously avoid, functioning as appraisers, at least when wearing their auditor hats.

The Asset Side of the Balance Sheet

The asset side of the balance sheet is divided into two parts—current assets and long-lived assets. Current assets are those expected to be converted into cash within a year, and long-lived assets are all other assets. The most important current assets are usually cash and cash equivalents, accounts receivable, and inventory, although there are a few other categories—most notably deferred tax assets, which will be described later.

Current Assets

Cash and Cash Equivalents

For purposes of simplicity, let's consider cash equivalents (usually U.S. government notes, marketable securities, certificates of deposit, and time deposits) as cash. Cash equivalents may or may not be marked to their market value rather than carried at cost, as discussed in chapter 1. In the case of short-term financial instruments, there is rarely a significant difference between cost and market values.

The amount of cash on hand at year-end may not be indicative of the amount of cash the company had on hand at other times during its year. By and large, management likes to submit the annual report to shareholders at a time when the company looks good—that is, as flush with cash as possible. Retailers, for example, usually have the most cash shortly after the Christmas rush. Not wanting to have the auditors underfoot during that rush, and wanting to count inventory at its low point, when it is easier to count, most retailers use a January 31 fiscal year. Similarly, tax return preparers, ski resorts, and other highly seasonal businesses may have a substantial hoard of cash at a particular time of year, but little at another time. If one were trying to understand the financial strength of a ski resort, for example, one would want to examine the balance sheet not only as of April 30, just after the resort finished selling lift tickets for the season, but also as of October 31, after the resort incurred expenditures for maintenance and repairs but before the new season's revenues had begun. Certain other companies—such as those that are young, highly leveraged, or in trouble—are likely to be very sensitive to their cash positions. Because the cash position can change quickly, such companies may have to monitor their cash positions and make careful cash projections, not only quarterly, but monthly, weekly, or, in some cases, even daily.

In analyzing the financials, it is worth noting how much cash a company has as a percentage of total assets. Some companies have a substantial amount of cash. At one extreme, Microsoft Corporation, with $6.94 billion in cash on total assets of $10.1 billion as of December 31, 1996, held 69% of its total assets in cash.[1] This put the company in a position to pay a substantial dividend, buy back its own stock, make a significant cash acquisition, or launch a new business—an enviable constellation of alternatives. Inasmuch as the cash is not the result of a recent securities offering or debt financing, this bespeaks the strength of Microsoft's business and its ability to generate more cash than is needed to reinvest in its current software business.

However, there is a downside to having such a large portion of the company's assets tied up in cash. During 1996, Microsoft earned $320 million, pretax, in interest on its cash. Given that Microsoft in 1996 accrued taxes at a rate of 35%, it earned $208 million after tax on its cash, a 3% return. Because the company began fiscal 1996 with $4.8 billion in cash and ended with $6.9 billion, and because the cash account grew so much, a more reliable measure is its return on average cash. On average it had $5.9 billion in cash, on which it earned $208 million after tax. Thus its return on average cash was 3.5%.[2]

Consider that Microsoft had a profit after tax (PAT) of $2,195 million. If $208 million of that was attributable to interest on the cash, then the balance of $1,987 million ($2,195 million in company-wide PAT less the $208 million after tax earnings on the cash) was attributable to earnings on the software business. Further, Microsoft had total assets of $10.1 billion, but it really needed only some $3.2 billion to be in the software business ($10.1 billion total assets less the $6.9 billion in cash). Actually, one would not want to run the business without enough cash on hand to meet the payroll and pay other bills as they come due. In 1996, Microsoft's total expenses—

---

1. MICROSOFT CORPORATION, 1996 ANNUAL REPORT.
2. *Id.*

Table 14	
Microsoft's 1996 Return on Assets Invested in the Software Business*	
Average total assets	$8.65B
Average cash and cash equivalents	$5.85B
Average assets used in software business	$2.8B
After tax interest earned	$208M
After tax return on software business assets	$2.0B
Return on average total assets	22%
Return on average cash	3.5%
Return on average software assets	54%
*Microsoft Corporation, 1996 Annual Report.	

cost of goods sold (CGS) plus research and development (R&D) and overhead—were $5.6 billion. If the company had wanted to keep a one-month supply of cash on hand, then it would want about $467 million in cash ($5.6 billion total expenses for the year divided by 12 months) in addition to the other operating assets of $3.2 billion. Thus, to be in the software business (as contrasted with the cash management business), Microsoft would have needed not $10.1 billion but only $3.7 billion. (Actually, on average during 1996, Microsoft had less than that in software business assets because it began the year with fewer assets than it ended with. Its average assets needed in the business were only some $3.5 billion.[3]) Suffice it here to note that in 1996, Microsoft was an amalgam of two companies: (1) the software business, which generated approximately $2.0 billion in after tax earnings on average operating assets of $3.5 billion (a 57% return), and (2) a cash management business, which generated a return of $208 million on average cash of $5.9 billion (a 3.5% return on its average cash). Microsoft's cash account was so substantial that it had a material adverse impact on the overall corporate performance.

This is not to say, however, that holding such a large amount of cash was necessarily imprudent for Microsoft. First, having such a large cash account reduced the overall risk of the company. Investors in Microsoft have what amounts to an interest in two businesses, a money market mutual fund (albeit one that pays no dividends) and a software company. The combination is less risky than a pure play in software. Thus the cash account reduces both the risk and the return for Microsoft. It has also enabled it to make acquisitions, as noted by its offer to buy Intuit, the creator of Quicken, although the offer was withdrawn due to antitrust problems.

Second, were Microsoft to pay its cash out as a dividend, its shareholders would have to pay income tax on the dividend. For every $1.00 received, the shareholder paying tax at the maximum federal income tax rate of 39.6% plus any state and local income taxes, may be left with less than $.60. Essentially, Microsoft's board would be saying to an investor, "Look, you are better off going into the stock market with your $.60 than you are leaving your dollar with us. To be sure, you will need to

---

3. *Id.*

generate a 67% return after taxes on your $.60 to get back to the dollar, but your odds of doing that are better than investing with us." Boards of directors don't like to do that. If nothing else, they find it embarrassing. To be sure, if the company has a large constituency of tax exempt investors (such as pension funds, retirement accounts, or universities), or if the company is privately owned and there are a lot of relatives trying to live on dividends, then the board might see this differently, but such cases remain exceptions. Of course, as retirement assets become a larger portion of the market, some companies may find that tax exempt investors are an increasingly significant part of their shareholder constituency.

In contrast to Microsoft, some companies have scant cash relative to their asset bases. This can be a cause for concern, or it can be a sign of strength. Bradlee's, the discount chain in the Northeast, illustrates the former. As of May 31, 1995, Bradlee's reported cash of $3.7 million, amounting to a mere 1% of its total assets and only enough to cover its costs for one day.[4] On June 23, 1995, Bradlee's filed for Chapter 11 bankruptcy protection. Here, a scant cash supply indicated severe financial stress.

Wal-Mart, which also has a small amount of cash relative to its total assets, provides a different example. As of January 31, 1995, its cash position was $45 million, amounting to barely one-tenth of 1% of its total assets.[5] Given that Wal-Mart's 1995 revenues of $83.4 billion averaged $228 million per day, the $45 million in cash represented far less than a one-day supply of cash. Wal-Mart was clearly sweeping the cash out of its point-of-sale terminals as rapidly as feasible (probably several times per day, leaving only enough on hand to make change for customers), knowing that it would be better off investing the cash in new inventory, real estate, or equipment. Moreover, if it were ever to need more cash, Wal-Mart is in a strong position to get it, for it is a highly creditworthy company, for reasons we will observe later.

How can one determine whether a low level of cash indicates that the company is weak and in trouble (Bradlee's) or is strong and merely reinvesting cash in the business where it can make a return in excess of the returns available on cash (Wal-Mart)? That determination is best made by examining the profitability of the company. If the company has solid earnings, then it has the ability to replenish its cash supply, as illustrated by Wal-Mart, which in fiscal 1995 had a return on average assets of 10.8%. However, if the earnings picture is marginal or rocky, as illustrated by Bradlee's, which in fiscal 1995 had a return on average assets of 0.6%, then a paucity of cash is a sign that the company may be facing financial difficulties. For a fuller discussion of performance, please refer to chapter 4.

During the 1980s, many companies abandoned the luxury of living with comfortable levels of cash and other current assets. What constitutes a necessary or advisable versus an excessive level of cash is at times open to debate, depending in part upon one's perspective.

In November 1996, Kirk Kerkorian wrote a letter[6] to Chrysler Corporation's management, arguing that a $6.6 billion cash account at Chrysler was excessive and

---

4. BRADLEE'S, INC., 1995 ANNUAL REPORT.

5. WAL-MART STORES, INC., 1995 ANNUAL REPORT. Lately Wal-Mart's cash position has been rising rapidly, reaching $1.4 billion as of January 31, 1998. Query whether you believe this is a sign of strength. In fiscal 1998, its return on average assets had declined to 8.3%, which is very good but less than 10.8%.

6. Douglas Lavin & Gabriella Stern, *Chrysler Seen Heeding Call from Kerkorian*, WALL ST. J., Nov. 16, 1994, at A-3.

ought to be paid out to the owners. Chrysler management saw it quite differently, observing that (1) at 1994's run rate, $5.1 billion would cover only 44 days of expenses—for CGS and selling, general, and administration (SG&A) expenses, and (2) with $50.4 billion in annual revenues from the automobile business, one or two bad months could use up the cash. In a cyclical business such as autos, management felt that it ought to conserve the cash for a downturn. Where one stands on that issue may well depend upon where one sits, but the clear lesson is that management teams who enjoy the comfort of too much cash or too much working capital run the risk of inviting a hostile takeover unless they are insulated from such an attack by a friendly party holding a control position, or close to it. At least one Fortune 50 management team makes a point of keeping its cash level just high enough to provide some comfort, but just below the level it believes would invite a hostile takeover attempt. Time will tell whether it has succeeded in identifying that point.

Accounts Receivable

Unless a company sells its goods or services exclusively for cash, which very few do, it will record revenues for sales for which it has not yet been paid. The right to collect payment for such sales creates an account receivable.

There are three things to look for when reviewing accounts receivable:

1. how substantial they are as a percentage of total assets,
2. how long it takes the company to collect on them, on average, and
3. how collectible they are.

In many industries, particularly cash businesses such as restaurants and entertainment (cinemas, gaming), accounts receivable are a minor—if not trivial—percentage of total assets. For example, Circus Circus Enterprises, Inc., the Las Vegas gaming company, has only 0.7% of its assets in accounts receivable, reflecting the cash nature of the business.[7] Indeed, its receivables would probably be an even lower percentage of assets if it did not have hotel rooms and restaurants and take several days to collect those revenues from credit card companies.

However, in other industries, the opposite is true. Many professional service firms must invest a substantial portion of their assets—often over half—in accounts receivable. When this is the case, one should carefully monitor the collectibility of the receivables. A quick overview can be obtained by checking the *days accounts receivable,* sometimes referred to as the *days sales outstanding* (DSO). This is determined by the following formula:

$$\frac{\text{Accounts Receivable}}{\text{Revenues}} \times 365 = \text{Days Sales Outstanding}$$

The formula tells us—at year-end or another point—the portion of the company's revenues still unpaid, what portion of the year that is, and how long it takes, on average, to collect the receivables. If you know the portion of the sales made for credit, then you would include only the credit sales in the above equation.

A more refined analysis of receivables involves an examination of their aging. Although the patterns vary across industries, generally there is cause to probe if one

---

7. *See, e.g.,* Circus Circus Enterprises, Inc., 1997 Annual Report 26.

sees receivables over 60 days, and almost certainly over 90 days, especially if receivables are growing faster than revenues. On the other hand, some companies that are entirely healthy have substantial portions (even around 50% for professional service firms) of their assets in receivables.

In some cases, a review of the age of receivables reveals merely that the most recent quarter was a terrific one, although the cash has not been collected. For example, in 1992, Powersoft had 47% of its assets in receivables, and 102 days of accounts receivable.[8] However, Powersoft was enjoying spectacular growth, with revenues rising some 33% every quarter. With fourth-quarter revenues of $8 million, the $5.9 million in receivables were not out of line and might have all been the result of recent sales.[9] One could not know this without seeing an aging of the receivables.

The major concern about the aging of the receivables is the possibility that some of the customers are not creditworthy. If the portion of the receivables that are uncollectible creeps above 3–5%, or if accounts receivable have recently risen more rapidly than revenues, there is reason to investigate. It may be that the company, in its eagerness to increase revenues, has extended credit to noncreditworthy buyers. In general, it is safer for a company to have receivables due from a large number of customers rather than a small number. When the number is large, the financial impact of any one or two customers encountering financial difficulty is minimized. By contrast, if the company has extended credit to a small number of customers, the consequences of any one of them being unable to pay can be material and adverse. Also, if any customer accounts for a high percentage of revenues, it may have so much bargaining power that it can get very good terms, such as lower prices or longer credit terms. Generally accepted accounting principles (GAAP) require disclosure in the notes to the financials if any customer accounts for 10% or more of revenues.

It is worth noting that generally, the further a company is from the ultimate customer, the longer the collection cycle is likely to be. For example, producers of cans usually have a longer days accounts receivable (Crown Cork & Seal's receivables run close to 2 months)[10] than the beverage producers (Anheuser-Busch's receivables run about 3 weeks).[11] The beverage producers usually have longer collection cycles than the retailers (Albertson's Inc.'s receivables are slightly less than three days).[12] The reason is that in the absence of bargaining power to offset the pattern, the retailer will look for credit from the beverage producer (or distributor, if there is one). The beverage producer knows that the retailer will sell the product for cash within about three weeks, and therefore will not extend credit for a longer period. The beverage maker will seek credit from the can producer to cover not only the few weeks of credit it has to extend, but also the period during which it holds the cans before filling and shipping them. Hence the can producer's receivables are usually longer than three weeks.

High or rising receivables can be a tip-off of warranty problems. Customers may be withholding payment as a result of dissatisfaction with the product or its failure, or perceived failure, to meet express or implied warranties. This problem is most likely to occur with new products or products built to specification for the particular customer.

---

8. POWERSOFT CORPORATION, 1992 ANNUAL REPORT.

9. *Id.*

10. CROWN CORK & SEAL COMPANY, INC., 1996 ANNUAL REPORT 7, 8.

11. ANHEUSER-BUSCH COMPANIES, INC., 1996 ANNUAL REPORT 48, 49.

12. ALBERTSON'S, INC., 1996 ANNUAL REPORT.

Inventory

As discussed in chapter 1, inventory count provides the critical link to CGS (cost of goods sold). Determining the carrying amount of inventory can be difficult, but important because it can be a source of fraud. Under GAAP, companies may choose numerous ways to measure their inventory. The two most common are FIFO (first in, first out) and LIFO (last in, first out). Many foreign countries do not permit LIFO inventory accounting. Indeed it was not permitted in the United States under GAAP until the late 1940s, and even then it was permitted only after the U.S. Supreme Court held that companies could elect to use LIFO for tax purposes.[13]

Sidebar 8

Calculation of Days Inventory

Days inventory can be calculated by dividing CGS by the inventory and multiplying the result by 365. If year-end inventory numbers are thought to be an unreliable gauge of average inventory, then one ought to use the average of the beginning inventory, first, second, and third-quarter inventory, and year-end inventory.

On December 31, 1996, Caterpillar, Inc., the earth-moving equipment company headquartered in Peoria, Illinois, had $2.22 billion in inventory, up from $1.92 billion at the beginning of its year, indicating an average inventory of approximately $2.1 billion. Its CGS for the year was $11.8 billion, indicating that it had a 65-day supply of inventory on hand at year-end at 1996 sales levels.[14]

$$\frac{\$2.1 \text{ billion in average inventory}}{\$11.8 \text{ billion CGS}} \times 365 \text{ days} = 65\text{-day inventory supply}$$

To refine this analysis slightly, the notes to Caterpillar's financial statements reveal that at year-ends 1996 and 1995, if it had used FIFO rather than LIFO, its inventory would have been 4,345 and 4,024, respectively. FIFO measures the economic value of the ending inventory more accurately than LIFO; hence a more accurate measure of inventory turnover would be based on FIFO:

$$\frac{\$4.19 \text{ billion in average inventory}}{\$11.8 \text{ billion in CGS}} \times 365 \text{ days} = 130\text{-day inventory supply}$$

There can be a material difference in a company's GAAP earnings depending on whether it uses FIFO or LIFO. Consider a retailer that buys 3 television sets for $200, $210, and $220, respectively, and then sells one of those sets for $300. Its reported gross profit depends on whether it uses FIFO or LIFO.

---

13. Hutzler Brothers Co. v. Internal Revenue Serv., 8 T.C. 14, 31 (1947).
14. CATERPILLAR, INC., 1996 ANNUAL REPORT.

Table 15 FIFO vs. LIFO Accounting	FIFO	LIFO
Revenues	$300	$300
Cost of goods sold	200	220
Gross profit	100	80

Clearly, if costs are rising, the retailer will show greater earnings by using FIFO rather than LIFO. Yet most companies use LIFO, and the reason is that it provides a tax shelter. To illustrate, let's carry the above example a step further.

Table 16 FIFO vs. LIFO as a Tax Shelter	FIFO	LIFO
Revenues	$300	$300
Cost of goods sold	200	220
Gross profit	100	80
Operating expense	40	40
Pretax profit	60	40
Tax @ 40%	24	16
Profit after tax	36	24

To be sure, by using FIFO the company shows a better profit after tax, as well as a better gross profit. However, it will also pay a higher tax ($24 versus $16) and the tax will be a cash expense, whereas the difference in GAAP PAT is purely a bookkeeping difference. Thus, if costs are rising, LIFO results in lower profits but higher cash flow, and FIFO results in higher profits but lower cash flow.

The conventional wisdom has been that privately owned companies focus more on cash flow (because the owners want cash) and publicly held companies focus more on earnings (because, it has been believed, the market wants earnings). However, there is increasing evidence that the market also prefers cash earnings, as discussed in chapter 6.

When inflation runs to double digits, this difference between FIFO and LIFO becomes more acute. Indeed, it is part of a larger picture concerning the subtle but potentially powerful ravages of inflation. In recent years inflation has been tamed, though in some foreign countries it remains an acute problem. On the chance that a return to the double-digit inflation of the early 1980s might recur, Sidebar 9 explains the impact of inflation.

_____ ***Sidebar 9*** _____

Effects of Inflation

Inflation tends to increase the cost of most supplies, plants, and equipment. Hence the company's cost of replacing inventory or other assets usually exceeds the cost of such assets on the books. There are two major consequences of this. First, as an economic matter, the real costs (both CGS and depreciation) as reported under GAAP accounting are understated. Second, taxes are imposed (and paid in cash) on earnings that are, in terms of economic reality, overstated. For an illustration of this, please refer to Sidebar 23 in chapter 6.

There is also a balance sheet difference between FIFO and LIFO. At the conceptual level, consider a copper company that has been around since the turn of the century and still has some pre-World War II copper on its books. Of course, that does not mean the same copper has been on hand since before World War II, but rather, that since that time the company has mined or bought more copper than it has sold. Inasmuch as copper prices—which due to the law of supply and demand tend to rise as housing starts rise and fall as the housing industry slumps (which in turn is geared to interest rates)—have risen over the past 50 years, the company may have some very "old" copper on its balance sheet. This would not be the case if the company used FIFO, for then it would have long since sold all its pre-World War II copper inventory. However, if it uses LIFO, it may still have some very "old," very low-cost copper in its LIFO inventory. That puts the company in a position, if and when management wants, to mine or buy less copper than it sells and thus increase earnings above what they would have been had the company mined or bought as much as, or more, than it sold.

To illustrate, consider once again our television retailer. When we left it, it had sold 1 of its 3 television sets during year 1. How much inventory it then had left on its balance sheet depends on whether it is using FIFO or LIFO. Remember, it bought 3 television sets, for $200, $210, and $220, respectively. If it is using FIFO, then it is deemed to have sold the first one, which it bought for $200. If it is using LIFO, then it is deemed to have sold the last one, which it bought for $220. Thus the respective balance sheets are as follows:

Table 17
Inventory Value under FIFO and LIFO

	FIFO	**LIFO**
Inventory	$430	$410

If during year 2 the retailer sells (at a price of $300) one television set more than it buys, then its income statement for the two years, if it is using LIFO, will be as follows.

Table 18		
LIFO Liquidation		
	LIFO	
	Year 1	**Year 2**
Revenues	$300	$300
Cost of goods sold	220	210
Gross profit	80	90
SG&A	40	40
Pretax profit	40	50
Tax @ 40%	16	20
Profit after tax	24	30

Thus, by not making or buying as many new television sets as sold during year 2, the retailer can sell off, or liquidate, "old" layers of LIFO inventory and thereby increase its earnings. Management often likes to keep some old inventory (remember, "old" here refers not to the actual age of the inventory but only to its accounting—that is, how it is reported on the books) on hand to delve into when it wants to increase earnings for a particular reason, such as making the company more attractive for an equity offering, for sale, for executive compensation purposes, or for some other reason. This happens quite commonly in the steel, aluminum, and chemical industries. Keep in mind that the older the inventory is, the longer LIFO has been used, and the greater the inflation rate has been since the inventory was built or bought, the more pronounced the effect of the LIFO liquidation—not only in terms of its impact on the company's earnings, but also (and this can be very important) upon its taxes due the Internal Revenue Service (IRS). This can be a trap for the unwary. For example, if Company A buys Company B, and the latter has considerable "old" LIFO inventory, the buyer may eventually get stuck paying higher-than-expected income taxes. Liquidating old LIFO inventory helps to raise GAAP earnings, but it also increases taxable income.

In industries where costs tend to be falling, such as electronics and communications, the above analysis is reversed: earnings will be greater but cash flow less if the company uses LIFO, and earnings will be less but cash flow greater if it uses FIFO. San Jose's Cisco Systems, Inc., for example, the worldwide leader in networking for the Internet, uses FIFO,[15] which is common in Silicon Valley. However, there is no corollary to the LIFO liquidation under FIFO because companies using FIFO do not have the same latitude. That is, even if they make or buy less (or more) than they sell, they are compelled to expense the oldest, and hence there is no room to manage earnings or cash flow in the same manner.

---

15. CISCO SYSTEMS, INC., 1997 ANNUAL REPORT.

Counsel should be watchful for LIFO liquidations if a company is being valued based on earnings or cash flow. How your client's interests may be affected will vary with the circumstances, but LIFO liquidations ought to be detected and, when appropriate, adjustments made in determining a value. The Securities and Exchange Commission (SEC) now requires that LIFO liquidations be disclosed in the footnotes,[16] which makes this easier than it used to be. Counsel should also be watchful for LIFO liquidations when reviewing the management discussion and analysis (MD&A) narrative. If material, its occurrence and impact merit discussion.

If the LIFO method is used, there may be a significant difference between what the inventory is worth and the cost at which it is being carried on the books. When this occurs, the company has, in effect, created value without that value passing through the income statement. Furthermore, the GAAP financials will understate the company's asset base, for the historic cost of the inventory as stated on the books is less than its real, or fair market, value.

When financials understate assets, it is useful to make two adjustments for purposes of analysis: one to the balance sheet and one to the income statement. The adjustment to the balance sheet is essentially to increase the inventory to reflect its replacement cost. An SEC rule[17] mandates disclosure of *LIFO Reserves*, which captures the concept. Under the SEC regulation, the replacement cost of the inventory is either (1) the cost the company would incur if it were to replace its inventory at current costs, or (2) the FIFO cost of the inventory. The LIFO reserve is the difference between the replacement (or FIFO cost, if that is used instead) and the LIFO inventory.

The replacement cost of the inventory more accurately reflects the economic realities than does the LIFO inventory number. One can think of this as the impact inflation has had on the inventory as the company has held it. For companies such as discounters whose inventory turns quickly, the LIFO reserves are usually minor (1% to 5% of LIFO inventory). However, companies whose inventories turn less rapidly may have material differences between replacement (or FIFO) cost and LIFO cost (that is, they have more material LIFO reserves). When LIFO reserves are material, analysts often add the LIFO reserve to the reported assets (and the equity) of the company in assessing its performance. Caterpillar, Inc., the Peoria, Illinois-based producer of earth-moving equipment, provides an illustration. As of year-end 1996, Caterpillar reported inventory (using LIFO) as follows.

Table 19		
Caterpillar Inventory		
Inventories	**1996**	**1995**
	($ million)	
At replacement cost	4,435	4,024
Less LIFO reserve	2,123	2,103
Inventories at LIFO cost	2,222	1,921

---

16. 17 C.F.R. § 211, Staff Accounting Bulletin No. 40 (Release No. SAB-40) (1981).
17. 17 C.F.R. § 210, 50 Fed. Reg. 49,533 (1985).

In Caterpillar's case, this means adding $2.1 billion to the company's assets and equity for purposes of analysis. This point is further illustrated in Sidebar 24, page 143, where LIFO reserves are discussed in another context.

Similarly, during any particular year, any increase in LIFO reserves indicates that the gross profit appreciated by the amount of the decrease in the LIFO reserves. This is the case even though that increase did not impact the economic income—it was a creation of value (at least in nominal, if not inflation-adjusted, terms). Some analysts will add this increase to the reported earnings of the company in assessing its performance. In Cabot's case, this means adding $6 million (the increase from $27 million to $33 million in LIFO reserves) to its 1994 earnings when measuring its performance. Thus, in assessing a company's performance, when LIFO reserves are material, cutting-edge analysts now add the total LIFO reserves to the company's assets (and equity) and the change in LIFO reserves to the company's earnings.

Other Current Assets

Occasionally companies have other assets that are expected to be converted into cash within a year. Although these are rarely material, they can be, and include such items as short-term notes if the company has made a loan (to an executive, for example), the current portion of any long-term loans the company has made, prepaid expenses, and deferred tax assets (discussed on page 44).

Long-Lived Assets

Assets that are not expected to be converted into cash within a year are considered long-term, or fixed, assets.

Property, Plant, and Equipment

The most common fixed asset is *property, plant, and equipment* (PP&E or P&E). Though the term is self-explanatory, there are a few matters to note.

First, the P&E is on the books at historic cost, and it may have appreciated substantially and have a market value far in excess of its carrying value. (Alternatively, it may have depreciated; witness the Japanese purchase of Rockefeller Center and the 1995 abandonment of its equity interest therein). Many savings and loan (S&L) institutions, for example, own street corner real estate that has been on the books for a century or more and may have a market value far in excess of its carrying value. McDonald's, which has been around for much less than a century, built many of its fast-food locations—including those it leases to franchisees—on what used to be open fields. As the suburbs have grown up around these locations, many have attained market values far in excess of their carrying values. The result has been value creation never reflected on the company's income statement, but which is real value nonetheless. Hence companies such as those S&Ls and McDonald's are in a position to sell off some real estate from time to time, recognize the gain (a disadvantage for tax purposes), and increase their earnings accordingly.

One should be aware of such value when it exists, but also be careful not to double count the value. Occasionally when a company is being sold, the seller will argue that the value of the company based on its earnings should be increased by the difference between the market value and the carrying cost of the P&E (and/or inventory if the difference between market and book value is material). However, this logic is flawed, for the correct method of valuation is either/or. If one is valuing a company based on its earnings power, then the difference between market and book values is irrelevant, for it is the ability to use the assets to generate earnings that drives the value of the company. A company cannot simultaneously over the long run operate the business and liquidate its assets. Only if the company is being valued on a liquidation basis is the difference between book value and market value of a particular asset relevant.

There are times when a company owns an asset that has a value in excess of the value of the company based on earnings. In that event, the board ought to give serious consideration to liquidating the company, or at least selling the assets. Alexander's, a New York City area department store chain catering to middle to lower income family budgets, illustrates this point. For years, Alexander's owned its own buildings or occupied them under long-term leases. By the mid-1980s, it suffered increased competition from other off-price retailers. In 1986, Alexander's stock—reflecting the company's value as a retail chain—traded in the mid-$30s. When Donald Trump began buying stock in the company in 1987, its market price quickly jumped to $46 per share, in anticipation that Trump would close the retail operations and sell the properties to third parties for purposes that would better reflect their highest and best use. Trump, however, was then too deeply in debt to seize the opportunity to buy a control position and effectuate this concept. The stock price languished and drifted down to $12 per share by May 1992, when Alexander's filed for Chapter 11 bankruptcy protection. As Alexander's began selling off its locations and leases to other retailers, its stock price continued to improve. By the time it received bankruptcy court approval to reorganize into a real estate company in September 1993, its stock price had reached a high of $61 per share. The buildings were still being used for their original purposes, but by more effective retailers, with the exception of the flagship store at 59th Street and Lexington Avenue in Manhattan, which Trump and investor Steve Roth wanted to make into a high-rise building.

In other words, over the decades Alexander's performance as a retailer had turned downward. In the meantime, the value of its real estate had appreciated to a point where the shareholders would have come out ahead if the company were to abandon the retail business, sell its real estate interests, and distribute the proceeds to the shareholders. Yet the market value of the company's stock reflected only its value as a retailer, because investors believed that the board would never sell the real estate. It was not until Donald Trump began buying stock in Alexanders's that the market price rose, reflecting the market's read that Trump would do what the board had not and liquidate the company, capturing for the investors the market value of the real estate.

Another factor worth watching is the rate at which P&E is depreciated. Although the IRS has rules on this, GAAP does not; this gives managements room to maneuver, which many readily do. (The IRS's allowance of more rapid depreciation under the Modified Accelerated Cost Recovery System (MACRS) than is often used under GAAP creates a deferred tax liability, discussed later in this chapter.) By extending the depreciation period for GAAP purposes, management can defer recognizing depreciation expense, but it also then recognizes a higher tax expense than is currently due. If an analyst or buyer believes that the company has used too long a depreciation period, then he or she might recalculate the earnings using a shorter depreciation period. Similarly, if depreciation is a material expense, then making an accurate comparison between or among companies may necessitate restating one or more of the company's depreciation schedules (and hence depreciation expenses) to place the company on the same footing as the one with which it is being compared. Many companies do not display the depreciation expenses on their income statements. However, the depreciation expense can almost always be found on the cash flow statement. When the depreciation and amortization are combined on the cash flow statement, the 10-K usually reports the depreciation expense in the case of publicly held companies.

Deferred Tax Assets

Until Statement of Financial Accounting Standard (SFAS) 109 was adopted,[18] deferred tax assets were as rare as two-dollar bills. The new rule, however, provides that deferred tax assets are created when a company has expensed a cost (such as a restructuring charge or a worker's compensation claim) under GAAP before it is entitled to take the deduction for income tax purposes. Until the rule was changed, companies could not book the deferred tax asset unless it was clear beyond a reasonable doubt that the company would have sufficient pretax profits in future years to enjoy the benefit of the deduction. Now, however, the standard has been lowered, and it need only be more likely than not that the company will have sufficient pretax earnings in future years to enjoy the benefit of the deduction. As a result, deferred tax assets are becoming much more common.

Because creating deferred tax assets is the opposite side of the coin of creating deferred tax liabilities (which are more common), please refer to the discussion of deferred tax liabilities on page 56 for an explanation of how deferred tax assets are created.

Goodwill

Most lawyers know that goodwill is created on Company A's books when Company A acquires Company B by purchase, and the purchase price exceeds the amount by which the fair market value (FMV) of Company B's assets exceeds the FMV of Company B's liabilities.

To illustrate, let's suppose Company A buys Company B for $300. Company B has assets and liabilities on its books, the FMV of which—immediately after the closing—is as follows.

Table 20
FMV of Assets and Liabilities

Assets		Liabilities	
Cash	25	Liabilites	
Receivables	75	Current liabilities	250
Inventory	100	Long-term debt	100
Fixed assets	300	Total liabilities	350
Total	500	Equity	150
		Total	500

---

18. SFAS-109 became effective for fiscal years beginning after December 5, 1992.

Company A essentially acquires, for $300, assets having a FMV of $500, less liabilities having a FMV of $350.

Table 21
Creation of Goodwill

FMV of Company B's assets	$500
FMV of Company B's liabilities	350
Net FMV of Company B's assets	150
Purchase price	300
Net FMV of Company B's assets	150
Goodwill	150

Thus Company A will have $150 of goodwill on its books after the closing.

Under Accounting Principles Board Opinion 16, which was adopted in 1970, that goodwill must be amortized over a period not to exceed 40 years. More specifically, the goodwill must be written off over the estimated useful life of the goodwill, and that estimate may not exceed 40 years. Many auditing firms are pressing companies to compress this period and amortize the goodwill over a much shorter period, typically 10 to 15 years. This reflects the belief that in today's rapidly changing environment, it is difficult to see more than 10 to 15 years ahead and hence have confidence that the goodwill of the acquired company will continue to have value after that period. To be sure, many managements resist such shortening, for the amortization adversely impacts GAAP earnings but has not historically been tax deductible. In 1993, however, President Clinton signed into law section 197 of the Internal Revenue Code (IRC).[19] The law permits taxpayers to deduct "any amortized section 197 intangible" ratably over a 15-year period. (The term *amortized section 197 intangible* is defined to include goodwill as well as certain other intangibles, including going concern value, and customer-based and supplier-based intangibles.) As a result, acquiring companies are beginning to ease up, but only slightly, on their determination that any acquisitions they make be treated as poolings rather than purchases. The tax deduction shelters only part of the goodwill expense, with the result that many managements still prefer pooling treatment. A more complete discussion of the financial and economic realities of goodwill, including purchase and pooling, is taken up in chapter 6.

Intellectual Property

Brand names, as well as trade secrets, patents, and other intellectual property, may have considerable economic value (witness the Coca-Cola name and formula), but they do not appear on balance sheets unless the owner of the intellectual property has been purchased, in which case the cost is capitalized. A minor exception to the rule that homegrown intellectual property is not on the balance sheet is that the legal costs and other direct expenses associated with filing, perfecting, and protecting a patent are capitalized. It is possible to estimate the value of a brand name, as described in Sidebar 10. Many foreign countries require that the value of brand names be included on a company's balance sheet.

---

19. Pub. L. No. 103-66, § 13261(a).

Sidebar 10

Valuation of Brand Names

It is possible to estimate the value of a brand name. Under GAAP, values of brand names and trademarks may not be included on a company's balance sheet unless specifically bought from a third party. In addition, in the event of an acquisition accounted for as a purchase, such values are indirectly included in the form of goodwill on the acquiror's balance sheet.

Yet the brand may have value. If so, a company ought to be able to borrow against it. For example, in the mid-1980s, Beatrice's GAAP earnings were only half its cash earnings (in its case, its PAT plus its goodwill expense)[20] because it had substantial goodwill deductions. Its stock price was low because the market feared it would continue to pay too much for more acquisitions. However, its cash earnings were strong enough to enable it to service much more debt than it had, and the strong brand names meant its assets had far more value than reflected on its balance sheet. KKR saw that, borrowed, and bought Beatrice. When stock prices are low, any company with significant brand names should watch for a predator looking to acquire those brand names.

The following methodology can be used to estimate the value of a brand. For example, consider Marlboro, which has worldwide sales of $15 billion and, based on industry estimates, an operating profit of 20%, which translates to $3 billion. If Marlboro had no interest expense and a tax rate of 33%, then its PAT would be $2 billion. The value of the brand is the value of the business in excess of the value of a no-name brand. If the no-name brand had 3% net margins on $15 billion of revenues, its profit would be $450 million. Thus Marlboro's $2 billion earnings exceed the unbranded product's $450 million earnings by $1,550 million. Putting a multiple of 15 on such spread indicates a $23.25 billion brand value. This is only an estimate, for other factors, such as better distribution networks or packaging, might also contribute to the superior margins.

Note again that the brand name value increases the company's capacity for debt. If every dollar in sales requires $.60 in assets, then $9 billion in assets are needed to support $15 billion in sales. Without giving value to the brand name, a typical way to finance this would be as follows.

Table 22
Financing without Brand Name Value

Assets	$9B	Current liabilities	$2B
		Long-term debt	$2B
		Equity	$5B

---

20. For instance, in its fiscal year ended February 28, 1983, Beatrice reported net earnings of $43 million and goodwill write-down of $187 million. In addition to the mandatory goodwill amortization, management concluded that Tropicana was worth much less than Beatrice had paid for it, and wrote down much of the goodwill. *See* BEATRICE FOODS CO., 1983 ANNUAL REPORT.

However, attributing a value to the brand name would indicate real values as follows.

Table 23 Financing with Brand Name Value			
Assets	$9B	Current liabilities	$2B
Brand name	$23.25B	Long-term debt	$2B
Total	$32.25B	Equity	$28.25B

Reflecting even partial use of the potential leverage for the same company indicates a balance sheet such as the following.

Table 24 Financing with Brand Name Supporting Debt			
Total assets	$32.25B	Current liabilities	$2B
		Long-term debt	$12B
		Equity	$18.25B

The most valuable brand name in the world is Coca-Cola, which in 1996 enjoyed a PAT of $3.5 billion on revenues of $18.5 billion, or 19% net margins.[21] Had the product been a commodity beverage and enjoyed only 3% net margins, the earnings would have been only $555 million, approximately $3 billion less. Even at a typical market average price/earnings multiple of 15, this implies a $45 billion value for Coke's intellectual property. Yet because of Coke's growth rate, which has averaged 12% a year for the past decade, its price/earnings multiple has been 25 and often considerably higher because investors are willing to pay a premium to get not only the current return, but also the future returns in excess of commodity levels. Yet nowhere on Coke's balance sheet does one find intellectual property, other than a comparatively negligible amount for goodwill and other intangible assets.

There is an important implication to valuing brand names in terms of evaluating management. Consider Viad Corp., the Phoenix-based company previously known as Dial Corporation. For its fiscal year ending October 31, 1994, it had earnings of $140 million on equity of $555 million.[22] However, the company enjoyed only

---

21. COCA-COLA COMPANY, 1996 ANNUAL REPORT.

22. DIAL CORPORATION, 1994 ANNUAL REPORT (for fiscal 1994). In fiscal 1996, the company spun off its Dial consumer products group (which took the Dial name) and changed its name to Viad Corp., keeping airline catering and services, convention services, and travel, leisure, and payment services.

a typical market price to earnings multiple of about 13. That is, on earnings of $1.61 per share, the stock was trading at year-end for some $21 per share. Given the 1994 growth rate of 18% and a return on equity of 25%, well in excess of market norms, some people wondered why Dial's price earnings multiple was not substantially higher. At least part of the answer lies in the fact that with the number-one market share for soap in the United States, the Dial brand had significant value (as did some of the company's other brands, such as Purex, Brillo, and its Armour Star line of canned meats). If one were to add the value of brand names to the company's assets and make the corresponding addition to the equity account, then the return on equity would drop to about 15%. Indeed, the company's price earnings multiple almost exactly reflected this calculation. For a more comprehensive discussion of performance measures, please refer to chapter 4. Suffice it for the present to note that brand names—as well as trademarks, trade secrets, and other intellectual property—generally do not appear on the balance sheet (except for the legal and related costs of perfecting and protecting the intellectual property rights, which are capitalized and carried on the balance sheet), but have value on which the owners are likely to expect a return.

Capital Leases

Included among fixed assets are capital leases. Before 1976, leases rarely appeared on balance sheets. Until then, rather than buy an asset and borrow the funds to finance it (thus cluttering the balance sheet with debt and increasing the leverage and perceived risk), companies would simply lease the asset. This was the classic *off balance sheet* financing.

Then in 1976 the Financial Accounting Standards Board (FASB) began requiring[23] that leases be capitalized if the lease has substantially the same economic characteristics as ownership; that is, if it confers upon the lessee substantially the same benefits and economic risks, or indicia of ownership, as owning the asset. Specifically, SFAS 13 provides that the lessee must capitalize the lease if any of the following criteria are met:

1. the lease contains a bargain purchase option, defined as a price so low that it makes the exercise of the option almost certain,
2. title passes automatically to the lessee at the end of the lease,
3. the term is equal to 75% or more of the estimated useful life of the asset, or
4. the net present value of the lessee's minimum lease payments under the lease equals 90% or more of the FMV of the asset at the inception of the lease.

Unless none of these four tests is met, the lessee must capitalize the lease. If any one of the tests is met, the lease is a capital lease. Otherwise, it is an operating lease. The distinction is for reporting purposes only; for tax purposes, there is no distinction.

Capitalizing a lease means that the net present value of the payments to be made under the lease must be recorded as both an asset and a liability of the lessee.

---

23. CODIFICATION OF ACCOUNTING STANDARDS AND PROCEDURES, Statement of Financial Accounting No. 13 (American Inst. of Certified Pub. Accountants 1976).

On the balance sheet the asset declines as the asset is depreciated, and the liability declines as the payments under the lease are made.

In determining the net present value of a capital lease, the payments the lessee must make are discounted at the rate of interest implicit in the lease. The discount rate is the rate that, when applied to (1) the minimum lease payments plus (2) the estimated fair value of the property at the end of the lease term, results in an aggregate present value equal to the fair value of the leased property at the beginning of the lease term, less any credit the lessor expects to realize.

There is an income statement reason why many lessees try to avoid capitalizing their leases. Under an operating lease, the lessee simply expenses the monthly rent. Under a capital lease, the lessee must recognize both (1) the implicit interest expense as it arises and (2) the depreciation expense. The former is higher in the early years. Over the life of the lease it does not matter, but because under capital leases a higher portion of the expense is incurred in the earlier years, many lessees seek to avoid capitalizing their leases.

There is also a balance sheet reason why some lessees want to avoid capitalizing their leases. Capitalizing a lease does not immediately impact a company's net worth, for the addition of the liability is offset by the addition of the capital lease as an asset. With time, however, the asset side declines slightly more rapidly than the liability side, because in the early years of the lease the depreciation of the capital lease exceeds the rate at which principal is reduced. Consequently, capital leases can have a major impact on a company's financial leverage. (Financial leverage is discussed at length in chapter 4.) For example, consider a lessee that has agreed to a loan covenant requiring that it maintain a debt to equity ratio of no more than 1.0. The addition of the capital lease is normally defined as debt, with the result that it will impact the company's leverage under this test. Consequently, many companies seek to have their leases treated as operating—rather than capital—leases; that is, they try to avoid all four tests set forth above.

Lenders and analysts may capitalize the operating leases (which must be disclosed in the notes to the financials) even though GAAP does not, in the thought that, although the company has avoided the GAAP provisions requiring lease capitalization, the economic realities are such that the operating leases may impose long-term obligations on the company, which—like capital leases—encumber its future operations.

Circuit City Stores, Inc., the Richmond-based retailer, has a balance sheet showing $2 billion in assets and no capital leases.[24] The notes to the financials reveal that the long-term debt displayed on the balance sheet includes the net present value of the company's obligations under capital leases of $13 million. The notes also disclose total minimum obligations under operating leases of $2 billion, indicating that the company is careful to structure its lease terms to avoid the strictures of SFAS 13.

The irony is that good analysts will capitalize the operating leases notwithstanding SFAS 13. There are two ways to do this. If possible, one might review each lease, determine the appropriate discount rate, and calculate the net present value of the future obligation as though each lease were a capital lease. The second way, which usually is far more practical, is simply to apply the same present

---

24. Circuit City Stores, Inc., 1997 Annual Report 43.

value multiple to the prediscounted obligations as the company applied to its capital leases. As an illustration, consider the future minimum fixed lease obligations of Circuit City as of February 28, 1997.[25]

	Table 25	
	Capitalizing Operating Lease Obligations	
Fiscal Year	**Capital Leases**	**Operating Lease Commitments** ($ thousand)
1998	1,541	206,825
1999	1,579	204,587
2000	1,662	202,486
2001	1,681	201,317
2002	1,725	198,164
After 2002	19,958	2,293,992
Total minimum lease payments	28,146	3,307,301
Less amounts representing interest	15,072	1,771,038*
Present value of net minimum capital lease payments	13,074	1,536,263**

*This number is derived by imputing the same discount rate to the $3,307,301 total minimum lease payments that $15,072 bears to the $28,146 total minimum lease payments under the capital leases.
**This number is the net of $3,307,301 less $1,771,038.

One could thus impute $1.5 billion of capital leases to the Circuit City balance sheet, as both an asset and liability. This would greatly impact the company's financial leverage. (Leverage is discussed in chapter 4.) If a simple debt to equity ratio is used, Table 26 shows the effect.

	Table 26	
	Impact of Capitalizing the Leases	
	Circuit City	
	Ignoring the Operating Leases	**Capitalizing the Operating Leases**
	($ million)	
All debt	181	1,046
Equity	877	877
Ratio	.21	1.19

The decision to use a capital lease or buy property is very much tax driven and can vary from location to location and from one transaction to the next. Each case must be analyzed carefully by the seller (lessor) and buyer (lessee) to see which way minimizes their combined tax liability. Then the terms are drafted to allocate the tax benefits based on the respective bargaining power of the parties. At times in the past it has been worth introducing third parties, such as limited partnerships, into the equation to take title to the property and borrow the long-term financing, but this, too, is a function of the tax laws in effect at the time and the particular circumstances of the case.

The Liability Side of the Balance Sheet

There are three parts of the right-hand side of the balance sheet: current liabilities, long-term liabilities, and equity. They are set forth in descending order of liquidity. Those payable within a year are current liabilities.

Current Liabilities

The most important current liability is usually accounts payable, but short-term debt, accrued liabilities, accrued taxes, and the portions of long-term debt and capital leases due within a year can also be important.

Short-Term Debt

Commercial paper and other short-term debt is usually the first item on the right-hand side of the balance sheet. The level of short-term debt usually varies over the course of the year. This is especially true for seasonal businesses, as it is used to cover buildups of inventory and receivables. In the seed business, for example, there ought to be scant short-term debt by November (depending on the crop) because the growing season has ended, collections should have been made, and inventory buildup for the next season has yet to begin. At this point seed companies ought to have negligible or no short-term debt. By contrast, in February their short-term debt levels are likely to be high because they have built up their inventories but have not yet sold them. Even in May their receivables may be high, but they have not collected the cash. As the receivables are collected, they pay down their short-term debt. Soon they start the cycle again. Partly to discipline the borrower, many lenders will often require that all short-term debt be fully paid off for a period of time each year.

The tax return preparation business constitutes such a large portion of H & R Block's business that the company as a whole is seasonal. On April 30, 1994 (its fiscal year-end), H & R Block had $514 million in cash and marketable securities and no short-term debt,[26] reflecting the fact that it rendered its services in connection with the April 15 income tax filing deadline, most of its customers being individuals

---

26. H & R BLOCK, INC., 1994 ANNUAL REPORT.

who pay within the quarter. Revenues during the other quarters are far lower, and the company draws down its cash waiting for the next tax preparation season. By January 31, 1995, its cash and marketable securities had declined to $170 million, and it had $90 million in short-term debt.[27] If H & R Block were exclusively a tax return business, this pattern would be even more extreme. The pattern is moderated by its CompuServe business, which is not geared to the tax season. H & R Block announced plans in 1996 to spin off its 80% interest in CompuServe, which would have amplified H & R Block's seasonal cash swings. However, it postponed such plans because of the unit's disappointing recent performance, apparently hoping the on-line computer service industry will rebound.[28]

Although generally companies should use short-term debt to finance current assets, some companies try to use it to finance fixed assets because short-term debt is usually cheaper than long-term debt. There are two risks in this. First, payment of the debt may be required at a bad time for the company, forcing it into serious difficulty. Second, occasionally short-term interest rates rise above long-term rates, as happened in 1980–81 when many S&Ls found themselves in the highly unenviable position of having made fixed-rate mortgage loans at 7%, but financing that debt by borrowing in the short-term markets. When the prime rate went to 20% in 1981, these institutions hemorrhaged cash, and many failed. Indeed, that experience gave impetus to the derivatives market, as companies in that situation wanted to swap their short-term debt for long-term debt and better match the duration of their rights with the duration of their obligations.

Accounts Payable

Accounts payable represent the amounts owed to vendors (other than accrued payroll) for goods or services rendered to the company. For example, if the company buys $100 in lumber from a supplier, the lumber is added to inventory and the $100 becomes an account payable. When the company pays for the lumber, its cash account on the asset side of the balance sheet and the accounts payable on the liability side of the balance sheet each decline by $100.

It can be useful to check how long it takes a company to pay its payables, although calculating days payables outstanding (DPO) is more difficult than calculating days sales outstanding (DSO). Ideally one would like to calculate the number of days it takes the company to pay for raw materials, supplies, and services rendered to it (other than by employees). Unfortunately, the amounts spent for purchases of materials, supplies, and services are buried in the CGS account and in the inventory account at the end of the period. In the absence of extensive information usually available only within the company, a crude approximation of DPO can be made by dividing the accounts payable by the CGS and multiplying the fraction by 365.

To illustrate, the following sets forth a calculation of days payable for Rubbermaid Incorporated, the Ohio maker of household products, as of December 31, 1996.[29]

---

27. H & R Block, Inc., 10-Q Report (Jan. 16, 1995).

28. James P. Miller & Jared Sandberg, *CompuServe Spinoff Plan is Postponed*, Wall St. J., Aug. 29, 1996, at A-3.

29. Rubbermaid Inc., 1996 Annual Report.

($ million)

$$\frac{\text{Accounts Payable}}{\text{Cost of Goods Sold}} \times 365 = \text{Days Payable}$$

$$\frac{\$155}{1,650} \times 365 = 34 \text{ Days Payable}$$

A calculation could be performed for a service company, but rather than using CGS in the denominator, one would use the costs of obtaining supplies or services used in the business. For example, in the case of AMR, the holding company of American Airlines, one would use the costs of fuel, food, and other supplies used in performing services rather than CGS. Although this measure is admittedly crude, it can be useful for watching patterns over time and comparing the company with others in its industry. In general, a high and rising days payable can be a tip-off of financial difficulty and an inability to pay vendors, although, as noted in the discussion of Gillette, pages 55–56, it can be a sign of a powerful buyer flexing its muscles with vendors. The most important aspects of accounts payable are discussed in this chapter's section on working capital, current ratio, and quick ratio on pages 54–55.

There is a hazard associated with deferring payment of payables for too long, for unless the buyer has exceptional bargaining power, most vendors will exact a price for doing so. The price might literally be in the form of higher prices, but it may take other forms, such as slower service, longer delivery times, reduced warranty protection, or favoritism toward other buyers in the event of shortages.

As a strategic matter, it can be important to know whether a company can obtain supplies from multiple vendors. If the company is dependent upon a sole vendor for a key component, supply, or service, then it is at risk of being compelled by the sole vendor to pay such high prices that it can barely stay afloat. Most vendors in that situation want to keep the company as a customer, so they will charge as high a price as they can without driving the company out of business. Sometimes a vendor does not realize that it is the sole source of an important component, supply, or service for a buyer. When that is the case, the buyer that is a publicly held company must draft its MD&A with extreme care, for it must comply with the disclosure rules without tipping its hand to the vendor, if at all possible.

When the buyer is a powerful party such as one of the Big Three automakers or Wal-Mart, it will pay as low a price as it can to take as much of the profits as possible for itself, without paying such a low price that it drives the hapless vendor out of business. It may also extend its payables. Price Costco, the Kirkland, Washington-based membership warehouse discounter, and Von's, the southern California grocery chain, both extend payables so long that they pay for the goods barely before they are sold.[30] One can detect this by seeing that inventories are almost matched by accounts payable. And one can learn by talking to vendors that these companies have at times been able to put goods on the shelf, sell them, and collect interest on the proceeds before they pay for those goods.

If a company has a very long accounts payable cycle, the clear possibility is that it is a highly powerful buyer. The major automotive companies, for example, are

---

30. Costco Companies, Inc.'s fiscal 1997 annual report shows inventory of $1.7 billion and accounts payable of $1.7 billion.

notoriously slow to pay. Lear Corporation, which makes auto and truck seats for the automotive industry, had 106 days accounts receivable on June 30, 1993, reflecting the power held—at least at that time—by its customers.[31]

Working Capital, Current Ratio, and Quick Ratio

There are three often-used measures of a company's liquidity: working capital, current ratio, and quick ratio (sometimes referred to as the acid test ratio). Working capital is current assets less current liabilities, the current ratio is current assets divided by current liabilities, and the quick ratio is current assets less the inventory, divided by current liabilities. The quick ratio is used by lenders, and sometimes vendors, who figure that if the company were to become insolvent then the inventory (whether it be Bavarian bird feeders, yesterday's fashions, or out-of-date software) might not sell and ought to be omitted from current assets in gauging a company's liquidity. If other current assets look as though they might be uncollectible (such as deferred tax assets), then many creditors would also net these out of the numerator in calculating the quick ratio.

There are two kinds of companies with very low working capital, current ratios, and quick ratios: those that are powerful and use their strength to exact great terms from their buyers and vendors (Gillette, Wal-Mart, and the Big Three automakers, to identify a few), and those that are weak and at risk of extinction (such as Bradlee's, as noted earlier). The difference can be best determined by examining performance.

To illustrate, consider Bradlee's and Wal-Mart's current assets and liabilities, as of January 28 and January 31, 1995, respectively, as set forth below.[32]

Table 27
Calculating Working Capital, Current Ratio, and Quick Ratio

	Bradlee's ($ thousand)	Wal-Mart ($ million)
Cash and equivalents	10	45
Accounts receivable	18	700
Inventory	306	14,064
Other current assets	12	529
Total current assets	346	15,338
Total current liabilities	313	9,973
Current ratio*	1.11	1.54
Quick ratio**	.13	.09
Working capital***	33	5,365

*Current ratio is current assets divided by current liabilities.
   For Bradlee's, it was $\frac{\$346}{\$313} = 1.11$

**Quick ratio is current assets net of inventory divided by current liabilities.
   For Bradlee's it was $\frac{\$346 - \$306}{\$313} = .13$

***Working capital is current assets less current liabilities.
   For Bradlee's it was $346 - 313 = 33$

---

31. Lear Seating Corporation, 1994 Prospectus (Apr. 6, 1994) (name later changed to Lear Corporation).

32. Bradlee's, Inc., 1995 Annual Report; Wal-Mart Stores, Inc., 1995 Annual Report.

First, note the difference in the amount of working capital at the two companies. Although Wal-Mart was about 40 times as big as Bradlee's ($83 billion versus under $2 billion in revenues in fiscal 1995, Bradlee's last full year of operation), it had over 160 times as much working capital. Wal-Mart manages its working capital very tightly, but Bradlee's was not simply managing its working capital tightly, it was running out of money. The critical difference could be noted quickly by looking at any one of a number of performance measures. (Performance measures are discussed in chapter 4.) Comparing their respective returns on assets (to choose one of the more potent performance measures), Wal-Mart enjoyed a very attractive 8% return on ending assets whereas Bradlee's had but a 3% return on ending assets. In retailing, the former connotes strength, and the latter connotes trouble.

The quick ratios of these companies are both remarkably low, reflecting that (1) they have low receivables because they are in cash businesses and (2) the overwhelming majority of their current assets is in inventory, which when deducted from current assets leaves little by way of current assets.

Historically it has been thought that companies, like families or individuals, ought to have a respectable degree of liquidity and that their current assets ought to exceed their current liabilities comfortably. Hence, at the risk of being too general, a current ratio of 2 and a quick ratio of 1 was thought desirable, although particular industries had their own, more specific benchmarks.

Much of the conventional wisdom, however, was reversed during the 1980s for the reasons noted in the discussion of cash on pages 31–35. Consider Gillette's balance sheet as of December 31, 1985.[33]

Table 28
Gillette 1985 Balance Sheet

Assets	($ million)	Liabilities	($ million)
Cash and cash equivalents	473	Short-term debt	199
Receivables	497	Payables	673
Inventory	469	Other current liabilities	29
Other current assets	92	Total current liabilities	901
Total current assets	1,531	Long-term debt	436
Fixed assets	893	Other long-term liabilities	189
Total assets	2,424	Equity	898
		Total liabilities and equity	2,424

The Revlon Group, a corporate predator from New York, launched a hostile attempt to take over Gillette.[34] Part of the reasoning was that Gillette had more current assets than it needed and fewer current liabilities (not to mention debt) than it was able to carry.

---

33. GILLETTE COMPANY, 1985 ANNUAL REPORT.
34. GILLETTE COMPANY, 1986 ANNUAL REPORT.

As for current assets, Revlon reasoned that it could run Gillette with far less cash than the $473 million Gillette had. It also reasoned that it could collect on Gillette's receivables more rapidly by extending less credit to buyers. If it could cut days receivable from Gillette's then level of 76 days to, say, 43 days (competitor Bic Corporation's level), then it could squeeze $281 million in cash out of the receivables and use that to service or reduce debt. (Although that would be a one-shot event, if Gillette's weighted cost of capital—see chapter 9—were approximately 8%, then going forward with $281 million less in receivables would cost the company $22 million less per year in capital cost.) Similarly, the predators reasoned that the company could squeeze down on its inventory and move toward a just-in-time system. If it could cut inventory from a 173-day supply to an 87-day supply, a level achieved by Bic, then $233 million could be squeezed out of inventory, saving Gillette some $19 million in annual capital costs. If nothing else, savings in the annual cost of capital for incremental inventory and receivables could amount to approximately $41 million.

Similarly, the predators planned on using Gillette's bargaining power with its vendors to obtain more attractive credit terms. If they could extend the days accounts payable from 66 days to 90 days, the company could extend the payables another $115 million and use that to reduce debt, or buy in stock and thereby cut annual capital costs.

Gillette succeeded in warding off the predators, but in 1988, the Coniston Group in New York made a hostile takeover attempt. Gillette borrowed heavily, bought in stock, and fought off this attempt as well,[35] becoming much more leveraged in the process, as discussed in chapter 12.

Long-Term Liabilities

Deferred Tax Liabilities

Deferred tax liabilities (DTLs) can be a fine source of financing. They arise from the government permitting companies to take more rapid depreciation of assets for tax purposes than for GAAP purposes. Essentially, by allowing accelerated depreciation, the government encourages investment in the socially desirable activity of investing in productive capacity in the form of new plants and equipment.

When a company depreciates an asset more rapidly for tax purposes than on its GAAP financials, the pretax earnings under the IRC are less, and therefore the tax due the IRS is less than the tax accrued under GAAP. Because the GAAP financials have a smaller tax shelter (due to the smaller depreciation expense in the early years, as the depreciation is not accelerated), they have a greater pretax income and hence a larger accrued tax expense. The accrued tax expense reduces net income, which in turn reduces the equity account on the balance sheet. To offset the reduction in the equity account (that is, the reduction compared with what the GAAP equity account would have been had the GAAP tax expense been the same as the tax due the IRS), the GAAP books show a DTL. During the later years in the useful life of the asset, the depreciation under the IRC becomes smaller than the GAAP depreciation. When that happens, the GAAP pretax earnings become less than the pretax earnings for tax

---

35. GILLETTE COMPANY, 1988 ANNUAL REPORT.

purposes, the IRC tax due begins to exceed the accrued tax, the GAAP earnings are more negatively affected by depreciation than the IRC earnings, and the DTL related to the particular asset begins to decline, eventually reaching zero. Because companies tend to grow, in most cases the DTL account on the GAAP books never reaches zero, but rather, tends to grow as well. Sidebar 11 illustrates the creation and handling of a DTL.

_____ *Sidebar 11* _____

Explanation of Deferred Tax Liability (DTL)

A DTL is created when (1) there is a temporary difference between an asset's or liability's GAAP basis and its tax basis, and (2) the tax treatment is to the taxpayer's advantage (for example, depreciating a machine with MACRS[36] for tax purposes versus straight line for GAAP). When the difference in basis is unfavorable, it creates a deferred tax asset (for example, nondeductibility of SFAS 106[37] accrued expense for post-retirement benefits other than pensions).

The major circumstances that cause a DTL to decline are (1) "reversals" in subsequent years that reflect narrowing of the GAAP/tax temporary difference (for example, by the time a machine is fully depreciated, the GAAP and tax depreciation amounts are the same and the machine's GAAP and tax basis have narrowed to zero) and (2) disposition of the asset or liability that created the DTL (when the machine is sold, there is no difference to account for).

Among other things, SFAS 109[38] addresses the case of an acquiror that uses the purchase method and, therefore, measures acquired assets and assumed liabilities at their fair value under GAAP. Even though the assets' fair values typically exceed their book values, for tax purposes the assets may retain their old, lower basis rather than the higher GAAP basis (because the IRS does not want greater CGS and depreciation expense amounts). SFAS requires that this be treated as a temporary difference, which means it creates a DTL.

Deferred tax assets (DTAs) operate the same way but in reverse. Whereas DTLs arise when the deductions are greater for IRC purposes than for GAAP purposes, DTAs arise when the deductions for GAAP purposes are greater than for IRC purposes. For example, if a company expenses a worker's compensation claim before it is paid in cash and deductible for IRC purposes, the company's GAAP pretax earnings and accrued tax will be less than the IRC pretax earnings and tax due. Consequently, the company's GAAP after tax earnings will be greater than if the GAAP taxes had been the same as the IRC taxes. The corresponding enhancement to the equity account is matched by a DTA on the asset side of the balance sheet. When the worker's compensation claim is

---

36. MACRS is the acronym for Modified Accelerated Cost Recovery System.
37. SFAS 106 was adopted for fiscal years beginning on or after December 15, 1992.
38. SFAS 109 was adopted for fiscal years beginning after December 15, 1992.

Table 29
Deferred Taxes—Timing Differences in Depreciation

Assume:
1. Asset bought for $100
2. Asset depreciation over 10 years for financial purposes
3. Asset depreciation over 5 years for tax purposes (accelerated)

	Year										Total
	1	**2**	**3**	**4**	**5**	**6**	**7**	**8**	**9**	**10**	**Total**
IRC											
1. Profit before tax and before depreciation	100	100	100	100	100	100	100	100	100	100	1,000
2. Depreciation	20	20	20	20	20	0	0	0	0	0	100
3. Taxable income	80	80	80	80	80	100	100	100	100	100	900
4. Tax due at 40%	32	32	32	32	32	40	40	40	40	40	360
5. PAT	48	48	48	48	48	60	60	60	60	60	540
GAAP											
6. Profit before tax and before depreciation	100	100	100	100	100	100	100	100	100	100	1,000
7. Depreciation	10	10	10	10	10	10	10	10	10	10	100
8. PBT	90	90	90	90	90	90	90	90	90	90	900
9. Tax due (IRC)	32	32	32	32	32	40	40	40	40	40	360
10. Tax expense (GAAP)	36	36	36	36	36	36	36	36	36	36	360
11. PAT	54	54	54	54	54	54	54	54	54	54	540
12. Cash flow (PAT and depreciation)	64	64	64	64	64	64	64	64	64	64	640
13. Tax expense	36	36	36	36	36	36	36	36	36	36	360
14. Tax due (IRC)	32	32	32	32	32	40	40	40	40	40	360
15. Deferred tax* (net change on balance sheet)	4	4	4	4	4	(4)	(4)	(4)	(4)	(4)	0
16. Accumulated deferred tax (as it appears on balance sheet)	4	8	12	16	20	16	12	8	4	0	—

*Amount by which the tax expense calculated in accordance with GAAP exceeds the tax due under the IRC.

in fact paid in cash and the deduction taken for IRC purposes, the DTA declines, with no additional effect on the equity account because it had been enhanced previously.

Long-Term Debt

The cost of long-term debt is discussed in chapter 7. The implication of long-term debt on a company's financial leverage is examined in chapters 4 and following.

Although capital leases are not, strictly speaking, long-term debt, they should for purposes of analysis (and loan covenant definitions) be treated as long-term debt, for they are its functional equivalent. As noted earlier, in some circumstances a company's operating leases should also be capitalized and treated as long-term debt.

Sometimes long-term debt has a market value different from its face value. If a company has borrowed long term and interest rates have risen, then the market value of its long-term debt will have declined. This is not recognized under GAAP unless the company is acquired in a transaction treated as a purchase. In that event the liabilities, as well as the assets, are brought onto the books of the acquiror at their FMVs.

Thus a company could have on its books a $100 debt that has a market value of $90. If the company refinances by borrowing $90 and buying in the debt at $90, it has realized an economic advantage of $10 (exclusive of financing costs). The after tax effect of the $10 is added to the company's net earnings as an extraordinary item. The company could have simply enjoyed the benefit of below market interest rates in future years. However, by refinancing it has agreed to pay higher rates in future years, which will adversely impact future earnings. By refinancing it is bringing that advantage to the present year. Conversely, if interest rates have fallen and the market value of the debt has risen to $110, then the company can refinance by borrowing $110 and buying in the debt. The net is a $10 disadvantage (exclusive of transaction costs). If interest rates have fallen and the company refinances, it will do better in future years than it would have had it not refinanced. However, it is paying for that advantage in the present year, which adversely impacts current earnings. Thus, by refinancing, management can move earnings from one period to another, although in the year of the refinancing the gain or loss will be extraordinary. In subsequent years, however, the consequences of the refinancing—whether in the form of interest rates that are higher or lower than they would have been in the absence of the refinancing—are ordinary.

GAAP requires companies to disclose in an accompanying note the fair value of their financial instruments (assets, liabilities, and unrecognized—that is, off balance sheet—financial instruments). This disclosure can be particularly important for financial institutions. For instance, American Express's 1995 financials include the following information in the notes (please see Table 30 on page 60).[39]

Changes in the value of the debt instruments under the held-to-maturity category do not impact either the income statement or the balance sheet unless the instruments are sold. By contrast, changes in the value of the instruments held on an available-for-sale basis directly impact the shareholders' equity on the balance sheet, even if the gains and losses are unrealized. Notice that in American Express's case, as of year-end 1995 there were $805 million of unrealized gains and $46 million of unrealized losses in the held-to-maturity category. This gave management the opportunity, should it choose, to sell such instruments and take out all or part of such gains or losses into 1995 earnings.

Equity

Stockholders' equity, subordinated debentures, and preferred stock are treated in detail in chapter 8 and elsewhere. Before getting there, however, there is one more major financial statement to analyze, namely the statement of cash flows.

---

39. AMERICAN EXPRESS COMPANY, 1995 ANNUAL REPORT 35.

Table 30
American Express Debt Instruments Held*

Held to Maturity

	1995				1994			
	Cost	Fair Value	Gross Unrealized Gains	Gross Unrealized Losses	Cost	Fair Value	Gross Unrealized Gains	Gross Unrealized Losses
			($ million)				($ million)	
U.S. government and agencies obligations	2,695	2,698	3	–	3,450	3,445	–	5
State and municipal obligations	1,560	1,638	78	–	4,816	4,841	115	90
Corporate debt securities	10,109	10,655	672	36	10,627	10,294	172	505
Foreign government bonds and obligations	63	69	6	–	104	105	3	2
Mortgage-backed securities	2,324	2,360	46	10	2,596	2,386	13	223
Other	129	129	–	–	316	316	–	–
Total	16,790	17,549	805	46	21,909	21,387	303	825

Available for Sale

	1995 ($ million)				1994 ($ million)			
	Cost	Fair Value	Gross Unrealized Gains	Gross Unrealized Losses	Cost	Fair Value	Gross Unrealized Gains	Gross Unrealized Losses
U.S. government and agencies obligations	370	377	8	1	355	344	–	11
State and municipal obligations	3,749	4,027	278	–	312	321	$10	1
Corporate debt securities	4,200	4,410	217	7	3,104	3,007	31	38
Foreign government bonds and obligations	1,655	1,664	25	16	1,618	1,592	11	37
Mortgage-backed securities	8,731	8,932	227	26	8,515	7,977	12	550
Equity securities	863	2,140	1,278	1	732	691	15	56
Other	884	885	1	–	1,366	1,361	8	13
Total	20,452	22,435	2,034	51	15,912	15,293	87	706

*American Express Company, 1995 Annual Report.

The Cash Flow Statement

Chapter

3

By and large, lawyers underuse cash flow statements. Yet they are worth knowing because, if one can see the forest through the trees, cash flow statements show us two things of great importance. First, they disclose whether the company is an absorber of cash or a generator of cash. Second, they give us important clues about what management is doing, wants to do, and—in some cases—must do. By revealing what management does with any discretionary cash, the cash flow statement sends a strong signal regarding the company's strategy.

First, let's have a look at some of the more important trees in the forest. Since 1988, the statement of cash flows (SCF) has consisted of three parts, namely the cash provided by (or absorbed in) operations, the cash provided by (or used in) investing activities, and the cash provided by (or used for) financing activities.

Operating Activities

The cash flow from operating activities shows how much cash (as contrasted with accrued operating profit) the operations generated. Usually the most important source of cash from operations is net income. Two major categories of adjustments to net income are used to determine cash flow. First, all non-cash expenses that were deducted in arriving at net income are added back. Of these, the most important is usually depreciation (see Sidebar 12 for an explanation of why depreciation is a source of cash), and the second most important is usually the increase in the deferred tax liabilities (DTL)—that is, that portion of the tax accrued during the period under generally accepted accounting principles (GAAP) that did not have to be paid in cash to the Internal Revenue Service (IRS).

_____ *Sidebar 12* _____

Why Depreciation Is a Source of Cash

The add-back of depreciation in determining cash flow stems from the asset (usually plant or equipment) being purchased and paid for in an earlier period, but capitalized rather than expensed at the time of purchase. (*Capitalizing* a cost means putting it on the balance sheet as an asset and subsequently depreciating it, rather than treating the full cost as an expense at the time of purchase. See the discussion of capitalization in chapter 1 and Sidebar 6.) During the second and subsequent years, until the asset is fully depreciated, the company accrues a depreciation expense but makes no cash payments. (They were made in the first year, when the asset was bought.) This, as you may have noticed, is a result of having capitalized the asset in the earlier period. Consider a rolling stock company that on January 1 of year 1 purchased a locomotive for $4 million, which it financed by borrowing the $4 million. The company capitalized the asset and depreciates it straight line over 10 years. Ignoring the other assets and expenses, if revenues are $5 million per year and all revenue is collected in cash, then the impact of the foregoing on income and cash flow will be as follows during years 1 and 2.

Table 31
Illustration of Why Depreciation Is a Source of Cash

	Year 1	Year 2
Income Statement		
Revenues	5,000,000	5,000,000
Depreciation	– 400,000	– 400,000
Income	4,600,000	4,600,000
Cash flow		
Income	4,600,000	4,600,000
Depreciation	400,000	400,000
Cash flow from operations	5,000,000	5,000,000
Cash flow from investing	(4,000,000)	0
Cash flow from financing	4,000,000	0
Total cash flow	5,000,000	5,000,000

The other adjustments to net income that are used to determine cash flow from operating activities adjust for the changes in current assets and current liabilities. The *funds flow system* involves the interplay between the company's operations and financing methods, as described in Sidebar 3. When a company first starts out, it raises capital from its shareholders and perhaps from lenders. With the cash thus raised, it buys raw materials (or finished goods in the case of retailers) and hires workers to make the finished goods inventory. To this point, the company is becoming less liquid and is taking the risk that its inventory will be worth more than the cash. When the company sells the inventory, it converts the latter back into cash and re-commences the cycle. Alternatively, if it extends credit to the buyer, it converts the inventory only into an account receivable, which ties up the company's cash until the buyer later pays for the goods. Then the company uses the cash to buy more raw materials, and the process iterates. This process is referred to as the *working capital cycle* or the *operating cycle*. As a company grows, it tends to make more and more inventory and extend more and more credit to its buyers, at a rate that ought to correspond to the company's growth rate. This is one of the ways that growing companies absorb cash. Mature companies tend not to absorb cash this way, as their cash received merely replaces the same levels of inventory with which they began.

As this is occurring on the left side of the balance sheet, a parallel process is occurring on the right side, although to a more limited degree. The company may get some trade credit from its vendors, which shows up on the balance sheet as an account payable—a liability. Every dollar in credit extended by a vendor is a dollar that the company does not have to raise from its shareholders or lenders, and thus it is a source of cash. As the company pays its payables, it uses cash. As it is extended more trade credit, it receives a source of cash.

See Sidebar 13 for a summary description of a SCF.

_____ *Sidebar 13* _____

Description of Cash Flow Statement

Consider Amalgamated Industries, a hypothetical company with $60 million profit after tax in 1997, and a balance sheet for 1996 and 1997 as in Table 32 on page 66.

At this point, you might want to look ahead to Tables 32 and 33 on pages 66 and 67. From the balance sheet and income statement on page 66 (all dollar amounts in millions) we can derive the SCF. First, note that the operations generated some funds, the most obvious source being the $60 in PAT. However, remember that the company calculated PAT on an accrual basis and recorded some sales that may not have been collected in cash. In fact, the accounts receivable are $100, as contrasted with the previous year's $80, which indicates that the company had to extend $20 more in credit to its customers than it did a year earlier. This incremental extension of credit absorbed $20 more cash than a year earlier. Hence the $60 in earnings must be adjusted to reflect this $20 absorption of cash. Another change we can see from the balance sheet is that the inventory rose from $90 to $120. If it had not risen, the company would not have been spending money (that is, using cash) to buy or make more inventory. The rise in the inventory account indicates that, to the tune of the $30 increment, management elected to use cash generated in the business to build or buy more inventory rather than hold the cash or pay it out to investors. Hence this $30 is another adjustment to earnings made in determining the cash flow.

While the receivables and inventory were absorbing cash, management obtained some cash from, among other places, its current liabilities. Specifically, the accounts payable rose from $40 to $75, indicating that suppliers extended more credit than they did a year ago. People refer to this as free money, and sometimes it is because the company does not pay interest on it. However, unless the buyer is extremely powerful, the supplier will at some point exact a price, whether literally in the form of higher prices to reflect the slower payments, or in other ways, such as slower service or favoritism toward other buyers in times of shortage. Further, it is possible that the increase in payables does not reflect slower payment, and the reasons for this are discussed in chapter 2. In any

Table 32
Amalgamated Industries

Balance Sheet and Income Statement for 1996, 1997

Assets	1996	1997	Liabilities	1996	1997
	($ million)			($ million)	
Cash	70	80	Short-term debt	125	150
Accounts Receivable	80	100	Accounts payable	40	75
Inventory	90	120	Other current liabilities	25	25
Total current assets	240	300	Total current liabilities	190	250
P&E	395	450	Long-term debt	195	225
Accumulated Depreciation	(125)	(150)	Deferred tax liabilities	75	85
Net P&E	270	300	Equity	125	140
Other fixed assets	75	100	Total liabilities and equity	585	700
Total assets	585	700			

Income Statement	1997 ($ million)
Revenues	$1,075
Cost of goods sold	650
Gross profit	425
SG&A	300
Operating profit	125
Interest	35
Profit before tax	90
Tax @ 33%	30
Profit after tax	60

> Depreciation is often not separately displayed on the income statement. Here the CGS includes $15 of depreciation on production plant and equipment, and the SG&A includes $10 depreciation on office equipment that is not used in production. Hence, the total depreciation expense is $25.

event, Amalgamated's payables rose by $35, and that was a "source" of cash. If creditors had not extended the incremental credit, management would have needed to find some other way to finance the incremental assets.

In addition to changes in the current assets and liabilities, there were changes in the fixed assets and long-term liabilities. The company invested another $55 in plant and equipment (P&E), in all likelihood reflecting a management judgment that business is good and merits further investment. (Additional investment in new P&E does not always reflect such a judgment. One company that had major investments in the oil and gas business in a third-world country made additional investments—which it did not really want—because the host government wanted new fields developed and threatened to expropriate, or raise the tax rates significantly on, the existing fields if the company did not make further investments in new P&E.) It is possible that the company actually spent more than $55 on new P&E, even though the increase on the balance sheet is only $55. This could occur if the company divested an asset or assets during the year, causing them to disappear from the balance sheet. In that case, the $55 increment is the net of the new expenditures less the divestitures.

The accumulated depreciation also rose $25, from $125 to $150. On the face of it, that would indicate that the accrued depreciation during the year was $25, and it may well have been. However, if the company divested assets during the year, it might have accrued some depreciation on such assets, with the result that its income statement would be impacted by such depreciation. However, as the assets were no longer on the books at year-end, the depreciation relating to such assets (as well as the assets themselves) would not be on the balance sheet. Thus it is entirely possible (even likely in the case of a large company) that somewhat more than $55 was actually spent on new P&E and more than $25 was actually accrued in depreciation. For present purposes, though, we will keep it simple and just use those numbers.

The incremental assets were financed not only with additional current liabilities, but also with some permanent capital. Specifically, the long-term debt increased by $30, from $195 to $225. This may have been a net of some debt repayment and new debt, but for cash flow purposes, what really matters is that on a net basis this was a $30 source of cash. Deferred taxes also rose, by $10. As discussed in chapter 2, DTLs can be a beneficial, and often virtually permanent, source of essentially free capital. Finally, the equity account rose by $15, from $125 to $140. The fact that it rose by less than the $60 PAT indicates that the company used some of its earnings for dividends or stock repurchases, either of which would have been a use of cash.

Putting the foregoing together, then, we can construct a SCF for Amalgamated, mindful that it may not tell the entire story for the reasons discussed above.

Table 33
Amalgamated Industries Cash Flow Statement

Cash Flow Statement		Comment
Cash flow from (to) Operations		
PAT	60	The starting point
Depreciation	25	Cash was not spent on this
Increase in deferred tax	10	Free money from the government
Increase in receivables	(20)	Added credit, absorbed cash
Increase in inventory	(30)	Adding inventory uses cash
Increase in payables	35	Vendors extended more credit
Net cash flow from operations	80	We will look at fixed assets and financing below
Cash flow from (to) investing		
Investment in new P&E	(55)	Company added to P&E
Investment in other fixed assets	(25)	Company added to other fixed assets
Net cash flow from investing	(80)	Total used for new fixed assets
Cash flow from financing		
Increase in short-term debt	25	Company added to current borrowings
Increase in long-term debt	30	Company added to long-term borrowings
Dividends	(45)	Company paid a dividend
Net cash flow from investing	10	
Net changes in cash position	10	
Beginning cash	70	
Ending cash	80	

Keep in mind that the SCF would not be needed if the books were kept on a cash basis. But GAAP seeks more accurate matching of revenues with the corresponding expenses that enabled the company to generate the revenues (and vice versa), resulting in financials prepared on an accrual basis. Because the income statement and balance sheet are based on accrual accounting, and because the SCF begins with net income, adjustments must be made to show how much cash the company generated and how it generated the cash. The SCF also explains how the previous year-end cash account changed to result in the current year-end cash account.

As a company grows it must usually invest, on average, more and more into accounts receivable, inventory, other current assets, fixed assets, and other assets (unless it gets better and better at managing its inventory or unless its costs are declining enough to offset the need for more receivables, inventory, and fixed assets). The incremental investments in such assets absorb cash, reflecting management's decision to invest in these assets rather than hold the cash it collects on sales. This decision reflects management's belief that such an investment provides a better return than (1) investing the cash in cash equivalents such as commercial paper or money market instruments, or (2) shareholders' investing of cash received (net of taxes) as a dividend or in stock repurchases.

Current Liabilities

Not only do current assets rise as the company grows, but so do current liabilities. The liability to watch most carefully is usually accounts payable. If payables are rising, that means the company is financing at least some of the growth in receivables and/or inventory with trade credit from its vendors. If the company were to pay its payables faster and reduce them, then that is a use of cash.

Hewlett-Packard Company, the Palo Alto-based electronics company, had payables at year-end 1994[1] that were $243 million higher than at year-end 1993, essentially reflecting incremental credit from its vendors. Although this represented a 20% increase, it is hardly surprising, inasmuch as revenues had grown 24% during 1994 compared with 1993. An increase of only 16% in Hewlett-Packard's 1994 year-end inventories indicates that the company was slower than it had been a year earlier in paying its vendors. By contrast, in 1996 Hewlett-Packard's accounts payable declined by 2%,[2] even though revenues and cost of goods each had risen during the year by over 2%. This indicates that in 1996, Hewlett-Packard was paying its vendors more quickly, perhaps in return for lower prices or other advantages.

Investing Activities

The second component of the SCF is the company's investing activity. This term usually refers to changes in noncurrent assets, but also encompasses investments in available-for-sale securities. Usually the most important thing to look for here is an increase in P&E, both in absolute terms and relative to prior years.

---

1. Hewlett-Packard Company, 1994 Annual Report.
2. Hewlett-Packard Company, 1996 Annual Report.

One expects companies to be continually reinvesting cash in new productive capacity. If the company is investing heavily in new P&E, that indicates that management sees future opportunities and wants to have the productive capacity available to meet the anticipated demand. Alternatively, if the new investment in P&E represents a smaller increase in P&E than the company's growth rate, one should ascertain the reason. It may be an indication that the company has recently completed a major capital spending campaign. If previous years' cash flow statements indicate a major capital spending campaign, perhaps it has ended, but that ought to be checked with other sources. A decline in capital spending may also mean that the company is not making the investments necessary to sustain and replenish its productive capacity.

It can be difficult to spot a migration of capital from one segment to another based on the financials alone, unless the patterns are extreme. However, even modest changes in these patterns can be a tip-off that a qualitative inquiry using other sources might be fruitful. If one is reviewing a management discussion and analysis (MD&A), the inquiry might involve no more than a call to management. However, a litigator may need to use other sources, such as industry publications or the client's knowledge.

If the investment is in new fixed assets that represent a transition away from the company's core business (such as AMR Corporation, the holding company for American Airlines, Inc., as discussed in Sidebar 14, on page 71), that is an important development that ought to be discussed in (or gleaned from) the MD&A or other narrative disclosure document. If a company is in multiple business segments, then the allocation of new P&E among those segments can be useful information.

GAAP requires disclosure of operating profits, revenues, and assets on a segment basis, as well as operating profits and revenues on a geographic basis. The segment numbers can be useful to detect a company deploying discretionary cash into one segment more heavily than others, reflecting a shift to different segments. For instance, from 1987 to 1989, Dow Chemical Company actually reduced the assets devoted to its chemical and performance products (such as caustic soda and coatings), while increasing by 39% the assets devoted to plastics; it generally has been committing more capital to higher margin businesses and migrating, albeit slowly, away from commodity chemicals.[3] Similarly, allocation of less cash into fixed assets than in the past indicates that a company is trying to migrate away from a particular business and seek better returns elsewhere.

Financing Activities

The third category of a source or use of cash is financing activities. This portion of the SCF shows how a company is financing its investing activities and any negative cash flow from operations. Usually this section reveals a combination of some dividends paid, some sale of stock on exercise of options, and some new debt.

---

3. Dow Chemical Company, 1989 Annual Report.

Table 34
Consolidated Statements of Cash Flows

Home Depot, Inc. and Subsidiaries*

	Fiscal year ended January 29, 1995 ($ thousand)
Cash provided from operations:	
Net earnings	604,501
Reconciliation of net earnings to net cash provided by operations	
Depreciation and amortization	129,609
Increase in receivables, net	(69,023)
Increase in merchandise inventories	(405,197)
Increase in accounts payable and accrued expenses	280,056
Other	(5,433)
Net cash provided by operations	534,513
Cash flows from investing activities:	
Capital expenditures, net of $31,183, $36,294, and $4,765 of non-cash capital expenditures in fiscal 1994, 1993, and 1992, respectively	(1,100,654)
Acquisition of Canadian partnership interest	(161,548)
Proceeds from sale of long-term investments	403,738
Other	104,184
Net cash used in investing activities	(754,280)
Cash flows from financing activities:	
Proceeds from commercial paper and long-term borrowings	100,000
Proceeds from sale of common stock, net	77,926
Cash dividends paid to stockholders	(67,792)
Other	10,790
Net cash provided by financing activities	120,924
Decrease in cash and cash equivalents	(98,843)
Cash and cash equivalents at beginning of year	99,997
Cash and cash equivalents at end of year	1,154

*Home Depot, Inc., 1995 Annual Report.

When new growth is being financed, usually the SCF reveals a sale of stock or debt. In some cases there are unusual wrinkles. For example, Home Depot, Inc., an Atlanta-based home improvement retailer, generated $535 million from its operations in fiscal 1995 but spent $1.1 billion on capital expenditures, in addition to making a $161 million acquisition. It financed this $700 million gap by selling some $500 million in securities and debt issued by other companies and by borrowing in the commercial paper markets.[4] Had it not had the securities and debt issued by third parties, it would have needed to sell some other assets (such as locations), borrow more, or make an equity offering. Home Depot's 1995 SCF is set forth in Table 34.

---

4. HOME DEPOT, INC., 1995 ANNUAL REPORT.

A Tale of Two Companies

One of the most critical distinctions among companies is whether they are generating cash or absorbing cash. This distinction is revealed most clearly in the SCF.

_____ *Sidebar 14* _____

Cash Generator or Cash Absorber?

A highly valuable piece of information to ferret out of a SCF is whether the issuer is investing more, less, or about the same amount of cash in its business than its operations generate.

As discussed in the text, in the early and mid-1990s, Home Depot was clearly a cash absorber, growing 35% a year and needing more cash for new locations and inventory than its operations were generating. Happily, in 1995 it generated earnings of $604 million on average assets of $3.2 billion, a 19% return on assets.[5] Any time a company can generate that kind of return it ought to commit as much capital as it can to the business. (Much more will be said about such matters in chapters 4 and following.)

Standing in contrast to Home Depot is Maytag Corporation, the Newton, Iowa, employer of the lonely Maytag repairman. In 1994 Maytag spent $79 million on capital expenditures, which is a lot of change, but not a lot compared with the $148 million generated by its operations.[6] The reason, in a nutshell, is that it did not need much more productive capacity. Whereas Home Depot was growing hand over fist, Maytag's sales grew a total of only 10% over the five-year period from 1990–1994, indicating that its revenues were not even keeping up with inflation. In response, Maytag in 1996 put on a push to grow.[7]

A slightly different story is told by AMR Corporation, the holding company of American Airlines, Inc. The airline industry has been chronically plagued by excess capacity and low profitability. AMR has the misfortune of competing against low-cost carriers, and the good fortune that UAL Corporation, the parent of United Airlines, Inc., did not respond affirmatively to American's call—taped by the FBI—seeking to initiate a price fixing agreement between the two airlines. In any event, in 1993, AMR adopted its *Transition Plan* to keep its options open in the airline business while building its other businesses, most notably its Sabre group in the information technology area and its management services group.[8] Although revenues for AMR grew only 2% in 1994, its Sabre group's revenues grew 13% and its management services group's revenues grew 18%; each enjoys substantially better operating margins and return on assets than does the airline business, at least in most years. Hence, although

---

5. *Id.*
6. MAYTAG CORPORATION, 1994 ANNUAL REPORT.
7. MAYTAG CORPORATION, 1996 ANNUAL REPORT.
8. AMR CORPORATION, 1993 ANNUAL REPORT.

AMR generated $2.7 billion in cash from its operations in 1996, it made only $0.5 billion in capital expenditures for new P&E. From 1992 through 1996 it drastically cut back its capital expenditures, and between 1991 and 1994 did not order a new jet aircraft, although in 1996 it placed firm orders with Boeing Company for 103 aircraft. A growing portion of its capital expenditures is in its nonairline businesses, where the company hopes to earn better returns. In short, AMR is a company that may very well be migrating, or at least threatening to migrate, from one business to multiple businesses.

In 1994, Gillette Company's revenues grew 12% and its operations generated $805 million. Gillette spent $400 million on new P&E and still had $405 million left over. It used that excess to increase its dividend payments from $183 million to $219 million. During 1994 Gillette's return on assets was $694 million on assets of $5.5 billion, or 13%,[9] which is excellent. One can surmise that if the company had been able to build more plants and buy more equipment on which it could have earned 13%, it would have done so. Yet consider Gillette's businesses—chiefly razors, blades, and toiletries. The only ways to grow revenues in these businesses more rapidly than the inflation rate (about 3% in 1994) plus the population growth rate (1% in the United States and close to 2% worldwide in 1994) are to (1) increase prices, (2) increase market share, (3) move into new geographic markets, or (4) move into new business segments.

Taking these in reverse order, Gillette has moved into new business segments over the years (a generation ago it was almost exclusively a blades and razors company), but moving into new business segments is risky, and the company's success in doing so has been mixed.[10] It has been more successful moving into new geographic markets; the opportunity for significant new growth there is modest, although not inconsequential, and is an important strategic thrust for the company. Taking market share from others is usually more difficult than growing businesses in new industries, and Gillette is in mature businesses in which its competitors are strong (such as Bic Corporation in disposable shavers and writing instruments, and Colgate-Palmolive Company and a host of others in toiletries). And raising prices more rapidly than the inflation rate poses the risk of business being lost to competitors. Gillette's 12% increase in revenues is commendable under the circumstances. But the point is that this growth rate did not require or permit enough incremental investment in fixed assets and working capital to absorb all the cash generated by operations—Gillette is a prototypical cash generator, or "cash cow," to borrow a phrase.[11]

A dramatic example of a company at the opposite end of the cash flow spectrum is provided by Reebok International, Ltd., in its halcyon days a decade ago. From 1980 to 1985 its revenues grew from $1.3 million to $307 million—a 236-fold

---

9. GILLETTE COMPANY, 1994 ANNUAL REPORT.

10. For instance, in 1996 Gillette's operating profit in blades and razors was $.41 for every $1.00 in assets, as contrasted with $.10 for every $1.00 invested in stationery and Oral-B products. Its operating profit in Latin America was $.19 for every $1.00 in assets in 1996, which was a below average year in Latin America for Gillette, although currency swings make comparisons difficult.

11. Gillette acquired Duracell, Inc. in 1996 and made other acquisitions in 1995 and 1996, which involved commitments of $300 million and $278 million, respectively.

increase. In 1985 its earnings were $39 million, but its incremental receivables and inventory alone were $58 million and $44 million, respectively, amounting to over $100 million. When one considers that Reebok also had to add to its other assets to support its expanding operations, it should come as no surprise that the company did a $42 million equity offering to finance its growth.[12]

By contrast, Intel Corporation is in a rapidly growing field and is using all the cash it can generate from operations—and then some—to finance its revenue growth, which averaged 35% from 1994 through 1996. In 1996 its net income was $5.2 billion, and its cash flow from operations was $8.7 billion.[13] Because its return on average assets was a handsome 25%, and because its industry was growing rapidly, Intel found ample opportunities to build new P&E to support projected future sales, as witnessed by its October 1995 announcement of plans to build three new semiconductor plants, estimated to cost some $4.5 billion.

Does Cash Flow Have to Be Positive for a Company to Be Creating Value?

Reebok raises a very important and interesting question. Clearly during the 1980–1985 period its cash flow was negative. Yet does that mean it was not creating new value for its owners? It began the 1980s with approximately $168,000 of capital invested by its owners, and by 1986 the shares owned by these individuals (plus those issued in its $42 million initial public offering)[14] had a market value of $615 million. More recently, in the early 1990s, a few individuals invested $11.3 million in Shiva Corporation, the Massachusetts builder of remote access networks. As late as 1995 its cash flow was negative, mainly because it was investing in new P&E and equipment.[15] But the value of the shares held by the early investors had risen to approximately $900 million (albeit the stock price dropped precipitously in mid-1997), which clearly indicates that the investing public believed that Shiva, like Reebok before it, was creating value despite its negative cash flow. The converse question also arises. If a company has a positive cash flow, does that necessarily mean it is creating value? These questions will be addressed in chapters 11 and 12.

Before leaving the discussion of cash flow, we ought to address some definitional questions. Specifically, though the terms *cash flow* and *free cash flow* are often used in financial parlance, there are no hard and universally agreed upon definitions of these terms. Hence in any particular context it can be important to identify exactly how the user of the terms is defining them.

Not infrequently, the term *cash flow* is used to refer to a company's after tax income plus depreciation and less any increase in working capital (or plus any decrease in working capital); *free cash flow* is used to refer to cash flow less any new capital expenditures. There are two refinements on these definitions, however,

---

12. REEBOK INTERNATIONAL, LTD., 1980–1995 ANNUAL REPORTS.
13. INTEL CORPORATION, 1996 ANNUAL REPORT.
14. REEBOK INTERNATIONAL, LTD., 1980–1986 ANNUAL REPORTS.
15. SHIVA CORPORATION, 1995 ANNUAL REPORT.

which may or may not be intended by the user of the terms. First, many—especially more sophisticated—people and institutions will unlever the company's after tax income; that is, calculate what it would have been had the company been debt-free. Second, many will reason that if the company is going to remain in business then it must constantly invest in new P&E, even if only to replace worn-out P&E. The upshot of this reasoning is that because such investment is not discretionary, depreciation (at least to the extent needed to sustain existing levels of production) should not be added back to determine free cash flow. These important and interesting refinements are treated in chapters 9 and following.

Interpreting the Financials

Chapter
4

Introduction

Companies serve multiple constituents, most notably customers, employees, and owners, but also vendors, neighbors, lenders, tax collectors, and others. From a financial standpoint, the primary constituent consists of the owners. Investors use a number of measures of financial performance, virtually all of which are explained below. Of these, the most widely used by investors is return on equity, as measured by profit after tax divided by shareholders' equity. (There are refinements on this measure that are being adopted by a growing number of sophisticated investors, and they are explained and examined in chapters 6 and following.)

The DuPont Formula

During the 1910s and 1920s, the legendary Alfred P. Sloane, CEO of DuPont and later of General Motors Corporation, developed the *DuPont Formula.* Some balk at the use of the term, contending that the financial realities it describes exist, just as gravity exists, and for DuPont to put its name on the formula is a misnomer. Be that as it may, the DuPont Formula asserts that return on equity is a function of three variables, namely net margins, asset turnover, and financial leverage, as shown in Table 35.

Margins

As explained in chapter 1, there are four kind of margins: gross margins, operating margins, pretax margins, and net margins. Each reveals something different about a company. Gross margins are the best place to look if one wants to know how much a company marks up the goods and to understand pricing policy (or how high or low a ceiling the market is putting on prices). Operating margins enable one to make the most accurate assessment of how well the company is running its operations regardless of how it is financed. Pretax margins reflect financing because they are net of interest expense. Finally, net (or after tax) margins show how well a company has done for its owners after taking care of all other claimants—including vendors, employees, lenders, and tax collectors.

Table 35
Summary of DuPont Formula

	Definitions
$\dfrac{PAT}{S} \times \dfrac{S}{A} = \dfrac{PAT}{A}$	PAT = Profit after tax
	S = Revenues
	A = Assets
$\dfrac{PAT}{S} \times \dfrac{S}{A} \times \dfrac{A}{E} = \dfrac{PAT}{E}$	E = Equity
	PAT/S = Net margins
	S/A = Asset turnover
$\dfrac{PAT}{A} \times \dfrac{A}{E} = \dfrac{PAT}{E}$	A/E = Financial leverage
	PAT/A = Return on assets
	PAT/E = Return on equity

As is intuitive, high net margins are better than low net margins. However, there are some very successful companies that have low net margins, and there are industries in which net margins are almost always low. Stop & Shop Supermarket Company, for example, the New England supermarket chain (which in 1996 was acquired by Royal Ahold, the Dutch global food retailer), is very successful, providing a 25% return on average equity in 1995, which was a rather typical year.[1] Yet its net margins were a mere 1.9%, which would be very poor in most industries but is outstanding in the grocery business. By contrast, pharmaceutical companies tend to have very high net margins. For the years 1992 through 1996, Merck & Company, Inc.'s net margins averaged 22% (ignoring the non-cash portion of the 1993 restructuring charge).[2]

This contrast between Stop & Shop and Merck reflects the difference in the underlying businesses. Food spoils if it is not sold, so the grocer prices the food low, figuring that he or she will make up for it with volume. By contrast, once a pharmaceutical firm has Food and Drug Administration (FDA) approval and/or a patent for a drug, it has a government-granted monopoly, which keeps out competitors, at least until another company gets FDA approval for a competitive drug and designs around any patent.

When in 1977 SmithKline Beckman (renamed SmithKline Beecham after its 1989 merger with the United Kingdom-based Beecham Group) received FDA approval for Tagamet, the first effective treatment for ulcers, SmithKline generated $1 billion in revenues from Tagamet and could price it high without fear of competition.[3] The company's earnings rose from $90 million in 1977 to $160 million in 1978, and to over $460 million in 1982, the year before Glaxo introduced Zantac, the first directly competitive product. The stock price rose from $20 per share in 1977 to $84 per share in 1981, when it declined some 25% in anticipation of competition from Glaxo. Once Glaxo received FDA approval for Zantac in 1983, SmithKline's margins declined. Whereas during the 1978 to 1982 period SmithKline's net margins were running as high as 19%, (reflecting its entire portfolio of pharmaceutical products, of course), they declined to 14% in 1986 in the face of competition from

---

1. Stop & Shop Supermarket Company, 1995 Annual Report.
2. Merck & Company, Inc., 1992–1996 Annual Reports.
3. This discussion of SmithKline Beecham is based on an internal Dickie Group research report dated December 21, 1995.

Zantac. Thus the pharmaceutical industry is competitive in terms of developing new products, which compels investment in research and development. The entire pricing strategy is different from the food industry, and the difference is reflected in the margins.

Asset Turnover

However, even with low margins the grocer may be highly successful—indeed more successful than some companies in the pharmaceutical business. Hence, if you knew only that a company had 3% net margins, you would not know whether it was a phenomenally successful grocer or a highly unsuccessful pharmaceutical company.

The difference lies in the asset turnover. Actually, the term is a bit of a misnomer. Though it might better be called something like *asset efficiency* because it is a measure of how wisely the company has deployed its asset base to generate a revenue stream, the term *asset turnover* is the one used.

Let's consider two retailers, each with the same goods, the same prices, and the same inventory turnover. One must do business in a very upscale building on Fifth Avenue to lure customers, whereas the other can generate the same revenues and the same net margins from a much more modest location. It may be counterintuitive, but the latter is almost surely getting the best return on its investment, assuming, of course, that it really generates the same revenues and margins as the retailer in the upscale location. The reason is that the investment in the Taj Mahal-like facility requires capital, which means that the retailer must either borrow and incur interest expenses or suffer equity dilution to enable it to occupy the facility that, in turn, enables it to generate the inventory turns. The other retailer needs far less capital and thus need not finance nearly as much in the way of noninventory assets, thus incurring far less interest expense or equity dilution.

To measure how effectively a company has deployed its assets to generate a revenue stream, boards, management, and financial analysts will consider a company's asset turnover, as measured by the revenue to asset ratio. Another way of looking at this is to reason that for a given asset base it is better that a company generate a higher—rather than a lower—level of revenues, or, conversely, that a company generate a given revenue level with a smaller—rather than a larger—asset base.

Return on Assets

Now that you understand return on sales and asset turnover, it is a short step to understand return on assets, an important measure of how well a company is running its business. To be sure, one can measure return on assets directly by dividing the company's profit after tax[4] (PAT) by its total assets.[5] For a more refined assessment, one can

---

4. When it is important to isolate the strength of a company's operations without the effects of financial leverage, such as when one wants to compare the operating strength of competitors, the better measure to use is operating profit divided by assets. For present purposes we will use the profit after tax figure, because we are not trying to compare the company with others in its industry.

5. Particularly if a company is growing rapidly, one ought to look at earnings relative to beginning or average assets or equity rather than year-end assets or equity. The same reasoning applies here. Especially if a company is growing rapidly, one ought to measure return based on beginning or average equity.

unbundle return on assets into its two component parts, return on sales and asset turnover. It does not really matter whether a company generates a good return on assets as a result of high margins, high asset turnover, or a combination thereof. But by unbundling the return on assets into its component parts, one can determine whether the company's key to success is in its margins or its asset turnover—that is, whether it is more like a grocer or a pharmaceutical firm.

For example, both Royal Ahold (the Dutch supermarket chain that bought Giant Food, Inc. in the Washington D.C. area, Stop & Shop in New England, and numerous other food retailers on four continents) and Wisconsin Energy Corporation (the dairy state's major utility) have a return on assets of 4% to 5%.[6] However, each achieves this result very differently. As shown in Table 36, Ahold has low margins, although at 1.7% its margins are very good for a grocer. Yet it is not very asset intensive, relatively speaking, and has a revenue to asset ratio of 2.5. By contrast, Wisconsin Energy's 12% margins are much higher, but its asset intensity is so great that its asset turnover is only 0.37. Thus Ahold achieves its performance with good turnover, Wisconsin Energy with good margins.

	Table 36				
	Return on Assets (1996)				
Company	**Net Margins**	×	**Asset Turnover**	=	**Return on Assets**
Royal Ahold*	1.76%	×	2.46	=	4%
Wisconsin Energy**	12.2%	×	.37	=	5%

*Koninklijke Ahold, 1996 Annual Report.
**Wisconsin Energy Corporation, 1996 Annual Report.

Before proceeding further, it is useful to check how the company has deployed its assets. This can be done quite simply by calculating for each category of assets the percentage of total assets it constitutes. An example of that is provided in Table 37.

Notice that the utility has 64% of its assets in plant and equipment (P&E), even after depreciation has been deducted. By contrast, Liz Claiborne, Inc., the woman's apparel company, has 83% of its assets in current assets and only 16% in P&E. This difference reflects the realities of the two businesses. Wisconsin Energy operates in a regulated world (though the utility business is rapidly becoming much more competitive because new technologies are making possible much wider geographical and economical distribution of power than previously). Although regulation limited the returns available to Wisconsin Energy, it historically reduced risk by insulating the company from competition, or at least limiting exposure to competition and providing the company with near monopoly power. Thus Wisconsin Energy has historically been able to invest heavily in P&E without being exposed to undue risk of having noneconomical assets. Even many companies in unregulated industries are P&E intensive due to the very nature of their businesses, such as steel production com-

---

6. Koninklijke Ahold nv in zaandam, 1996 Annual Report; Wisconsin Energy Corporation, 1996 Annual Report.

Table 37
Allocation of Assets (1996)

Capital Intensive versus Non-Capital Intensive Companies

	Wisconsin Energy*** (%)	Liz Claiborne**** (%)
Cash	—*	38
Receivables	6	12
Inventory	4	25
Other current assets	1	8
P&E**	64	16
Other fixed assets	25	1
Total assets	100	100

*Less than 1% but not zero
**Net of depreciation
***Wisconsin Energy Corporation, 1996 Annual Report.
****Liz Claiborne, Inc., 1996 Annual Report.

panies, cruise lines, cable television companies, or hotel chains. In general, a heavy investment in P&E is riskier than not having such investment, as will be examined below on pages 90–96 in the discussion of operating leverage.

By contrast, Liz Claiborne's balance sheet is much more nimble. The company anticipates that 83% of its assets will be converted to cash within a year.[7] As the

Table 38
Examples of Capital Intensive Businesses*

Industry	Company	P&E** as a Percent of Total Assets
Airlines	Southwest Airlines Company	80
Auto rental	Avis, Inc.	77
Casinos	Circus Circus Enterprises, Inc.	67
Cruise ships	Kloster Cruise Lines***	88
Freight	CSX Corporation	80
Paper	International Paper Company	47
Pipelines	Williams Companies, Inc.	76
Steel	U.S. Steel Group****	61

*1996 data
**Net of depreciation
***1994 data (company has since gone private)
****A unit of USX

7. Because 83% of Liz Claiborne's assets are classified as current assets (see Table 37), under GAAP management must anticipate that all such assets will be converted into cash within 12 months.

current assets are converted to cash, management will have frequent opportunities to decide whether it wants to shift direction and deploy its cash doing something other than designing and marketing women's clothing, and consequently it could become quite a different company in a few years. Such flexibility makes sense in an industry as fickle as clothing, where fashions and consumer preferences change rapidly. Thus there is, as there ought to be, a careful match between the nature of a business and the way the company deploys its assets.

Sidebar 15

Return on Assets in the Professional Services Firm

Usually the return on assets in professional services firms is quite high, at least as measured by generally accepted accounting principles (GAAP). An important reason for this is that their assets tend to be low, usually consisting of telecommunications and electronics equipment, furniture, perhaps some paintings and other tangible assets as well as a minor amount of inventory, an often all-too-large investment in receivables, and varying amounts of cash. However, what GAAP does not seek to measure or put on the books is the professional services firm's most important asset—its people.

In assessing the performance of the professional services firm, one ought to try to capitalize the human resources of the professionals, or at least the partners or (if it is incorporated) the owners of the firm. To date, the accounting profession has not developed a system for doing so, although in the early 1980s several companies began developing present value measures for their human capital and including them in footnotes to the financial statements.

Return on Division Assets

Many companies are in more than one business, and each business may have a very different profile in terms of margins, turnover, and return on assets. In analyzing a company, whether for internal purposes or from the outside, it can be highly useful to determine where the company is generating its earnings. The task is certainly easier with internal company documents but, to a degree, depending upon the company, it can be done from the outside with some effort. GAAP requires that segment data be reported if 10% or more of either income or assets is derived from the segment.

The usefulness of segment-reported analysis is well illustrated by Dial Corporation, the Phoenix-based maker of soap and other consumer products. In 1994, Dial (which later changed its name to Viad) had net income of $140 million on revenues of $3.5 billion and assets of $3.8 billion. That looks simple enough—net margins of 4% and nearly the same return on assets.[8]

The segment data,[9] however, reveals an interesting pattern that has major implications in terms of Dial's return on assets and its corporate strategy. Dial had

---

8. DIAL CORPORATION, 1994 ANNUAL REPORT.
9. *Id.*

	Whole Corporation	Consumer Products ($ million)	Travel, Leisure and Payment Services
Operating profit	286 (100%)	160 (56%)	58 (20%)
Assets	3,781 (100%)	887 (23%)	1,830 (48%)
Operating profit / Assets	8%	18%	3%

Table 39
Dial Corporation Segment Data 1994*

*Excludes service businesses

$286 million in operating income, over half that amount ($160 million) from its consumer products. Yet only 23% of its assets were invested in consumer products. Nearly half its assets (48%) were invested in the travel, leisure, and payment services businesses, most of it in the cruise ship business, which generated operating income of $58 million, a poor 3% operating return on assets.

Moreover, it may well be that the cruise lines actually lost money but that this was obscured by solid earnings in the payment services business, a small credit card and travel check business owned by Dial. To be sure, it is possible that the cruise lines made a little and that the ships made such good collateral that Dial could make up for the thin margins with heavy financial leverage. Yet the returns are so much better in consumer products than in travel, leisure, and payment services that one would expect Dial to invest as much as it could in the former and still get the same level of return on assets. In sum, as Dial shows, segment data can tell us, or at least give us an important indication concerning, where a company is making money and where it is not.

Segment data can also help ferret out management decisions to migrate from one business to another. Dow Chemical Company illustrates this point, even though its asset base has considerable P&E that depreciates over a long period and thus makes it slow to change directions. As shown in Table 40, Dow Chemical has four business segments, namely chemicals and performance products (mostly chemicals such as chlorinated solvents, caustic soda, and de-icing fluids), plastic products (mostly thermoplastics used in a wide variety of markets, such as packaging, flooring, and automotive), hydrocarbons and energy (petroleum derivatives such as olefins, styrene, power, and steam, mostly used by Dow's other businesses), and consumer specialties (agricultural products, pharmaceuticals, and products such as Ziploc bags and Saran Wrap).

In 1987 Dow's chemicals and performance business accounted for 34%, and consumer specialties accounted for 19%, of Dow's assets (excluding corporate level assets unallocated to the divisions). By 1994, however, these ratios had more than reversed, and consumer specialties had become the heavier area of investment, with 37% of the company's assets, as contrasted with only 19% invested in chemicals and performance products. Over that seven-year span, Dow had increased its asset base in the chemical and performance products business by a mere 2% (not even keeping up with inflation), but had more than tripled its investment in the consumer specialty

Table 40

Dow Chemical Company's Industry Segment Data

Dow Chemical 1987 versus 1994*

(Percent of corporate total excluding corporate and unallocated assets)

		Chemicals and Performance		Plastic Products		Hydrocarbons and Energy		Consumer Specialty	
				($ million)					
Operating income	1987	708	(31%)	1,036	(51%)	173	(9%)	385	(17%)
	1994	592	(25%)	1,131	(48%)	74	(3%)	762	(32%)
Assets	1987	3,966	(34%)	3,676	(32%)	1,737	(15%)	2,175	(19%)
	1994	4,051	(19%)	5,782	(28%)	3,455	(17%)	7,582	(37%)

*May not add to 100% due to roundings and corporate eliminations; Dow Chemical Company, 1994 Annual Report.

business.[10] This appears to reflect a management decision to migrate the business away from cyclical and generally low-margin commodity chemicals that have been Dow's historic meat and potatoes, to the less cyclical and higher-margin consumer products business. However, appearances can be deceiving. The above reasoning, though compelling, is not quite conclusive for two reasons, both having to do with segment earnings.[11] First, the allocation of corporate overhead can be handled in a way to gross up the earnings of one segment at the expense of another. For instance, if Dow wanted to make its consumer specialty segment look stronger, it could allocate a disproportionate share of the corporate level overhead to the other businesses. The second way it might do so is to have other segments sell to consumer specialty units at below market level prices (or buy from those units at above market level prices, though this is unlikely simply because consumer specialty products are sold to distributors or retailers, not chemical businesses).

A parallel analysis can be made for geographic segments, although the conclusions regarding profitability are more tenuous because many companies go to considerable effort to allocate expenses and use transfer pricing (that is, the prices at which products and services are exchanged among divisions or other operating units) to minimize overall tax liability. For instance, assume a company might otherwise enjoy its best returns in France but France has a particularly high tax rate. If the French unit purchases materials from other units, the prices might be set high, to enjoy the revenues and profits at the vendor unit's level rather than at the French unit. Over the past 10 to 20 years, tax treaties and exchange of information among governments have made this practice more difficult and have forced companies to be relatively realistic, but the practice still occurs, although to a much lesser degree than a generation ago. Nonetheless, drawing inferences—especially about earnings—from

---

10. DOW CHEMICAL COMPANY, 1987–1994 ANNUAL REPORTS.

11. More recent information confirms the inference. Although subsequent restructuring and acquisitions make longitudinal comparison of segment performance more difficult, management has been positioning Dow more heavily in higher-margin specialty chemicals and less in basic chemicals. *See, e.g.,* Susan Warren, *Dow Chemical Aims to Escape Industry's Down Cycles*, WALL ST. J., Dec. 17, 1997, at B-4.

public data concerning segment information must be done carefully. It is still often worth examining the geographic data, partly because in some cases the patterns are dramatic, and also because at least the allocation of assets numbers can indicate a decision to migrate assets from one part of the world to another.

Sometimes the matter of where a company is making money is quite subtle. A great example is Brad Regan, Inc., a tire retailer in Charlotte. Its 1995 income statement was as follows:

Table 41	
Brad Regan, Inc.	

1995 Income Statement*

	($ thousand)
Net sales	236,975
Miscellaneous income	14,167
Total revenues	251,142
Cost of goods sold	165,850
Selling, general, and administration expenses	80,397
Interest expense	2,485
Total costs	248,732
Pretax profit	2,410
Provision for income taxes	1,054
Net income	1,356

*Brad Regan, Inc., 1996 Annual Report.

This looks rather simple—a tire discounter making 0.6% net margins. But tucked away in Note 3 was material revealing that the $14,167 in miscellaneous income included $11,902 in finance charge revenue, apparently on the company's average accounts receivables of some $69 million.[12] That means the company was selling the tires approximately at cost and making money by extending credit and charging credit card rates. How much the company was making or losing on tires— and it certainly was not making much, if anything, and may well have been losing money—depended upon how the company allocated selling, general, and administration (SG&A) expenses between its tire and lending businesses.

The notes further revealed that Brad Regan was majority owned by Goodyear Tire & Rubber Company.[13] So one of two things may have been occurring. First, Goodyear may have been charging Brad Regan above market level prices, taking the profits at the tire maker's level, and using Brad Regan to get into the lucrative credit card rate lending business. (If this was the case, then consider whether the minority shareholders' rights were being abridged.) The other possibility was similar in terms of Brad Regan making money as a lender, but different in that Goodyear may have

12. *Id.*
13. *Id.*

been charging Brad Regan discount prices to get volume and allocate its fixed cost at the tire-making level across more units, a topic that we will explore further in our description of operating leverage later in this chapter.

Managements find segment and similar data highly useful. Before turning to the particulars, however, a bit of background may be useful. Since World War II, a great many American companies have adopted a divisional structure. Briefly, the history of this goes back to the period between World War I and World War II, when the improving transportation system enabled companies to grow. Some executives decided it would also be wise to diversify, to insulate their core corporate earnings from downturns associated with the business cycles inherent in the core businesses. As geographic expansion and diversification occurred, many headquarters managements found themselves too physically remote from the individual businesses to be effective decision makers in each of them. In addition, with responsibility for a large and expanding number of product groups, they found themselves inundated with too much information to make good decisions on a timely basis. Accordingly, they created divisions and pushed profit responsibility down. In many cases, the changes became a great deal more complex than mere division creation. Some companies, such as General Electric Company (the largest highly diversified company in the country), have become so large that they have sectors, each of which has multiple groups, each of which has multiple divisions. Because a thorough review of corporate structure is beyond the scope of this book, suffice it here to observe that many companies have gone to division-type structures, pushing profit responsibility down from headquarters closer to the markets. Sometimes the terms *divisionalize* or *divisionalization* are used to refer to the segments, groups, divisions, or other units below headquarters to which profit responsibility has been given.

Beginning in the 1970s, some companies, later followed by many others, measured division performance by tracking the earnings before interest and taxes (EBIT) relative to the assets of (or sometimes by the capital deployed in) each division. This measure was useful for two reasons. First, companies wanted to allocate their next dollar of investment where previously invested capital had done the best. Only by measuring this return would management be able to do so. Even then, at times the best performance was in businesses that could not effectively absorb significantly more assets, as illustrated by Dial's consumer products division and by Gillette, discussed earlier.

Second, the measure was useful for evaluating and developing managers. Making line managers responsible for return on assets has often had a powerful effect. FMC Corporation, a large diversified company based in Chicago, implemented this change in the late 1970s and found that division performance improved markedly.[14] Division management found they could improve performance not only by getting earnings up, but also by getting their asset base down; that is, by not asking for a new plant unless they were sure they could earn a good return on it.

Although the change had a positive and lasting impact on division performance at FMC, within two or three years such impact had run its course. The next step the company took was to mark assets to their market value when it was not prohibitively expensive to do so, with land being the prime example. Previously, one division man-

---

14. Interview with Dial's inside counsel, in Phoenix, Arizona (Dec. 7, 1994).

ager always argued that the division's largest plant really needed all the many acres the company owned, on the chance that the division might at some point want to expand and use the land. After division management found that its compensation was impacted by having the excess land in its asset base for purposes of calculating the division's return on assets, it took a fresh look at the land, concluding it could be sold and that any future growth could be handled by using a fraction of such land and perhaps adding another story to the existing plant. The company then sold the land and used the proceeds to invest in other of its businesses.[15] Simply removing the idle land from the division's asset base improved its return on assets.

Having measured divisions based on EBIT divided by assets employed, FMC then put two refinements on this, one designed to calculate a division's capital cost and the other to impute an income tax to the divisions. As for the former, FMC headquarters began to impute a cost of capital to the business. (The details of how to calculate a cost of capital are discussed in chapters 7, 8, and 9. Important here is simply whether headquarters assesses divisions a charge for use of capital.) This meant that division management's evaluation would be based on earnings after a capital charge but before tax divided by capital employed, rather than on earnings before interest and taxes divided by capital employed.[16]

The second refinement on gauging division performance based on EBIT relative to invested capital is that, rather than measure returns before taxes, one can impute the corporate tax rate or, preferably, determine what the income taxes would be if the business were a freestanding company. Thus one can derive an after tax return on assets for each segment.

Except in those rare cases where these two refinements have been implemented, counsel will find that division managements are far more conversant with concepts and measurement of EBIT (or EBITDA, discussed in chapter 1) to capital employed (or an equivalent measure—terminology and details vary slightly among companies) than PAT divided by equity. That is because headquarters has, in effect, said to divisional managers, "We will be your banker, Internal Revenue Service, and Securities and Exchange Commission. You just run the operations." Consequently, if counsel is representing division management in, say, a leveraged buyout or litigation, counsel ought to remain mindful that the managers are likely to be unfamiliar with concepts of financial leverage, tax considerations, or expectations of equity investors.

Financial Leverage

The difference between return on assets and return on equity lies solely in the way a company is financed. There are many measures of financial leverage. For loan covenant purposes, leverage is usually measured in terms of debt to equity

---

15. *Id.*
16. Two schools of thought exist about whether a cost of capital ought to be imputed to a division. One school of thought holds, logically enough, that the cost of capital ought to be imputed and ought to reflect the business of the division. For instance, if a utility holding company with a low cost of capital acquires a software company with a high cost of capital, the utility managers ought not be charged with the high capital costs of a software business. The other school of thought holds that the differences in capital costs are rarely significant enough to justify the internal squabbling that often accompanies an attempt to distinguish among businesses.

ratios, because lenders are less interested in the overall performance of the company than in having a cushion of equity or other junior securities subordinated to their debt.

There can be some adjustments to GAAP accounting in defining debt and equity. For example, some lenders will capitalize operating leases, and some borrowers may argue that deferred tax liabilities are equity. Hence, in writing loan covenants, counsel for the lender and borrower may disagree on the appropriate definition of debt and equity.

In assessing a company's performance, one can look simply at a company's return on equity, and one often does. However, for a more refined and penetrating analysis, it is useful to identify how a company makes its money—is it via high margins, high turnover, or high leverage (or some combination thereof)? Banks, for example, have thin margins and are asset intensive, but are very highly leveraged, usually with assets of 15 to 20 times their equity bases. (Their degree of leverage is regulated by the Federal Reserve or other federal or state authority, depending upon where they are chartered.) Citicorp, for example, had $281 billion in assets and $16.3 billion in equity as of year-end 1996,[17] amounting to an asset to equity ratio of 14.

The amount of leverage suitable for a company is an extremely complex and important issue, and there is no universally correct answer. The subject is treated in detail in chapters 9 and following. It is important to note here that, although higher leverage means higher returns to equity holders, some companies would be ill-advised to become financially leveraged and ought to be financed purely with equity (except perhaps for some short-term credit against approved accounts receivable).

For example, Powersoft Corporation, a software company founded in the late 1980s in Concord, Massachusetts, and bought in 1994 by Emeryville, California's Sybase Inc., did not even have revenues until 1990. It was financed with $8 million from venture capital sources and went public in 1993, taking in $38 million more in equity.[18] Even after it had revenues, Powersoft financed itself virtually exclusively with equity because it was so unproven, and its industry so volatile, that it did not want to risk not being able to service the debt if it had any. That is, the core business was simply too risky to take on financial leverage. To be sure, many ventures are financed heavily with debt, often with equity kickers. The reasons for this vary but often have to do with tax considerations and/or the wish of outside investors to exercise tight control, even without a majority stake, should the venture falter.

By contrast, as explained in more detail in chapter 12, Gillette Company took on an enormous debt load in 1988, but its business was so stable there was little chance Gillette would be unable to service the debt. As a result of borrowing an incremental $1.2 billion and using the proceeds to buy in stock and reduce the equity account, Gillette's return on equity rose dramatically[19] (see Sidebar 16).

---

17. CITICORP, 1996 ANNUAL REPORT.
18. POWERSOFT CORPORATION, 1993 ANNUAL REPORT.
19. GILLETTE COMPANY, 1988 ANNUAL REPORT.

_____ **Sidebar 16** _____

Gillette Company's Performance from 1987 to 1991

From 1985 to 1988, Gillette, seeking to ward off a pair of hostile takeover attempts, borrowed $1.2 billion and used the proceeds to buy in shares of its stock—essentially substituting debt for equity on its books. It successfully warded off the takeover attempts, and in the ensuing years it used its cash flow to pay down its debt, thereby reducing its financial leverage.

Throughout the period its business remained stable, as reflected in its margins and turnover remaining almost constant. As the company paid down the debt its interest expense decreased, thereby slightly increasing its net margins. However, as Gillette used the cash flow from its business to pay down debt from 1988 to 1991, its leverage declined, and, along with it, its return on equity declined.

Table 42
Gillette Company's Performance*

	1985	1986**	1987	1988	1989	1990	1991
Net margins	6.7%	5.2%	7.3%	7.5%	6.8%	8.5%	9.1%
Asset turnover	1.01	1.11	1.16	1.25	1.23	1.18	1.21
Return on assets	6.6%	5.7%	8.0%	9.3%	8.45	10.0%	11.0%
Financial leverage	2.70	5.51	4.56	inf.***	44.5	13.9	3.4
Return on equity	18%	32%	38%	inf.***	373%	138%	37%
Long-term debt	$436M	$915M	$839M	$1,675M	$1,041M	$1,046M	$742M

*Gillette Company, 1985–1991 Annual Reports.
**After reversing the effect of the non-cash portion of a restructuring charge in 1986.
***Infinite due to the book equity being negative.

Note that in 1988 Gillette's equity account became negative. That was because the company used the proceeds of $840 million in new debt to buy in stock. As it bought in stock, its cash account on the left side of the balance sheet declined and its retained earnings account on the right side of the balance sheet declined in identical amounts. Because the sums spent to purchase shares exceeded the equity account, the latter became negative, albeit only for GAAP purposes. The shares continued to have value. When the takeover attempts began in 1985, Gillette had 31 million shares outstanding at a market price of $64 per share, a market capitalization of $2 billion. By year-end 1988, when the second hostile takeover attempt was over, Gillette had 137 million shares outstanding (the stock repurchases had been more than offset by a series of stock splits) at a price per share of $35, a market capitalization of $4.8 billion, and shareholders had received $1.5 billion from the company in return for shares sold back to it, a combined value of $6.3 billion.[20]

Other companies, including FMC Corporation, Shoney's, Inc.,[21] Service Merchandise Company, Inc.,[22] and others have done comparable refinancings of a nature described in chapter 11. In such cases, when GAAP equity becomes negative, boards of directors and counsel must exercise extreme caution, for the laws of many states impose personal liability on board members—of companies incorporated in those states—who approve paying dividends or redeeming stock if the company is insolvent or would thereby be rendered insolvent. When Shoney's paid its extraordinary $583 million dividend, each member of its board was subject to personal liability under the Tennessee Business Corporation Act if, after giving effect to the dividend, the company would not be able to pay its debts as they came due in the usual course of business, or if the company's assets would be less than its total liabilities.[23] As is the case under the corporation laws of many states, under the Tennessee law the balance sheet test may be based,[24] in the discretion of the corporation, on either the financial statement prepared in accordance with GAAP or on a fair valuation or other method that is reasonable under the circumstances. Service Merchandise's board used the latter balance sheet test and relied heavily on the opinion of a real estate appraiser regarding the fair market value of the corporate real estate. Based on such opinion the board approved a massive dividend, even though for GAAP purposes its equity account was rendered negative by the dividend payment.

The effects of a negative net worth (for GAAP purposes) on a company's position relative to the federal bankruptcy laws and the applicable state fraudulent conveyance statutes must be considered with extreme care in situations such as these. As illustrated by Service Merchandise, some state laws use the book value test, and some permit a company to measure net worth based on fair market values. Even in the latter cases, boards and counsel must act with extreme caution, from both a substantive and procedural standpoint.

Measuring Return on Equity

There are two situations in which measuring return on equity requires particular care and specific adjustments in addition to those explained in later chapters. These situations occur if the company is growing fast or if the company did an equity offering during the year.

Fast-Growing Companies

A good example of some simple calculations needed to determine return on equity for a fast-growing company is provided by Reebok International, Ltd., the Massachusetts-based athletic shoe company, during its rapid growth in the mid-1980s.

---

20. Gillette Company, 1985–1988 Annual Reports.
21. Shoney's, Inc., 1988 Annual Report.
22. Service Merchandise Company, Inc., 1989 Annual Report.
23. Shoney's, Inc., Proxy Statement for Special Meeting of Shareholders to be Held June 23, 1988 26 (1988).
24. Tennessee Business Corporation Act, Tenn. Code Ann. § 48-16-401 (1988).

Table 43
Reebok Return on Equity 1984

	1983	1984
	($ thousand)	
Net income	667	6,145
Equity (year-end)	771	6,832
Return on beginning equity	647%**	790%
Return on average equity	153%**	162%
Return on ending equity	87%	90%

*Reebok International, Ltd., 1984 Annual Report.
**1983 beginning equity was $51 million.

One can see from Reebok's financial data, set forth in Table 43, that in 1984 Reebok earned $6.1 million on shareholders' equity of $6.8 million, constituting a return on shareholders' equity of 90%. Because the company increased its revenues nearly tenfold and its equity account from $771 thousand to $6.8 million, management surely would have argued that it would be unfair to measure its performance based on year-end equity, for the equity account achieved that level only by virtue of the hard work and fine performance of management, and management and the company ought to be evaluated by the return on the equity that management was given to work with, namely the beginning equity. This line of reasoning would indicate a return of $6.1 million on beginning equity of $771 thousand, or a return on beginning equity of 790%. Though Reebok's returns by any measure were spectacular, there is a material difference between its return on ending equity and return on beginning equity. A counter to the management perspective is that on average during the year, management had something more than the beginning equity to work with, because rather than pay dividends from the earnings as they accrued, the owners left the earnings in the business. Hence a compromise position would be to evaluate management and the company based on the return on average equity (here 162%). For average equity, one can use (1) the average of the beginning equity and ending equity, (2) the average of the beginning equity and ending equity of each of the four quarters, or (3) the average equity measured at other points in time, such as every business day of the year, if one has that information.

If a company is growing rapidly, management could contend that it may take six months, a year, or even more, depending on the business, from the time the company commits new assets to the business until the time such assets generate revenues and earnings. If, for example, the company begins on January 1 to build a new plant for the manufacture of semiconductors, it may very well be some 18 months until the plant is generating revenues and profits. In such event, it may indeed be unfair to evaluate management even on the basis of returns on average equity; the yardstick of return on beginning equity may be reasonable.

More important than taking sides on this issue, the purpose here is to recognize it and suggest that whichever measure is used, it ought to be used consistently. However, that is not to suggest that the shareholders are indifferent about how long it takes a plant to get up and running, for the time value of money favors rapid action.

Accordingly, to align the incentives of management and the shareholders, it makes sense to evaluate management on the basis of the return on owners' capital even if the new plant is not yet operational. The problem then is to avoid deterring management from requesting capital for good projects. The way to encourage management is to have incentive plans that prompt long-term, rather than short-term, planning.

Equity Offerings

One must also exercise caution in measuring return on assets or return on equity if a company did an equity offering during the year. To illustrate, Powersoft Corporation, the software company discussed earlier, had earnings of $8 million in 1993 on year-end equity of $50 million, a 16% return. However, it did a $38 million stock offering during the year and was not able to put most of the new cash to work in the business in time to earn a return on it during the year. To be more precise, if we subtract the interest income from Powersoft's 1993 earnings and subtract the proceeds of its initial public offering (IPO) from its equity, the earnings drop to $7.5 million but the equity drops to $12 million. Thus the return on equity invested in the business is not merely a solid 16%, but a nearly spectacular 63%.[25]

Operating Leverage

There is another variable at work that can mightily impact the amount of financial leverage a company ought to have, and it is known as operating leverage. Operating leverage is high if a company's fixed costs are a high percentage of total costs, and low if they are a small percentage of total costs. Of course, fixed costs can be anywhere on the spectrum from low to high, and pinning down precisely which costs are fixed and which are variable is difficult, if not impossible, even for skilled cost accountants inside the company.

Understanding operating leverage helps us understand the impact that changes in sales volume have on profits. The critical variables are price per unit sold (P), the number of units sold (N), the variable costs per unit sold (VC), and the total fixed costs (FC). Keep in mind that all these are on a per unit basis, except fixed costs and profits, which are firm-wide numbers. The relationship is captured by the following formula:

$$\text{profit} = N\ (P - VC) - FC$$

(Profits can be pretax or after tax, depending upon whether one has built taxes into the formula.)

To see how this works in practice, consider an airline with fixed costs of $10 million per year (consisting primarily of depreciation on the aircraft, fuel, personnel, and interest costs), and average variable costs and revenues per passenger of $50 and $250, respectively. Thus each ticket sale contributes $200 toward covering fixed costs and, once the company has reached the break-even point, to profits. For any given volume of ticket sales, one could use the above formula. For instance, if 60,000 tickets were sold, then the profit would be as follows:

---

25. Powersoft Corporation, 1993 Annual Report.

profit = 60,000 ($250 − $50) − $10 million

profit = $12 million − $10 million

profit = $2 million

By contrast, if only 40,000 tickets were sold, then the same formula would tell us that the company would lose $2 million.

One could chart these relationships, as illustrated below.

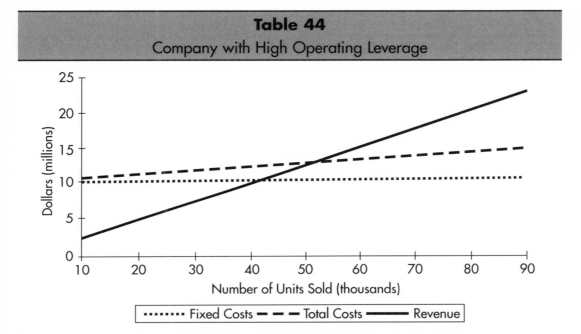

Table 44

Company with High Operating Leverage

.... Fixed Costs ▬ ▬ ▬ Total Costs ▬▬▬ Revenue

Table 45

Impact of Volume Changes on Profits

Volume (units)	Volume (% increase)	Profits ($)	Profits (% increase)
10,000	—	(8M)	(33)
20,000	100	(6M)	(50)
30,000	50	(4M)	(100)
40,000	33	(2M)	(infinite)
50,000	25	0	—
60,000	20	2M	infinite
70,000	16	4M	100
80,000	14	6M	50
90,000	12	8M	33

At zero volume, fixed costs of $10 million are incurred and remain constant regardless of the number of units sold. By contrast, variable costs start at zero, for if no customers appear, no variable costs are incurred. Revenues begin at zero and rise in increments of $250 until full capacity is reached.

The point at which the total revenue and total costs lines cross is the break-even point, the point at which the company experiences neither profit nor loss. This is a crucial point for management and investors to discern. The break-even point can be determined mathematically by applying the following formula:

$$\text{Break even volume (in units)} = \frac{FC}{P - VC}$$

A critical point regarding break-even analysis is that the impact a change in unit volume has on profits is magnified as operating leverage rises. In other words, once a firm with high operating leverage is above the break-even point, another unit of sales makes a greater contribution to profit than is the case for a company with less operating leverage. For instance, notice in the above example that if the number of tickets sold rose by 16%, from 60,000 to 70,000, the profits rose by a larger proportion, from $2 million to $4 million, or 100%. Contrast that with another airline that has lower operating leverage—using older aircraft, nonunionized personnel, and no-frills service—driving its fixed costs down to $5 million. Let's assume there was no impact on variable costs, but to attract passengers the company offers lower prices, an average of $150 per passenger. Its volume to profitability relationship is as follows, in Table 46.

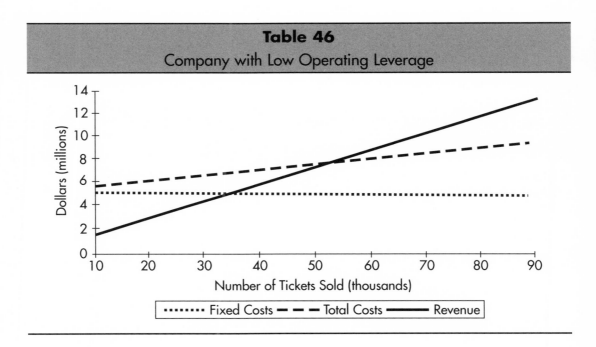

Table 46
Company with Low Operating Leverage

Table 47			
Impact of Volume Changes on Profits			
Volume (units)	**Volume** (% increase)	**Profits** ($)	**Profits** (% increase)
10,000	—	(4M)	(33)
20,000	100	(3M)	(50)
30,000	50	(2M)	(100)
40,000	33	(1M)	(infinite)
50,000	25	0	—
60,000	20	1M	infinite
70,000	16	2M	100
80,000	14	3M	50

Comparing the volume/profitability charts of the two airlines, each has the same break- even point at 50,000 passengers, but the no-frills airline has less operating leverage. If each airline sells 60,000 tickets, the upscale airline enjoys a profit of $2 million, whereas the no-frills airline enjoys a profit of only $1 million. That is the beauty of operating leverage. Above breakeven, each dollar in incremental revenue contributes more to the bottom line than is the case with less operating leverage. The downside, however, is equally potent. If only 40,000 tickets are sold, the no-frills airline holds its losses to $1 million, whereas the upscale airline loses $2 million.

The closer a company is to breakeven, the greater the profit impact of volume changes. For instance, when the upscale airline increases the number of tickets sold from 60,000 to 70,000, its profits double. However, when it increases the number of tickets sold another 10,000, from 70,000 to 80,000 (effectively moving away from the break-even point), the profits increase only 50%, and so on, and the same is true on the downside. In short, the closer a company is to the break-even point the more sensitive the profits are to changes in revenues, and higher operating leverage magnifies this phenomenon.

As an aside, the analogy of the airlines to law firms is interesting. As many lawyers know, the profitability of a firm can be captured by the following formula, each component of which can be managed to influence the net income per partner:

NIPP = (1 + L) (U) (BR) (R) (M) The firm must manage all 5 factors.
NIPP = net income per partner
L = leverage, as measured by the number of nonpartners per partner
U = utilization, as measured by the average number of hours billed per lawyer
BR = average billing rate per lawyer
R = realization, as measured by the percentage of billings collected
M = margins, as measured by revenues less expenses

You can see that as a law firm's leverage (L) rises, its net income per partner rises. This is intuitive once one realizes that the most important assets of a law firm are its partners; leveraging them is akin to a company leveraging its assets. Once a firm establishes its degree of leverage, the challenge becomes to increase its utilization, billing rates, realization, and margins. Pricing by firms has also become more complex than previously.

Returning to the airline example, there are three elements of the operating leverage relationship, namely price, variable costs, and fixed costs, which are under the influence, if not the control, of a company's management. Price has an impact on the volume of revenues, of course, and is a highly important element of a corporate strategy, albeit often the least well understood. Suffice it here to note that changes in prices often impact the competitive environment. Competitors might meet price cuts (causing the industry to lose money or earn less than before), match price increases (causing all competitors to make more unless demand drops), or decline to go along with price increases (likely causing the price change initiator to either roll back the price increase or lose volume).

$$profit = N\ (P - VC) - FC$$

The above formula tells management what it must do to meet earnings targets; the levers it can use to influence the outcome are all embedded in that formula. Changes in any variable can be charted or run through the profitability formula to determine their impact on profits. For instance, if the upscale airline is operating at break-even volume of 50,000 passengers and wants to increase its profits to $2 million, clearly one way is to sell 10,000 more tickets. However, if the marketing specialists advise senior management that increased sales are unlikely and that the company should plan on ticket sales and prices remaining at the 50,000 and $250 levels, respectively, then management must work the other levers, namely fixed and variable costs. One can test how much each of these would need to be reduced to meet the earnings targets by turning the formula around and asking, in effect, "If we want profits of $2 million, and if price and volume are not going to change, how much do we have to reduce fixed and variable costs, respectively?" In the case of the upscale airline, one could first test for the extent to which fixed costs must be held down.

$$\$2\ million = 50,000\ (\$250 - \$50) - FC$$

Solving the equation for the new, necessary fixed cost level shows that the company would have to drive its fixed costs down by $2 million, from $10 million to $8 million. Management's job then becomes translating that mandate into action, such as by trimming routes, negotiating better and less costly contracts with labor or port authorities, or the like. If that is not feasible or is undesirable, the other alternative is to drive down the variable costs. The profitability formula

$$\$2\ million = 50,000\ (\$250 - VC) - \$10\ million$$

tells management that it must reduce variable costs by $40, to $10 per passenger. Such a conclusion also translates into an imperative to cut costs, in this case variable costs such as food service and travel agents' commissions. To be sure, these variables operate simultaneously and management can use several levers at once. Rather than managing only one lever, financial planning can incorporate multiple simultaneous changes.

Although the term *variable* cost is often used, it is more accurate to speak and think in terms of *incremental* costs. The reason is that at some point companies must make major investments to service one more customer. At some point the hotel cannot accommodate another guest, the airline cannot fly another passenger, and the steel mill cannot produce another ton without adding fixed costs. Thus, in practice, the break-even charts are as follows.

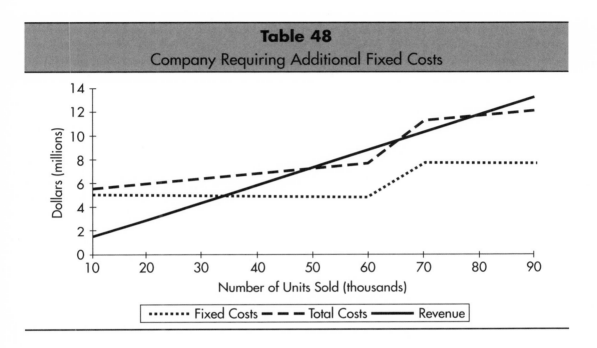

Table 48

Company Requiring Additional Fixed Costs

Although the pricing formula has difficulty distinguishing between variable and incremental costs, spreadsheets—such as those described in subsequent chapters—can do so. The distinction is particularly important in terms of pricing policy, where management must be very cognizant of the points at which significant increments in fixed costs must be undertaken to serve the next customer.

The degree of operating leverage can have major implications for how a company ought to be financed. Some businesses—such as hotel chains, cruise lines, airlines, and pipelines—almost inevitably have high operating leverage, simply because the business requires a large asset base and huge costs that must be met even if no customers turn up. By contrast, some companies—such as real estate managers and providers of janitorial services—have comparatively few fixed costs. If customers do not turn up, the companies can lay people off and hunker down until times improve, which puts the company in a much less risky position.

Thus, if a company has high operating leverage, adding financial leverage might be particularly unwise. Not only do interest expenses add to the fixed costs and hence the operating leverage, but if revenues turn down, the company has far less slack (because lenders can push the company into bankruptcy) and is at greater risk of going bankrupt. Companies with high operating leverage are generally not advised to take on much financial leverage unless they can be confident they will be operating above breakeven.

However, companies that can find ways to squeeze the risk out of having operating leverage are wise to take on both financial and operating leverage. For example, if a company can use contracts with customers to assure itself of having a revenue stream that will be above breakeven, build patent protection that will lock out competitors, or develop a market share so large that it virtually assures break-even volume, then not only is high operating leverage advisable, but so is high financial leverage.

Thus, there are three categories of risk: pure business risk (which is the risk that customers will not buy enough of the company's products and services to provide the company with a sufficient revenue stream to cover all its expenses), operating leverage (which may or may not be controllable, or may be controllable only at the margins), and financial leverage (which magnifies the PAT on the upside, but also the risk of bankruptcy on the downside). As the one easiest for management to control, financial leverage ought to key off the other two. The incentive to use high financial leverage is there, as the companies with the highest return on equity are those with high operating leverage and high financial leverage. Yet that is a position only for a company confident that the revenue stream will enable it to operate above its break-even volume.

Introduction to Valuation

Chapter
5

Measuring value is one of the most interesting, important, and challenging tasks in finance. Value is defined here to mean the fair price that a willing buyer would pay a willing seller for a company or a portion of a company (such as a division).

Nearly everything said in chapters 1 through 4 pertained to the past—that is, the historic performance of the company. We could logically take that very same analysis and apply it to the future for purposes of valuation. Most measures of value involve estimating or projecting future returns to the business's owners and then assessing the present value of those returns. That involves a combination of three factors:

1. the size of the future returns,
2. when those returns will be received, and
3. the risk the investor takes to get those returns.

Each of these elements will be examined in detail in the following chapters. What makes the valuation process difficult is that it pertains to the future, which involves uncertainties. There are numerous techniques of valuing companies, and some are more suitable in certain situations than others. This chapter provides an orientation for some basic techniques, while chapters 6 through 11 discuss more advanced and widely used methods.

The Legal Context

Valuing companies has taken on greater significance in recent years in the legal arena. Under the corporate laws of most states, the business of the corporation is to be managed by or under the direction of a board of directors. *The Corporate Director's Guidebook*[1] suggests that the board has a duty to evaluate the performance of the corporation, senior management, and the board itself. The Delaware chancellor has indicated

---

1. AMERICAN BAR ASSOCIATION, CORPORATE DIRECTOR'S GUIDEBOOK (2d ed. 1994).

his belief that the board has a duty to monitor the performance of the corporation and senior management on a continual basis and "should have an active role in the formulation of long-term strategic, financial and organizational goals of the corporation and should approve plans to achieve these goals."[2]

When litigation arises or is threatened, it often involves the sale or proposed sale of a business, and the allegation is usually that the board or its members had a conflict of interest or were grossly negligent. To be sure, it is no defense for a director to maintain that the value of the business was, let's say, $300 million, even if that is correct, for the adversary's point will be that but for the directors' actions the value would have been higher. Having said that, there may well be times when a director would like the opportunity to point to a good analysis, done by the company before the alleged misconduct, calculating the value of the business and identifying the factors to which such value was the most sensitive. If the conduct or inaction complained of could be shown to have had comparatively little, or very doubtful, impact on value as seen prospectively, the directors might well be on firmer legal ground than if the ability of the board to identify the impact of its action on shareholder value were exclusively qualitative and conceptual. That is not to say that qualitative thinking cannot be powerful and valuable; rather, when coupled with good quantitative analysis, qualitative thinking can be even more compelling. Chapters 11 and 12 illustrate this point.

Lawyers and board members are often interested in methods for valuing companies because of the large volume of transactions in which companies, or parts of companies, are being purchased and sold. For instance, consider what happened in late 1995 when Moore Corporation, a Toronto-based office supply company, made a hostile offer to acquire rival Wallace Computer Services, Inc., of Hillside, Illinois, at $30 per share (adjusted for a 1996 stock split), which was above Wallace's market price.[3] Wallace's board rejected the offer, and a year later its stock was languishing at some $28 per share. Although the shareholders overwhelmingly supported the acquisition and tendered three-quarters of all the outstanding shares, because the board rejected the offer they are out (1) the premium (some $74 million), (2) the possibility of a bidding war, and (3) the opportunity to invest the proceeds of the sale in a market that has risen 20%. Moore filed suit in Delaware against Wallace, but the federal court ruled that the Wallace board had acted within its discretion and may overrule shareholders in a takeover battle as long as it made a reasonable assessment of the company's value. Wallace's board had relied on an opinion of Goldman Sachs & Company, but critics argue that it was a "bought" opinion, a point dismissed by the trial judge; though one is left to wonder why, if Goldman Sachs was right that the $30 offer from Moore was too low, the stock is still trading below that level in a bull market. Even though this case, which has not been appealed, seems to suggest that boards would be protected by relying on an expert's opinion of value, board members might be better off if they have the ability to assess the expert's valuation methodology.

---

2. William T. Allen, *Defining the Role of Outside Directors in an Age of Global Competition*, 16 Director's Monthly 4 (Nov. 1992) (National Association of Corporate Directors).

3. *See* Reed Abelson, *When Boards Say "No Deal" to Holders*, N.Y. Times, Oct. 6, 1996, at 3-1 (contains excellent discussion of this case).

Further Background

The most widely used measure of corporate performance is return on shareholders' equity. This is an important and useful measure, for it tells the reader of the financials how much the company earned with the capital that the shareholders entrusted to it.

There is a subtle but powerful and interesting assumption or axiom in using this measure, namely that earnings correlate with share prices. (Share prices reflect investors' assessment of the value of the issuer.) If you had a choice between earnings and value, which would you choose? Both are important, but of the two, most investors would choose value. Part of the reason why value has been a less preeminent measure is that it has been much harder to measure than earnings. Earnings are important and comparatively easy to measure, and people tend to manage to achieve that which gets measured. Further, earnings usually are a good surrogate for, and generally (but not always) move in tandem with, value creation. In the past five to ten years, the methodology for measuring and monitoring value creation has been improving considerably, even dramatically, due to the aid of computer technology.

Before turning to the leading-edge techniques of valuation, some further preliminaries may be helpful. First, one often encounters an element of ambiguity concerning what is being valued. Ordinarily, one who speaks about the *fair value of a company* means the value of all the company's outstanding securities. (Although most bank debt and other loans do not involve securities as defined in the Securities Act of 1933 and in the law generally, we include them in the definition of securities for purposes of this chapter and following chapters.) That is, one is attempting to determine the value of the interests of all the parties who have provided capital or other consideration to the company and expect a return on it. Although a difficulty arises when the parties have different interests, motivations, or perspectives that cannot be easily reconciled, from a financial standpoint the enterprise has a specific economic value.

Placing a value on a company is an inexact science. Although the methods applied in the attempt are usually mathematically elegant and have many of the indicia of precision, at best one gets only an approximation—an estimate. As will become evident later in this book, it is easier to estimate the value of debt instruments than equity, for their value is likely to be less volatile, if for no other reason than the amount of return is usually fixed in the note or debt instrument. Equally important, one can estimate the value of some companies with much greater confidence than others. If a company has been in the same business for decades, has a growth rate that approximates the rate of inflation plus the population growth rate, faces few but well-known competitors, and occupies an industry with technology that rarely changes, then most sophisticated valuers of the company will not differ very much in their valuations. By contrast, if a company is young, growing quickly, facing an ever-changing list of competitors, and using new technologies, then the difference among the values that are likely to be placed upon the company may very well be considerable. Having said that, let's turn to the basic ways in which companies can be valued.

Valuation Methods

Book Value Method

Usually, the simplest method of valuing a company is the book value method. This involves summing the book values of the capital provided by lenders, equity holders, and any other investors (such as holders of subordinated debentures, preferred stock, and any other hybrid securities), as illustrated in Table 49. An alternative way to calculate the value based on the book value method (which provides exactly the same result) is to begin with total assets and deduct those that are not financed with capital on which any party expects a return; that is, non-interest-bearing liabilities, including deferred tax liabilities, as shown in Table 50. All other assets must be financed with capital on which the company is expected to provide a return, sooner or later.

Quaker Oats Company's 1996 balance sheet (Table 51) can be used to illustrate the book value method. The first way to calculate the book value of its capital is to sum the book value of all investor claims.

Table 49	
Measuring Total Capital—Direct Method	
Short-term debt	$517.0
Current portion of long-term debt	51.1
Long-term debt	928.6
Preferred stock	83.9
Deferred income taxes	238.4
Common equity	1,229.9
Total capital	$3,048.9

The other way, which produces exactly the same result, is to begin with total assets and deduct non-interest-bearing liabilities.

Table 50	
Measuring Total Capital—Indirect Method	
Total assets	$4,394.4
−Trade accounts payable	−210.2
−Accrued payroll, pension, and bonus	−111.3
−Accrued advertising and merchandising	−130.2
−Income taxes payable	− 42.4
−Other accrued liabilities	−292.5
−Other liabilities	−558.9
Total capital	$3,048.9

Table 51
Quaker Oats Company

Balance Sheet, June 30, 1996*

	($ thousand)
Current assets:	
Cash and cash equivalents	110.5
Trade accounts receivable—net of allowances	294.9
Inventories	274.9
Other current assets	209.4
Total current assets	889.7
Property, plant and equipment—net	1,200.7
Intangible assets—net of amortization	2,237.2
Other assets	66.8
Total assets	4,394.4
Current liabilities	
Short-term debt	517.0
Current portion of long-term debt	51.1
Trade accounts payable	210.2
Accrued payroll, pension, and bonus	111.3
Accrued advertising and merchandising	130.2
Income taxes payable	42.4
Other accrued liabilities	292.5
Total current liabilities**	1,354.7
Long-term debt	928.6
Other liabilities	558.9
Deferred income taxes	238.4
Preferred stock	83.9
Common shareholders' equity	1,229.9
Total liabilities and shareholders' equity	4,394.4

*Quaker Oats Company, 1996 Annual Report.
**Net of $69.4 in ESOP-related deferred compensation.

The book value method has several shortcomings, as explained below. Because of these limitations, the book value method is rarely used except when statutorily mandated. Most notably, many state regulatory bodies permit utilities to earn a fair rate of return on their rate base, which is often defined as total capital (that is, debt plus equity, these terms being defined broadly to include hybrid securities), or as the historic cost of the assets less depreciation and deferred taxes.

A significant shortcoming of the book value method is that due to inflation, the cost of the same assets might be greater at present than when the company acquired them (or lower in some cases, such as computing power). Further, even if one were to use replacement cost rather than actual historic cost, the company might not actually buy the very same assets were it to replace them currently. Clearly in the case of telecommunications equipment and computers, a company would generally not do so. Even in more stable industries such as shipping, the company might acquire more up-to-date assets. Hence, even adjusting for present costs of the assets requires judgment calls not universally agreed upon.

Moreover, if the assets have a recoverable amount (that is, the net value realizable from liquidation plus the discounted cash flow from any assets that might be used in any further operations of the business) in excess of their costs, a question arises about whether the liquidation values ought to be used. Consider, for example, a producer of wine, champagne, or brandy, which may have its inventory on its books at cost. Yet, if the fermenting liquor was laid down decades ago at the then cost of grape juice, the liquidation value will be far in excess of its book value. If the appraiser can make a reasonable estimate of its market value, then this estimate will represent a more realistic measure of value than the book value. If the assets are the type that trade on a commodities exchange or other active secondary market, then it might be reasonable to use market value, depending upon the purposes for which the appraisal is being conducted and the constraints under which the appraiser must work.

The single greatest limitation of the book value method is that it ignores the value management may have added to the assets. The whole point of management is to make the assets worth more than their cost. By building and training a work force, by developing a reputation in the marketplace, by learning how to produce the goods or services at low cost, by creating opportunities for expansion, and in other ways, management (and past managements) should have—and in most cases have—created value in excess of the cost or book value of the assets.

If the Securities Are Publicly Held: The Market Approach

If a company's securities are all publicly held, then the sum of the values placed on the securities in the public markets should be close to the value of the company. This method, often referred to as the market approach, is premised on the belief that the market's assessment of value is, on average, more accurate than that of any particular appraiser. To be sure, there are the Peter Lynches, Warren Buffetts, and George Soroses, but, as the efficient market hypothesis has it, they are statistical aberrations. On average, even institutional investors, which are paid to do better, underperform the major indexes because of their fees and brokerage commissions. Only two of five equity mutual funds have outperformed the market over time, and only one of five has done so when sales charges are factored into the calculation of returns. The difficulty lies in knowing in advance which investors or appraisers will be wiser than the market in the future. Thus, in the case of publicly held securities, because the likelihood of any particular appraiser being more accurate than the market is slim, the market approach has much to recommend it.

Though use of the market approach is fine if one is an outside investor, if the valuation is done by the company itself, then looking to the market for valuation is unduly deferential. After all, the market, although in theory endowed with all the material information about the company, does not have as much of this information as management. Hence, management should be able to render a more accurate valuation of the company than the market approach can provide. How management can do so will be explained in greater detail in chapters 10 and following.

You might also hear about internal rates of return in the valuation context. These are not particularly useful, for the reasons discussed in Sidebar 17.

Sidebar 17

The Internal Rate of Return

To calculate the internal rate of return (IRR), one projects the future cash flow of the project or company for as many years into the future as is feasible and for the terminal year. Such cash flow is earned on capital invested. Then one finds the discount rate that makes the present value of the future cash flows equal the amount of capital invested. That discount rate is the IRR.

One drawback to using the IRR is that it does not take into account the amount of capital being used. True, it does reveal whether the rate of return is 20% or 25%, for example, and by itself would steer one to the project that promises a 25% return. However, the project that holds the prospect of a 25% return might earn such a return on a much smaller capital base than the 20% project, and therefore create significantly less value. Thus, by telling us only the rate of return, the IRR methodology stops well short of telling us enough about values.

A related drawback is that the IRR methodology assumes the cash flow from the project can be reinvested at the same rate of return, when in fact this is often not possible.

Minority Discounts and Control Premiums

Regardless of whether a company is publicly or privately owned, or whether one has the benefit of comprehensive inside information, if a transaction involves the purchase or taxation of shares, then a minority discount or control premium may be involved. These are explained in Sidebar 18.

Sidebar 18

Control Premiums and Minority Discounts
by Philip Saunders, Jr., Ph.D.

All shares are equal, but some are more equal than others, to borrow a phrase from George Orwell. The value of the company can be estimated, as described in chapters 10 and 11, but do stockholders share equally in that value? Are the shares of controlling stockholders worth more per share than the shares of the minority? The answer, as will be seen below, is, it all depends.

Reasons for Control Premium

Control confers value. Stockholders holding a controlling interest in a company can determine the nature of the business; select management; enter into contracts; buy, sell, and pledge assets; borrow money; issue and repurchase stock; register stock for public offering; and liquidate, sell, or merge the company. The controlling party can also set management compensation and perquisites, declare (or not declare) dividends, make capital distributions, and control contracts and payments to third parties. In privately held companies, the ability to set compensation is critical, for owner/managers frequently distribute proceeds as compensation rather than dividends, in order to avoid double taxation. Minority stockholders often have minimal influence on these important activities.

Amount of Control Premium

Whether anyone will pay a premium for a controlling interest (a control premium) depends largely upon whether the potential buyer believes he or she can enhance the value of the company. If the company is being run satisfactorily by current management and new ownership could neither do better nor create synergies to increase value, what extra value could be created through acquisition? It is the potential for a new owner to increase value that makes buyers willing to pay a premium for control. Obviously, the size of the premium will depend upon how much incremental value buyers believe can be created.

Following the above reasoning, one would expect variation in the sizes of control premiums, depending upon the particular circumstances of the target companies. That is what one finds in practice. A study of 1997 acquisitions reported 487 purchases of major blocks of stocks in publicly traded companies for which a premium was paid.[4] The premiums ranged from zero to 733% with a median of 27.5% and mean of 35.7%.[5] In addition, premiums were not paid in all cases. Another 49 acquisitions were made at a discount from market.[6] The discounts ranged from zero to 67% and had a median of 6.8% and mean of 12.2%.

Of course, acquisition premiums are not only affected by the potential for increasing the value of the acquisition target. A premium may simply reflect a more sanguine view by the buyer of the prospects of the company than the current owners hold. In addition, depending upon the depth of the market for a particular stock, competition from other potential buyers, and the views and financial needs of the existing stockholders, a buyer may not have to pay as much as he or she estimates the company is worth in order to acquire it. Similarly, low or negative acquisition premiums may be the result of specific needs of the sellers.

In short, the mere fact of control does not lead to any specific premium. In fact, it does not necessarily lead to any premium at all. Logic and the data support the courts in their position that the existence and size of a control premium depends upon the facts of the specific case. If a control premium is to be

---

4. 1998 Mergerstat Review 23 (Los Angeles: Houlihan, Lokey, Howard & Zukin, 1998).
5. *Id.* at 23, 88–151.
6. *Id.* at 88–151.

added in the valuation of a company, the basis for adding it must lie in some identified potential for increasing value in the company, and the size of the premium depends on how much the value can be increased.

There are several ways that a new owner might enhance value. There may be potential synergies between the company and the buyer's other activities, although these synergies are often overestimated (see chapter 12). Perhaps the company is mismanaged, and profitability could be increased by new management. If current management is overcompensated, stockholder value can be enhanced by reducing compensation costs. Another possibility is that the sum of the company's parts is worth more than the whole, and the company can be liquidated at a profit.

In valuing a company, care must be taken to avoid double counting premiums. In the case of publicly traded companies, the market frequently anticipates changes that will enhance value, either because the market expects current management to make the changes or because it expects new management following a buyout. Similarly, in the valuation of private companies, financial statements are routinely adjusted to eliminate revenues or expenses that relate to current ownership but would not exist for a new owner. For example, reported earnings of a company might be $500,000, but the analyst might conclude that the CEO/owner is overpaid and that adjusting the CEO's salary to market would add $100,000 to earnings. The valuation would then be done based upon $600,000 of earnings. Suppose the valuation was being done on the basis of a price/earnings ratio of 5X. The company would be worth $2.5 million based upon unadjusted earnings but $3 million based on adjusted earnings. The extra $500,000 would be the value of a control premium, but would only be a premium over the $2.5 million. Adding it to the $3 million would be double counting. Any control premium should reflect only those enhancements not already taken into account.

Minority Discount

While a premium may be appropriate in acquiring a controlling block of shares in either a public or private company, a minority discount will be relevant only when valuing shares in a closely held company. Publicly traded shares are already priced as minority holdings, requiring no discount from the quoted value of the stock. This is not so for minority shares in a private company.

Reasons for Minority Discount

For all the reasons that a controlling stockholder may enjoy power and economic benefit, the minority stockholder may not. This is not to say that the minority stockholder cannot benefit from the actions of the majority. If the majority sells out at a control premium to a new owner who buys all the stock or succeeds in enhancing the value of the company, the minority owner will share in the gain. However, the minority shareholder in a private company is not generally able to control his or her own destiny, and the value of the minority shareholding is discounted. The depth of the discount will depend on the circumstances.

There are two reasons that the discount can vary. First, there are differences in the ability of minority stockholders to fend off majority oppression or exert influence on the company. In some cases, government regulations, indenture restrictions, contractual obligations, the financial condition of the company, and the realities of the competitive marketplace can restrict the freedom of action of those in nominal control. Moreover, the minority may have more power than the size of its holding would indicate. Statutes, articles of incorporation, or bylaws may require the consent of more than the usual 51% to approve certain actions. A minority shareholding may be enough to constitute a majority when combined with blocks of other shares; having the swing vote can confer power. Cumulative voting for directors can enhance minority power.

The second cause of variation in minority discounts is differences in the extent to which the minority stockholders are economically disadvantaged. In circumstances where a company is well run (that is, management is fairly compensated, financial information is provided, all stockholders receive the same pro rata returns to capital, and in general the minority stockholder enjoys the same benefits as the stockholder in a public company), the minority discount will be less. At the other end of the spectrum, when the minority stockholder has been frozen out, a substantial discount is required.

Minority interests of private companies typically lack marketability. A publicly traded share is in the minority, but it has liquidity. A share in a private company is both in the minority and lacks a market. Conceptually, lack of marketability is a separate attribute from merely being in the minority. However, the data frequently does not allow us to distinguish between minority and lack-of-marketability discounts; the two often become rolled together in analyses and by the courts.

Amount of Discount

Usable statistics on the size of minority discounts are scarce. A variety of types of data have been put forward as measuring minority discounts, and some types are more credible than others. Much of the data does not clearly indicate whether it measures minority discounts—or at least minority/lack-of-marketability discounts—as opposed to something else.[7] Studies in which it is reasonably clear that minority/lack-of-marketability discounts are being measured are of private sales of minority interests in real estate and in private companies.

Although not a perfect fit, minority interests in real estate are comparable to minority interests in corporations, in the sense that they share similar problems of lack of control and illiquidity. Two studies of sales of fractional interests in real estate indicate a wide range of minority discounts (zero to over 80% at the extremes), with the bulk of the discounts clustering in the 25% to 40% range.[8]

---

7. For example, it is argued, in a view not shared by the author, that premiums paid in acquisitions of publicly traded companies measure the value of control per se and that minority discounts can, therefore, be calculated as the mirror images of the premiums.

8. Don L. Harris et al., *The Valuation of Partial Interests in Real Estate*, ASA VALUATION, Dec. 1983, at 66–72; Peter J. Patchin, *Market Discounts for Undivided Minority Interests in Real Estate*, REAL EST. ISSUES, Fall/Winter 1988, at 15.

The other data come from a study of 49 sales of minority stockholdings in private corporations. Unfortunately, the minority discounts reported were from adjusted book values, not from estimates of market values. Although book value is frequently unrelated to market value, the author of the study reported that all the companies in the study had substantial tangible assets, in which case book value was probably close to being a floor for market value. The study showed discounts ranging between zero and 78%, with a median of 39% and a mean of 40%; approximately half were clustered in the 20% to 50% range.[9]

Minority Discounts and Case Law

A minority discount will be relevant in estate and gift tax cases but usually not in minority buyout cases. In tax cases the objective is to establish fair market value, and the courts have long recognized that "minority stock interests in a 'closed' corporation are usually worth much less than the proportionate share of the assets. . . ."[10]

Tax courts have allowed discounts for minority interests, but it has frequently been difficult or impossible to determine whether the discount was being allowed because the shares represented a minority interest, were unmarketable, or both. A survey of selected decisions shows discounts of one kind or another ranging from 10% to 65%.[11] The range for minority discounts, in those few cases in which it was clear what the award was for, was 20% to 35%.[12]

In minority buyout cases the courts have not tried to determine *market value* or *fair market value* of a minority interest, but rather, *fair value*, which is usually only broadly defined in the statutes. Not surprisingly, there has been substantial variation among courts regarding the determination of fair value. In general, the concept of fair value incorporates the notion that the minority shareholder should receive his or her pro rata share of the value of the company.

The rationale is that the need for a judicially ordered buyout is usually triggered by a situation that cannot otherwise be resolved without dissolution of the corporation or by oppressive behavior on the part of those in control. In the first instance, liquidation and distribution of the proceeds would lead to each stockholder receiving a pro rata share, without any discount; when mandating a buyout the court attempts to leave the minority stockholder in no worse position than he or she would have been had the

9. *Survey Shows Trend toward Larger Minority Discounts*, 10 EST. PLAN. 282 (1983).
10. Cravens v. Welch, 10 F. Supp. 94, 95 (S.D. Cal. 1935).
11. IRS VALUATION TRAINING FOR APPEALS OFFICERS at 9-57 to 9-59 (Commerce Clearing House, Inc., 1998).
12. *Id.*

corporation been dissolved. In the second instance, the oppression by the majority would be rewarded, if the minority stockholder did not receive a pro rata share but was subjected to a minority discount instead. Although the courts are not unanimous, minority discounts have not generally been taken in minority stockholder buyout cases.[13]

Bottom-Up Method

In valuing minority interests we have, up to this point in the discussion, valued the company first, and then calculated the minority discount. An alternative approach is to value the minority interest directly, which is sometimes referred to as the *bottom-up method.* In direct estimation, the analyst looks at the stock simply as another investment. The stock pays a dividend, or not, with some degree of regularity. Capital distributions may or may not be expected in the future. The company is in an industry and has a history, financial condition, assets, management, and other attributes that make one confident, or not, that the dividends and the distributions will be paid. The cash from future dividends and distributions can be estimated, and there is some degree of risk that the estimate may be wrong. The projected cash flow can be discounted back to a present value. The discount rate should reflect the degree of risk associated with the projections, as well as the facts that the instrument is unmarketable, lacks control, and is issued by a private company.

In this manner the minority, nonmarketable share is valued by the discounted cash flow method directly as a financial instrument without the need to value the company as a whole or estimate discounts. Although the method sounds neat and clean, it relies upon the correct choice of a discount rate, which can be subjective because, by definition, there is not a market of nonmarketable securities from which to derive the relevant discount rate. Nevertheless, the bottom-up method has considerable appeal, especially when the minority gets very little benefit from its shareholdings or is far removed from corporate control.

Example

A simplified example to illustrate the application of control premiums and minority discounts may be instructive.

---

13. For discussion of the issues and the cases, see Charles W. Murdock, *The Evolution of Effective Remedies for Minority Shareholders and Its Impact upon Valuation of Minority Shares,* 65 Notre Dame L. Rev. 425, 484 (1990) and Christopher Vaeth, *Propriety of Applying Minority Discount to Value of Shares Purchased by Corporation or Its Shareholders from Minority Shareholders,* 13 ALR5th 840 (1993, current through Sept. 1997 Supplement).

Fred Founder owns 60% of Intergalactic Enterprises, Inc. Cousins Larry and Liz own 20% each, but do not work for the company. The company pays dividends. When Larry dies, Intergalactic is valued at $10 million for estate tax purposes.

Table 52	
Minority Discount When Dividends Are Paid	
Company value	$10,000,000
Larry's pro rata share value	2,000,000
Minority discount	20%
Larry's estate's discounted share value	1,600,000

Note: The discount is relatively modest because the company is paying dividends, giving the minority stock an investment value based on yield.

The company stops paying dividends, and soon thereafter Liz dies of unrelated causes.

Table 53	
Minority Discount after Dividends Cease	
Company value	$10,000,000
Liz's pro rata share value	2,000,000
Minority discount	50%
Liz's estate's discounted share value	1,000,000

Note: The discount is greater because the minority holding has lost its investment value derived from the dividends.

Heirs Larry II and Liz II and Fred Founder are now stockholders. Fred sells his 60% to AcquisitionCo. AcquisitionCo is an independent third party, the price is set in arm's-length negotiation, and Fred gets no consideration other than payment for the shares. AcquisitionCo pays a premium because it can enhance the value 20% by making operations more efficient. AcquisitionCo anticipates only arm's-length intercorporate transactions and, thus, has no means of capturing the entire increase in value for AcquisitionCo; the gain in value will be shared with Intergalactic minority stockholders. Consequently, AcquisitionCo pays a premium based only upon Founder's shares (that is, the shares it will actually own), not on the whole company.

Table 54	
Minority Values Increase with Company Value	
Old company value	$10,000,000
Founder's share value	6,000,000
Control premium	20%
Founder's sale price	7,200,000
New company value	12,000,000
AcquisitionCo share value	7,200,000
Larry II's pro rata share value	2,400,000
Minority discount	50%
Larry II's discounted share value	1,200,000
Liz II's pro rata share value	2,400,000
Minority discount	50%
Liz II's discounted share value	1,200,000

Note: The minority shareholder values increase with the value of the company and thus benefit from the acquisition, even though they do not share directly in the control premium and still suffer the same percentage minority discount. Had AcquisitionCo been able to siphon off all the gain in value for itself, there would have been no gain for Larry II and Liz II, and AcquisitionCo could have paid a higher premium for Fred's controlling block. On this different set of facts, however, AcquisitionCo and Fred Founder might have been open to charges of looting, and Larry II and Liz II might have had grounds for suit.

AcquisitionCo brings in Larry II and Liz II to manage the company, which they do for several years, but then Larry II and AcquisitionCo have a falling out and AcquisitionCo fires Larry II, whereupon Larry II sues. The court finds AcquisitionCo breached its fiduciary duty to a minority stockholder and orders AcquisitionCo to buy Larry II's stock with no discount.

Table 55	
Effect of Judgment for Minority Shareholder	
Company value	$12,000,000
Larry II's pro rata share value	2,400,000
Minority discount	0%
Larry II's discounted share value	2,400,000

AcquisitionCo decides it can further enhance value by achieving synergies with its own operations. To that end it wants to own 100% of Intergalactic. Liz II does not want to sell. AcquisitionCo pays a premium for her minority shares just to buy her out.

Table 56	
Minority Value in Buy-Out	
Company value	$12,000,000
Liz II's pro rata share value	2,400,000
Premium	10%
Liz II's share value	2,640,000

If it was not obvious before the example, it should be now: control premiums and minority discounts depend upon the purpose for which the premium or discount is being calculated and the facts of the specific situation. As with so many things in life and the law, God and the devil are in the details.

Use of Comparables

Although the market approach is directly applicable only to companies with publicly traded securities, the method can be used derivatively for private companies, including those that are about to do their initial public offerings. It can also be used for divisions of public or private companies. Specifically, the securities of such private companies can be compared with those issued by companies that are already publicly owned. The concept is simple. If the companies are similar, then the multiples the market puts on their securities ought to be comparable.

Chief executive officers are very familiar with the use of comparables. Many a CEO of a publicly owned company monitors very closely his or her company's performance, especially its return on equity and price/earnings multiple, relative to its competitors. Once I met with the CEO of a conglomerate who had on his entire desk only one sheet of paper. It showed the performance of his company relative to about 20 competitors and look-alikes based on six financial criteria. The measure on which he was focused was the price/earnings multiple. His company's was the lowest. In a plaintive voice he said to me, "I was just up on Wall Street and explained our story to all the big houses, and our stock price didn't move. Why don't they like me?" Like many CEOs, he took the price/earnings ratio very personally.

Not only do CEOs look at comparables, so do the courts. Congress specifically approved the use of comparables in the estate tax area. The Internal Revenue Code (IRC) provides that for purposes of determining the value of the gross estate of a decedent, the value of "stock and securities" of a privately owned corporation "shall be determined by taking into consideration, in addition to other factors, the value of stock or securities of corporations engaged in the same or a similar line of business which are listed on an exchange."[14] The Internal Revenue Service (IRS) Commissioner has ruled that the factors to be considered in each valuation case are as follows:[15]

1. the nature of the business and the history of the enterprise, including the date of incorporation,
2. the economic outlook in general and the condition and outlook of the specific industry in particular,
3. the book value of the stock and the financial condition of the business,
4. the earning capacity of the company,
5. the dividend paying capacity,
6. goodwill,
7. sales of stock and the size of the block to be valued, and
8. the market price of stocks of corporations that are engaged in the same or a similar line of business and are listed on an exchange.

The judicial interpretation of these rules has emphasized the book value, earning power, and dividend capacity of the company, with particular emphasis on the latter two measures.[16] Dividend capacity may, of course, be less than the earning power if a company must use the earnings to finance its growth. Also, the willingness of control parties to declare a dividend may impact the degree to which minority interests ought to be discounted.

In the case of bonds, IRS regulations provide that the value of bonds of privately owned companies should take into consideration the "soundness of the security, the interest yield, the date of maturity, and other relevant factors."[17] The regulations regarding valuing stocks and debt securities of private companies in the gift tax area are virtually identical to the above regulations concerning estate taxes.[18]

Though the legal foundation for using comparables in the estate and gift tax context is clear, using comparables in other areas can present several complications.

Finding Comparables for Debt and Preferred Stock

Happily, the task of finding comparables is far less difficult for debt than for equity. In the case of debt, assuming there is no significant risk of default, the only risk is the interest rate risk. Consequently it is sufficient to find securities, and not necessarily companies, that are comparable. Because the prices and values of debt instruments are a function of the soundness of the security, interest yields, the period until maturity, and the size of the debt, their value can be determined by reference to debt instruments that are comparable by these criteria.

---

14. I.R.C. § 2031(b).
15. Rev. Rul. 59-60, 1959-1 C.B. 237. *See also* Rev. Rul. 83-120, 1983-2 C.B. 170, 26 C.F.R. 25.2512.2.
16. Bader v. United States, 172 F. Supp. 833 (N.D. Ill. 1959); Estate of Victor P. Clarke v. Commissioner, Tech. Mem. 1976-328 (1976); Central Trust Co. v. United States, 62 T.C. 2 (1962). *See also* B. Mandelbaum, 69 T.C.M. 2852 (CCH) 50,687, T.C. Memo 1995-265 (1995).
17. Treas. Reg. § 20.2031-2(f) (Internal Revenue estate tax regulation).
18. Treas. Reg. §§ 25.2512-2, 25.2512-3.

Which Companies Are Comparables?

If one is valuing a company's equity based on comparables, finding comparable companies can be extremely difficult. Ideally the comparables will be pure plays in terms of product lines (and the same mix), capital structure, management strength, competitiveness, earnings, book value, creditworthiness, size, riskiness, growth rates, and, if technology is important in the industry, technological strength. Often it is extremely difficult—if not impossible—to get even two or three comparables that meet most of these criteria. Courts have rejected comparability on the grounds that a company was less diversified,[19] and on the grounds that the companies proffered as comparables to a tannery made a different kind of leather and also had chemical operations.[20] When it is difficult to develop the list, it is best to focus on those variables that are most likely to influence future cash flow.

Price/Earnings Ratio and Other Measures

Using comparables requires choosing a financial measure by which to compare the companies. The one most often used in common parlance is the price/earnings ratio (P/E), which is the price of a share of stock divided by the issuer's earnings per share. The P/E may use either the reported earnings from the latest year (called a *trailing P/E*), or an analyst's forecast of the next year's earnings (called a *forward P/E*). For instance, a stock selling for $20 a share that earned $1 last year has a trailing P/E of 20. If the same stock has projected earnings of $2 next year, it will have a forward P/E of 10. The P/E gives investors an idea of how much they are paying for a company's earning power. The higher the P/E, the more investors are paying, and, therefore, the more earnings growth they are expecting.

The implication of using a P/E is that the company is worth a multiple of its earnings, and it frequently is not a bad measure. However, though a price/earnings multiple has the advantage of being widely understood, it is really derived from a valuation rather than a reliable determinant of value. Moreover, P/Es ignore differences in financial leverage. If one company is more leveraged than the other, then it is riskier and ought to be accorded a correspondingly lower price/earnings multiple, as explained in greater detail in chapter 8. It is possible to adjust for the leverage differential by unlevering the companies and making the comparison on an unlevered basis. (For an explanation of how to unlever the capital structure, please see chapters 8 and 9.)

An alternative to the P/E is to use measures other than profit after tax (PAT). Keep in mind that one is looking to fill in the missing element in the following equation:

$$\frac{\text{Price of Comparable}}{\substack{\text{Financial Measure} \\ \text{(such as PAT, EBIT)}}} = \frac{\text{Price of Company}}{\substack{\text{Finanacial Measure} \\ \text{(such as PAT, EBIT)}}}$$

Occasionally total sales are used as a financial measure. To be sure, the virtue of this approach is that sales are easy to measure (although the revenue recognition issues discussed in chapter 1 should be borne in mind). In addition, there is no need

---

19. Estate of Victor P. Clarke v. Commissioner, Tech. Mem. 1976-328 (1976).
20. Gallen v. Commissioner, Tech. Mem. 1974-284 (1974).

to deal with various expenses—such as executive compensation, research and development (R&D), or marketing expenses—which may have been "managed" by one of the companies under review. Evaluating on the basis of total sales avoids the capital structure issue. Indeed, sales may be a good measure for partnerships (at least those in which expenses are comparatively easy to control or manipulate), and for royalty obligations under license agreements. However, for valuing most companies, sales are too crude a benchmark, for the measure ignores differences in efficiencies, cost structures, and capital structures.

Caveats to Using Multiples of EBIT or EBITDA

Because differences in capital structures can be troublesome in the use of comparables, two other measures are often used—earnings before interest and taxes (EBIT), or earnings before interest, taxes, depreciation, and amortization (EBITDA). EBIT and EBITDA (discussed in Sidebar 7 as well as elsewhere in chapter 1) enable the appraiser to sidestep differences in capital structure. There is an important caveat here, however. If measures other than PAT are used (especially sales, EBIT, or EBITDA), they must be used to measure the value of the entire company, not merely the value of the equity.

Further, and very importantly, EBIT and EBITDA ought not be used as measures of the value of the company or the equity alone on a prospective basis, because if the capital structure of the company changes, the multiple chosen may turn out to be entirely inappropriate and even highly unfair. One entrepreneur, the owner of a growing company needing capital, caused the company to sell a substantial amount of stock to an investor, extending to the investor the right to put his stock to the company at any time over the ensuing five years at a multiple of six times its then most recent year's EBIT. To facilitate growth, the entrepreneur then caused the company to take on debt, using the new capital to build the business and accelerate the growth rate. When the investor exercised his put in year 5, the result promised to be highly unfair to the entrepreneur, because the agreement neglected to subtract the debt from the value of the company determined in accordance with the multiple of EBIT. That is, the agreement ignored the fact that the multiple of EBIT gave a value for the company when the parties were trying to value only the equity. The matter went to litigation and was settled.

_____ **Sidebar 19** _____

Illustration of the Danger of Using EBIT to Measure the Value of Equity Prospectively

Let's assume the following:

1. The company begins year 1 with equity of $1,000.
2. The year 1 EBIT is $250. (All earnings are paid out as dividends.)
3. At the end of year 1, the company raises $1,000 of new equity for half the company. It grants the investor the right to put the stock back to the company at a valuation of 6 times EBIT.
4. The year 2 EBIT is $500.

5. Six times EBIT indicates a value of $3,000.
6. At the end of year 2, the company adds $2,000 of debt at 10%.
7. The year 3 EBIT is $1,000.
8. Six times EBIT is $6,000.

Methods of Valuing One-Half Interest in the Equity:

A. The apparent terms of the put contract: one-half of 6 times EBIT

   6 × EBIT of $1,000 × 50% = $3,000 Value of a 50% equity interest

B. 50% of the equity value based on valuing the capital (including both debt and equity)

   6 × EBIT of $1,000 = $6,000

   $2,000 debt

   $4,000 value of equity

   ×   50%

   $2,000 value of a 50% equity interest

If equity value is based on a multiple of EBIT without appropriate adjustment to reflect changing degrees of financial leverage, another error creeps in. As leverage increases, the remaining equity is exposed to greater risk. To be sure, the return on the equity should rise, but the multiple accorded to earnings after interest and tax ought to decrease to reflect the increased level of risk. For a more complete discussion of this, please refer to Sidebar 19 and to the examination of the cost of capital in chapters 8 and 9.

Adjustments to the Financial Data

Before we turn to other methods of valuation, another problem merits our attention. What if the most recent year's financial performance appears to be an aberration? This problem arises no matter which financial measure is used, whether it be price/earnings, price/EBIT, price/EBITDA, or price as related to some other measure.

At first blush it would appear that one should simply use the most recent year's numbers and base comparisons on those. For example, if the company being appraised is unlevered and has EBIT of $50 million, and an exact look-alike company, which is publicly held and widely traded, is also unlevered and has EBIT of $100 million and a market capitalization of $600 million, then (assuming the companies are close comparables) it would appear that the price/EBIT ratio of 6 to 1 is appropriate. This would suggest that the company being appraised, by virtue of its $50 million EBIT and the 6:1 multiple, ought to be valued at $300 million, as shown in Table 57.

However, what if the company being valued, unlike the comparable, had an atypically bad or good year? Or what if its most recent year's EBIT was significantly

Table 57
Use of EBIT as a Comparable for Valuation Purposes

	Comparable Company ($ million)	Company Being Valued ($ million)
Market capitalization	600	300*
EBIT	100	50
Market capitalization/EBIT	6	6**

*Company's EBIT times the multiple derived from the comparable.
**Ratio of comparable company used here.

and adversely impacted by a $100 million restructuring charge, only $50 million of which was incurred in cash? Or what if the comparable company has announced that it will incur similar restructuring charges in the future?

To some degree this problem can be handled by restating earnings into cash earnings, as explained in chapter 6. Particularly when there are significant non-cash charges such as goodwill, amortization, non-cash restructuring charges, write-offs (in the case of banks' bad loans or other write-offs), or changes in the accounting rules governing deferred tax liability, the adjustments described in chapter 6 are worth making to base the comparison on cash earnings.

Yet even after earnings are restated into cash earnings, a further adjustment might be in order if the most recent year was unusually good or bad. One approach is to base the comparison on more than one year; for example, compare the company with its comparable based on a five-year average EBIT for each firm. This can be refined by weighting the average more heavily toward the recent years. One way to do this is to sum the 5 years' digits (1+2+3+4+5 = 15) and weigh the most recent year's EBIT 5/15, the prior year's EBIT 4/15, and so forth, with the first of the 5 years being weighted only 1/15.

Another way to adjust for swings or cycles in earnings or EBIT is to normalize them. This is a statistical technique that is different from averaging and that regresses the earnings on EBIT to a trend line, calculating what the numbers would have looked like if the company had grown at a consistent, rather than uneven, rate. This is illustrated in Table 58.

Table 58
Normalizing Five-Year EBIT for XYZ Corporation

Year	EBIT	Normalized EBIT
1991	1000	600
1992	250	800
1993	1250	1000
1994	750	1200
1995	1750	1400
	5000 ÷ 5 = 1000 average	

Table 59
Adjusting Earnings to Eliminate Excess Compensation

	As Reported ($ thousand)	Adjusted to Reflect Compensation at Market Value of Control Party ($ thousand)
Pretax profit excluding control party's compensation	8,000	8,000
Control party's compensation	1,500	500
EBIT	6,500	7,500
Multiple	5	5
Value of company	32,500	37,500

Normalizing minimizes the effects of swings in earnings and the undesired concomitant windfalls or unfair adverse effects of the cycles in a cyclical business. If one uses this method, however, one must normalize the earnings of not only the company being valued, but also the comparable companies.

Another type of restatement of financials is often necessary for private companies. It is not uncommon for senior management to own a control block of the company's stock, and perhaps all the stock. This being the case, it would rather take earnings out in the form of tax deductible compensation than in the form of dividends. Any spread between an owner/manager's compensation and what it would cost the company to replace that person with someone of comparable talent ought to be treated as a return on capital. Thus, any such excess (adjusted for taxes if the valuation is based on after tax earnings) ought to be added to the company's earnings before valuing the company.

One private company thought it was making this adjustment but made a potentially costly error in doing so. It sold stock to an investor and granted a put at a multiple of earnings. The mistake was that it agreed that the owner/manager's compensation would be added back, in its entirety, to pretax earnings before valuing the company. This is blatantly incorrect if one is trying to value the company accurately. Only any excess of the compensation over the fair market value of the employee's services ought to be added back to earnings in valuing the company's capital.

Indeed, there is a small but growing body of anecdotal evidence suggesting that once public companies earn more than an average benchmark, senior management takes a portion of such above average earnings not only in the form of higher compensation but, more importantly, in the form of perks such as company planes, larger and more upscale offices, and the like. One reason why minority interests trade at a discount is that minority shareholders have a difficult time detecting and combating this. In extreme cases, such as Borden, Inc. and Kmart Corporation, institutional investors eventually weigh in, put the wood to the board, and force changes in management.[21] In

---

21. *See, e.g.,* Allison Leigh Cowan, *Borden's Board Ousts Chief to Appease Investors,* N.Y. TIMES, Dec. 10, 1993, at D-1.

those cases, which are probably the exception, when a portion of the earnings in excess of market average returns are consumed by management, the excess cannot be added to earnings in determining value until there is reason to think any such excess will be left for investors.

Although many valuations rely on the use of comparables, the method is inherently circular. After all, if every company is valued on the basis of comparisons with other companies, then nothing is at work but a set of mirrors. Otherwise stated, if one is valuing a company based on how other companies are valued, then by what method are the comparable companies valued? This brings us to two other methods of valuation, namely the discounted cash flow method, which was initially developed in the 1960s, and the economic value added method, which is of more recent vintage but is rapidly gaining adherents among both executives and investment analysts. But first we need to understand two major building blocks of valuation, namely calculating a return on capital and calculating a cost of capital.

If the reader (1) is uninterested in the details concerning the calculation of return on capital and cost of capital and/or (2) knows all that he or she wants to know about the subject for the present, then the reader is encouraged to proceed directly to chapter 10.

Calculating a Return on Capital

Chapter

6

As noted at the outset of chapter 5, one of the determinants of a company's value is the return the owners receive on their investment. The return is important not only in and of itself but, more importantly, relative to the size of the investment made.

In the case of equity, that return generally takes two forms, namely cash dividends and share price appreciation. (The share price appreciation occurs because, if and as the issuer's fortunes and prospects improve, buyers will pay more to own a share of the expected future value created by the company.) The combination of dividends and share price appreciation is the total return to shareholders (TRS).

Publicly available research is fairly clear that share prices are a function of future earnings if (1) they can be predicted, and (2) expected earnings under generally accepted accounting principles (GAAP) and cash earnings are substantially similar. Beyond that, the research about what drives share prices is inconclusive, although it is known that annual earnings reports are part of the information used in forming stock prices and that the market does not usually react significantly, in short time intervals, to annual earnings announcements.[1] The result is that only a small part of annual movements in stock prices is explained by earnings announcements. This may be because the market has already anticipated the earnings news, or because numerous factors in addition to current earnings, such as growth prospects, risk, new product introductions, industry developments, and the like, also impact share prices.

A 1992 study found that over long time intervals, earnings calculated in accordance with GAAP correlate with share prices, although the tightness of the correlation is low (r^2 less the 20%).[2] There is also debate concerning whether *earnings* for these purposes ought to be primary or fully diluted, or pre- or post-extraordinary items.[3]

Although the evidence is inconclusive about whether GAAP earnings or cash earnings correlate more closely with TRS, most valuation systems currently used are

---

1. For instance, our research has found that announcements of asset write-downs, even if material for the year in question, have minimal impact on the issuer's share price except when the write-down is accompanied by a hint of fraudulent conduct on the part of management.

2. The r^2 is a statistical measure to determine the tightness of the correlation and thus the power of the relationship between variables (here earnings and share prices).

3. *See* Michael J. Brennan, *A Perspective on Accounting and Stock Prices*, 8 Bank Am. J. Applied Corp. Fin. 43–52 (Spring 1995) (includes good discussion of this topic).

geared to cash return on cash invested. Since the 1960s, the traditional method of valuing businesses has been the discounted cash flow (DCF) method, which holds that the value of a company's equity is the present value of its future cash earnings stream. As discussed in greater detail in chapter 11, the DCF method is being successfully challenged by other methods, most notably the economic value added method, which is being adopted by a large and growing number of companies. In a nutshell, the economic value added during any period, such as a year, is the company's cash earnings less a charge for the cost of the capital used to finance the company's asset base. As discussed in chapter 11, projections of current as well as future economic value added can be used as valuation tools.

The field of valuation is changing very rapidly, indeed at a pace analogous to the rate of change in medical and telecommunications technology. With that background and caveat, let's turn to some fundamentals of valuation as it is practiced.

Fundamentals of Valuation

Investors provide cash to the enterprise and expect that sooner or later they will receive cash back from the enterprise—and more than they put in. How high a return they expect depends upon how risky they gauge their investment to be. If it is highly risky, they will want a high return to compensate them for the risk to which they are exposed. If the investment is low risk, they will settle for a lower return, again reflecting the degree of risk. You can see that the risk/return relationship will influence the price at which stock is sold and, in the case of new issues, the amount of dilution. We will return to this point later.

You may have heard business men and women, usually in the course of raising capital, contend that their business is "different from other businesses." A principal who was raising capital for a new television station asserted, "You cannot value this business the same way you value other businesses." On another occasion, the treasurer of a professional sports franchise said, "We are different from other businesses and cannot be valued by the same measures." Both are right in the sense that some elements of every industry are unique. However, across every industry the common fact is that investors expect cash back, and, subject to ethical and legal bounds, the investors do not care whether it is from a television station, a sports franchise, or any other business. Further, apart from tax considerations, they generally do not care whether they get their return from the issuer or from a buyer of their shares.

As indicated above, there remains considerable debate—not only among scholars, but even among some investment bankers and CEOs—about whether the market rewards GAAP or cash earnings. Neither side on that debate has emerged victorious, and more research is needed. Often the two are closely correlated, and GAAP earnings are a good surrogate for cash earnings. Over the short term, cash earnings may well be a better guide to value than GAAP earnings, if for no other reason than that management has less room to manage the cash earnings. (Over the long run, of course, they are often the same, with the notable exceptions of amortization expenses and foreign currency translations, which are only a matter of timing. Maybe that is why, over the long term, GAAP earnings often correlate so closely with cash earnings and with share price.) One might do well here to keep in mind a case that is rarely, if ever, cited in the finance literature. In the landmark case[4] involving the management discussion and analysis (MD&A) portion of a disclosure document, the stock price of the company, Caterpillar, Inc., dropped some 15% the day after a press release announcing, in effect, that 1989 earnings had been very favorably impacted by a foreign currency adjustment that might not be repeated in 1990. Yet the foreign currency translations that impacted Caterpillar's income statement were not cash items. The market in that case was clearly reacting to GAAP rather than cash earnings. Lawyers preparing or reviewing MD&As or other disclosure documents might want to remember that event when considering the debate about whether the market reacts to cash or GAAP earnings.

Following are the major adjustments to GAAP earnings that are needed to calculate cash earnings. In fact, one could find over a hundred adjustments that might be made, although in any given company's case, only a few are likely to be material—usually those discussed in the following sections.

Major Adjustments to GAAP Earnings

Calculation of Cash Earnings

Cash earnings should not be confused with cash flow or free cash flow. Cash flow is usually defined as earnings plus depreciation. Free cash flow is often, but not always, defined as net operating profit after tax (NOPAT), discussed later, plus depreciation and minus increases in working capital and fixed assets. Yet, in practice, the terms are used in a variety of different ways, amounting to a Wall Street and financial executive Rorschach test. When discussing either term, one should clarify how it is being defined and then make sure that such definition suits the purpose for which cash flow or free cash flow is being measured.

Goodwill

Most lawyers know that when a purchase (versus a pooling) acquisition is done, the acquired company's assets and liabilities are marked up (or down) to their fair market values and brought onto the acquiror's balance sheet at such fair market values. The excess, if any, of the purchase price over the net of the fair market value of assets over the fair market value of liabilities is then recorded as goodwill on the acquiror's books.

Most lawyers also know that such goodwill must be amortized over its expected useful life, and that although the amortization period may not exceed 40 years, it is usually much shorter—often 10 to 15 years. Because this adversely impacts earnings, most lawyers take it as axiomatic, as do most managements, that purchase treatment is undesirable. The point is hardly academic. In an increasingly service oriented economy, the spread between book values and market values is widening. Further, the numbers are huge. In 1997, $1 trillion in mergers took place involving American companies, up some 50% from 1996, the previous record year.[5]

---

4. *In re* Caterpillar, Inc., Exchange Act Release No. 30,532 (1992).
5. Leslie Wayne, *Wave of Mergers Is Recasting Face of U.S. Business*, N.Y. Times, Jan. 19, 1998, at A-1.

Of the $1 trillion, approximately $850 billion involved U.S. companies acquiring other U.S. companies, $100 billion involved U.S. companies acquiring foreign companies, and $50 billion involved foreign companies acquiring U.S. companies. Often much of the purchase price must be allocated to goodwill. For instance, in the largest acquisition of 1995, the $19 billion Walt Disney merger with Capital Cities/ABC Inc., $16 billion was allocated to goodwill.[6] Even if Disney uses the maximum allowable 40 years to amortize the goodwill, it will incur a $400 million goodwill expense every year until 2035.

To avoid the creation of goodwill, the acquisition must qualify as a pooling of interests, which means meeting all 12 of the conditions set forth in Accounting Principles Board (APB) 16 and the additional interpretations of those requirements adopted by the Securities and Exchange Commission (SEC). The conditions are summarized in Sidebar 20, and the most important one is that the transaction be a stock-for-stock transaction. Another condition prohibits the acquiror from repurchasing its own shares for a period beginning two years before the merger and ending six months after it. (The idea is that both transactions, namely the acquisition and the use of cash to repurchase shares, will be deemed as one, as though the acquiror used its cash to do the acquisition.) When an acquisition qualifies for pooling treatment, the buyer merely adds the seller's assets and liabilities to its own balance sheet, using the same numbers as were on the seller's books. No goodwill is recorded or amortized, which makes the subsequent GAAP earnings of the company look better than if the acquiror had used purchase accounting. Not only do earnings look better with a pooling, but so does return on equity, because the equity account is lower.

Sidebar 20

Conditions That Must Be Met to Qualify for Pooling Treatment

The GAAP requirements for using the pooling of interests method are detailed and quite restrictive. All the following 12 criteria must be met:[7]

1. Each of the combining companies must be autonomous and not have been a subsidiary or division of another corporation within two years before the plan of combination is initiated.
2. At the date of initiation of the plan and at the date of its consummation, the combining companies must be independent of each other. An intercorporate ownership of 10% or less of the total outstanding voting stock of the other is acceptable.
3. The plan of combination, once initiated, must be completed within a year. There are various exceptions to this requirement. For instance, if litigation or government action is beyond the control of the parties and delays the implementation of the plan, then the one-year period is extended.

---

6. WALT DISNEY COMPANY, 1996 ANNUAL REPORT.
7. APB 16, adopted in November 1970.

4. At the date the plan is consummated, the acquiring company must offer and issue shares having voting rights in exchange for no less than 90% of the voting common stock interests of the company being acquired. This requirement has a number of specific rules concerning which shares are counted for measurement purposes. It also has rules permitting the assets of the acquired company to be transferred to the acquiror after the transaction.

5. For a period beginning two years before the initiation date of the plan of combination and ending six months after the plan is consummated, there may not have been any changes in the equity interests of the voting common stock of either combining company.

6. Neither company may have reacquired more than 10% of its voting common shares for purposes of the combination. However, pooling is permitted as long as any stock purchases are consistent with normal levels of repurchase, such as for stock option plans.

7. Each of the acquired company's shareholders must maintain the same proportionate equity interest after the combination.

8. Shareholders must have the same voting rights after the combination as before.

9. The entire plan must be effectuated on the date of combination. There must be no contingent or further consideration.

10. The combined enterprise may not reacquire any of the shares it issued to effect the combination.

11. The combined enterprise may not offer special financial arrangements to the acquired company's shareholders.

12. The combined enterprise may not dispose of a significant portion of the acquired assets within two years after the combination.

If the market prefers cash earnings to GAAP earnings, then whether an acquisition is accounted for by purchase or pooling ought to have no impact on the value of the postmerger acquiror. One way to test whether the market, when faced with a choice, prefers cash or accrual earnings is to see how the market treats goodwill. When an acquisition is accounted for as a purchase, goodwill is usually created and must be amortized, which reduces earnings. If an acquisition is treated as a pooling, no goodwill is created and there is no adverse impact on future earnings. In each case the cash earnings are the same. Thus, if the market punishes a company for doing a purchase acquisition but does not punish it for doing a pooling acquisition, we would have useful evidence regarding whether the market prefers accrual earnings (that is, favors the pooling acquisition) or is indifferent.

This issue was tested in two studies. In the first,[8] researchers at Carnegie-Mellon studied the share prices of a large sample of companies that made acquisitions in the 1960s. They divided the companies into two groups: those that used pooling treatment and those that were required to use purchase treatment. (Keep in mind that

---

8. Hai Hong et al., *Pooling vs. Purchase: The Effects of Accounting for Mergers on Stock Prices*, 53 ACCT. REV. 31–47 (1978).

during the pre-APB 16 era—before 1970—it was easier for an acquiror to get pooling treatment than it is today.) The study found that there was no significant difference in the performance of the stock prices of the two groups of companies, strongly indicating that the market was ignoring the amortization deduction from earnings. This study lends support to the hypothesis that accrued non-cash expenses (such as goodwill) have no bearing on a company's value.[9] In the second study,[10] involving 177 mergers completed between 1971 and 1982 (that is, after the adoption of APB 16), the researchers found that the market had little reaction to acquisitions accounted for as poolings and a statistically significant strong positive reaction to acquisitions accounted for as purchases.

The issue was also analyzed indirectly in a third study of acquisitions made from 1970 through 1989.[11] Although this study did not specifically address the issue at hand, it found that companies making acquisitions for cash saw their stock prices rise 113%, on average, over the five years following the acquisition—a compound annual appreciation of 16%. By contrast, companies making acquisitions by using their stock rather than cash saw their stock prices rise only 61% over the following five years—a compound annual appreciation of only 10%. Although not all acquisitions made with stock were accounted for as poolings, there were undoubtedly many more poolings in the latter group than the former. The disparity in returns indicates, though stops short of proving, that the market has a preference for acquisitions that are accounted for as purchases.

Thus many managements may have wasted undue expense and effort to avoid purchase treatment. Unfortunately, some have even turned their backs on otherwise sound mergers merely because they could not qualify for pooling treatment. Apart from the obvious reason that GAAP earnings are likely to be higher if an acquisition is accounted for as a pooling rather than a purchase (even though cash earnings will be the same or lower), there are two possible reasons why managements tend to prefer poolings. First, management compensation is more likely to be impacted by GAAP earnings than by cash earnings. Second, debt covenants might be such that skirting the adverse impact of goodwill amortization would be desirable.

Whatever the motivation, going to heroic measures to avoid purchase treatment is not unusual, although one study[12] found that of some 5,000 mergers and acquisitions by 600 companies from 1970 through 1994, poolings never constituted more than 43% of the total number, and that was in 1971. From 1986 through 1994, purchases constituted at least 90% of the transactions every year.[13]

An interesting example of a company that went to extraordinary lengths to avoid purchase treatment was AT&T Corporation when it sought to acquire NCR Corporation in 1991. Because NCR had taken several defensive steps to make pooling treatment unavailable to AT&T and thus deter AT&T from its acquisition effort, once NCR acquiesced and a merger agreement was reached, AT&T incurred

9. *See* John R. Robinson & Philip B. Shane, *Acquisition Accounting Method and Bid Premia for Target Firms*, 65 ACCT. REV. 25–48 (1990) (includes good discussion of this topic, though before enactment of the Rostenkowski bill).

10. Michael L. Davis, *The Purchase vs. Pooling Controversy: How the Stock Market Responds to Goodwill*, 9 BANK AM. J. APPLIED CORP. FIN. 50–59 (Spring 1996).

11. Roger Lowenstein, *Why All Takeovers Aren't Created Equal*, WALL ST. J., Mar. 6, 1997, at C-1.

12. Davis, *supra* note 9, at 50–59.

13. *Id.* at 51.

expenses of $50 million simply by helping NCR take steps to meet the conditions of APB 16. In addition, AT&T paid a premium of about $350 million in incremental AT&T shares issued in the pooling to consummate the transaction, and that does not count the $4 billion decline in market value of AT&T stock that took place while the merger was being conducted. In short, companies at times pay more to get less.

Now that the Internal Revenue Code (IRC) allows limited tax deductibility of goodwill over 15 years, there will be a net of taxes cash advantage to the acquiror using purchase accounting for an acquisition.[14] To be sure, the anecdotal evidence suggests that managements usually still seek to avoid purchase treatment on the grounds that the tax shelter protects them from only part of the adverse impact of the amortization expense. As noted above, at times the motivation to maximize GAAP rather than tax earnings comes from contracts, such as earn-outs, executive compensation agreements, or loan covenants, which can exert a powerful influence. Yet, by providing a cash tax advantage for using a non-cash deduction, purchase acquisitions ought to be more attractive now than poolings—affording the decision makers more than a mere toss-up. Although formal research on this has not yet been done, there is evidence that some managements are beginning to prefer purchase acquisitions (at least when imbedded contracts do not create the opposite incentive), because they can result in higher cash earnings than poolings. It is possible for a company to do a tax-free, stock-for-stock acquisition, to enable the seller to avoid recognizing a gain for tax purposes but still get purchase treatment. This is done by intentionally running afoul of a condition of APB 16, other than the requirement of a stock-for-stock deal. Table 60 summarizes the GAAP and tax treatment of acquisitions.

In any event, the market, seeking to reflect economic realities, apparently treats goodwill in a different way than the accountants. Specifically, lead investors make two adjustments in calculating return on investment, one to the earnings and another to the investment. As for earnings, top performing investors add to them any non-cash amortization expense. Although that is good news for management, the investors also gross up the equity account, not only by the most recent year's amortization expense, but also by previous years' amortization for as many years back as they can see (usually about three to five years), so they can restore the original goodwill amount. The rationale is that if Company A acquires Company B for

14. In passing the bill providing for the deductibility of goodwill over 15 years, Congress was seeking to resolve uncertainty resulting from the U.S. Supreme Court's 1993 opinion (5 to 4) in *Newark Morning Ledger Co. v. United States,* 734 F. Supp. 176 (D. N.J. 1990), *rev'd,* 945 F.2d 555 (3d Cir. 1991), *reh'g en banc denied,* 1991 U.S. App. LEXIS 24707 (3d Cir., 1991), *cert. granted,* 1992 U.S. LEXIS 2141, *rev'd,* 1993 U.S. LEXIS 2979. In *Newark Morning Ledger,* the taxpayer had acquired all the stock of Booth Newspapers, Inc., which published 8 newspapers in Michigan, for approximately $328 million in cash. The buyer allocated $67.8 million to an intangible known as "paid subscribers," consisting of 460,000 identified subscribers to the Booth newspapers, representing the present value of future profits attributable to the at-will contracts with these subscribers. The buyer also allocated $26.2 million to goodwill.

On its federal tax return, the buyer sought to deduct the amortization of the "paid subscriber" intangibles. The Internal Revenue Service challenged the deduction on the ground that the paid subscribers were indistinguishable from goodwill and hence not deductible, because under Treasury Regulation § 1.167(a)(3), goodwill is not depreciable. The Supreme Court agreed with the taxpayer and held that the amortization of the paid subscriber intangible was tax deductible. Fearing the loss of some $8 billion in revenues in similar cases, Congress amended the Internal Revenue Code, as described in the text. *See* I.R.C. § 197(a), (c), (d).

Table 60
Treatment of Goodwill

Nature of Transaction	GAAP Treatment	Federal Tax Treatment
Stock for stock	Pooling available if other conditions are also met. No goodwill created on buyer's books. However, if other conditions of APB 16 are not all met, goodwill is created.*	Likely to be a tax free reorganization under IRC. (See section 368.) If so, then no creation or recognition of goodwill for tax purposes; buyer inherits target's tax basis in assets. Seller recognizes no gain or loss, but buyer cannot amortize goodwill.
Stocks for assets	Must be treated as a purchase. Goodwill is created on buyer's books.** The goodwill has an adverse impact on buyer's GAAP earnings, but positive impact on buyer's cash earnings.	Can be a tax free reorganization if IRC section 368 conditions are met. Otherwise seller, unless target is a subsidiary in a consolidated tax group, can face double taxation, once at the top corporate level upon the sale of the assets and second upon the receipt of the sales proceeds. The selling shareholders may be able to avoid double taxation if the corporation is a subchapter S corporation or if certain other forms of organization, such as limited partnerships or limited liability companies, are used. If taxable, goodwill is created on the buyer's tax books if the fair market value of the target assets exceeds the fair market value of its liabilities; buyer can amortize such goodwill for tax purposes over 15 years.
Cash for assets	Same as the treatment described above in the case of a stock for assets transaction.	Cannot be tax free. Seller can face double taxation and buyer can amortize goodwill as described above in the case of a stock for assets transaction.***

*The conditions that must be met to qualify for pooling treatment are set forth in Sidebar 20.
**As explained in the text, this is true only if the purchase price exceeds net of the fair market of the seller's assets less the fair market value of its liabilities.
***The selling shareholders may be able to avoid double taxation if the corporation is a subchapter S corporation or if certain other forms of organization, such as limited partnerships, are used.

$10 million in cash, the investor expects a return on the $10 million, not on $10 million less amortized amounts.

The market may also make an adjustment to the balance sheet in the case of a pooling acquisition. Although GAAP does not recognize the creation of goodwill in a pooling acquisition, the market may do so. Under GAAP accounting, a pooling acquisition is accounted for by simply combining the companies' assets and liabilities. Thus, if Company A has $125 in equity and Company B has $50 in equity, GAAP accounting says that the combined entity has $175 in equity. However, if Company

A bought Company B by issuing 20 shares having a market value of $5 each, then the consideration is $100. Although the GAAP balance sheet will show $175 in post-merger equity, the market will calculate returns based on an equity value of $225 (that is, Company A's premerger equity of $125 plus the $100 in new consideration equity paid for Company B), as discussed in Sidebar 21.

_____ **Sidebar 21** _____

Pooling Goodwill

Suppose Company A acquires Company B in a stock-for-stock transaction, paying 20 shares at a market value of $5 per share for all B's stock, and that under GAAP the transaction is accounted for by combining the companies' balance sheets. Thus A + B = New A, as shown below. Notice that A's equity has increased by the amount of equity on B's books before the acquisition; that is, by $50. However, A paid for B with stock worth $100 (20 shares at $5 each). In terms of economic substance, A could have sold the shares to the public for $100 and used the $100 to buy B's stock. Had it done so, then A's equity account would have risen by $100, not by $50. Consequently, many analysts will gross up A's equity by an additional $50, to a total of $225 (that is, the $125 with which A began plus the $100 value of the stock issued by A), and expect a return on the full $225—not merely the $175 equity shown on A's GAAP books. In effect, the incremental $50 is placed by such investors on the left side of A's balance sheet as pooling goodwill and is not amortized.

(1) A	
CA 225	CL 100
	E 125

(2) B	
CA 100	CL 50
	E 50

(3) The GAAP treatment of the acquisition

New A	
CA 325	CL 150
	E 175

(4) The acquisition as grossed up to reflect purchase of goodwill:

Definitions
CL = current liabilities
CA = current assets
E = equity

New A		
A's assets	225	CL 150
B's assets	100	E 125
Pooling goodwill	50	+ 100
	375	375

Though there are many other areas in which accountants accrue non-cash expenses but the market does not, three of the most significant and common merit particular mention.

Restructuring Charges and Write-Offs

In the early 1990s, a great many companies recorded restructuring expenses. During this period, in the face of intense competition and cost pressure, many companies pared their number of employees, closed plants, idled equipment, and took other steps to reduce their fixed and variable costs. Caterpillar, Inc., Scott Paper Company, Digital Equipment Corporation, AT&T, and IBM are but some of the many examples. In some cases these restructurings made the companies more competitive. However, in many cases the amount of the restructuring charge taken by the company considerably exceeded the cash expenses incurred. All well and good, you might say—they were just being conservative.

Consider a company that in year 1 takes a $500 million restructuring charge. In year 2 it discovers that the $500 million charge was overly pessimistic and exceeded the expenses actually incurred. Does it go back and restate the year 1 financials? No. In year 2 the company merely reverses the unused restructuring charge, thereby diminishing year 2's expenses and correspondingly increasing its year 2 pretax earnings. If, for instance, in year 2 it realized that the actual expense was only $300 million, it will use the $200 million difference to reduce year 2's expenses. Thus, the $500 million expense in year 1, having been overstated by $200 million, enables the company to reverse the $200 million expense, correspondingly increasing the pretax earnings for year 2. This creates some devilish incentives for managements, especially new managements who want to look good in future years. By taking the "big bath" in year 1, they can blame the woes on their predecessors and bank some earnings for future years, thus amplifying the recovery. Because of this phenomenon, the market tends to ferret out and add back to net income those restructuring charges that were expensed but not paid in cash.

For example, in 1993 Apple Computer Inc. recognized a $321 million restructuring charge in connection with consolidating operations, closing or relocating certain facilities, and firing or relocating employees.[15] Essentially, the company took the familiar "big bath," with the thought (or at least the hope) that from then on the upward slope of the trajectory would look even steeper than it would otherwise, and the market would view the company's stock more favorably than it would otherwise. Then, in 1994, management concluded that the restructuring charges had been overestimated by $127 million and thus added $127 million to its 1994 pretax earnings, as shown in Table 61.[16] This practice of stashing away a source of future earnings, very common in Europe, is known among accountants as *sugarbowling*. The SEC has been challenging this type of accounting legerdemain, and in so doing, it is pursuing the same line of reasoning that the market apparently does.

---

15. APPLE COMPUTER, INC., 1993 ANNUAL REPORT.
16. APPLE COMPUTER, INC., 1994 ANNUAL REPORT.

Table 61

Apple Computer, Inc. 1993–1994
Restructuring Charges*

	1993	1994
	($ million)	
Earnings as reported	87	310
Earnings as adjusted to eliminate non-cash restructuring charges**	285	231***

*Apple Computer, Inc., 1994 Annual Report.

**Net of income taxes.

***1994 earnings would not have been as high as reported had the company not received $127 million pretax ($79 million after tax) in restructuring charges accrued in 1993.

There is an added benefit to this practice. By reducing earnings, restructuring charges also reduce shareholders' equity. By reducing shareholders' equity, management can later crow more loudly about its return on equity. Here, however, the interests of management and the interests of the owners diverge. The owners may well remark, "Wait a minute. That's our equity you wrote off. You may say it's gone, but we still expect a return on that." Absent such a chorus, whether explicit or through the silent but powerful message of the market, management might be tempted to write book equity down to a very low number. The market, however, has a rather long memory. Although research is needed to determine how long it will keep such practices in mind and gross up the equity accordingly, the market probably restates the equity account (as well as the earnings, as noted earlier) to offset the non-cash charges.

A similar rationale pertains to write-offs of assets. In 1987, Citicorp took $4.4 billion in non-cash write-offs, $3 billion of which was for foreign loans,[17] chiefly in Brazil, which appeared to have diminished dramatically in value. The foreign loan write-off of $3 billion alone reduced net income from a positive $1.8 billion to a negative $1.2 billion, and caused year-end equity to drop from what would have been $11.8 billion to $8.8 billion. In 1988 Citicorp did better and had earnings of $1.9 billion on year-end equity of $9.9 billion, ostensibly a 19% return on equity. However, the market apparently treated the equity account as being $12.9 billion (that is, the $9.9 billion plus the $3 billion that had been written off). On this basis the return on equity was only 15%, as shown in Table 62. The market price lost nearly half its value on the news of the write-off, but the sellers only created a buying opportunity for others, as the stock price hit an all-time high in mid-1989.

17. CITICORP, 1987 ANNUAL REPORT.

Table 62
Citicorp Performance 1987 and 1988 with and without Adjustments for Write-Offs*

	1987		1988	
	As Reported	**Offsetting the Write-Off**	**As Reported**	**Offsetting the Write-Off**
	($ billion)		($ billion)	
Net income	(1.2)	1.8	1.9	1.9
Equity	8.8	11.8	9.9	12.9
Return on equity	(14%)	15%	19%	15%
Year-end stock price	20		25	

*Citicorp, 1987 and 1988 Annual Reports.

By analogy to write-offs of restructuring charges and long-lived assets, consider a hypothetical oil and gas company that raises $10 million from investors to drill ten wells. Seven years later, management reports to the shareholders that it has great news. Although it has written off $9 million spent to drill nine dry wells, the tenth well was a big success. It cost only $1 million to drill but generated cash earnings of $10 million. Feverishly patting itself on the back, management reports a 10 to 1 return on investment for the investors—their $1 million has earned them a handsome 10 to 1 return. Not so, say the investors. Management may have written off the $9 million spent on dry wells, but the investors did not. From their standpoint, the company has not even earned its cost of capital. So too with goodwill. The market does not write it off, and from the market's standpoint, goodwill should have no impact on the income statement and should be left, unreduced by amortization, on the balance sheet.

In 1996, the Financial Accounting Standards Board (FASB) adopted a rule[18] providing that if management determines the value of a long-lived asset (such as a plant or an intangible asset) has been impaired, then it must write down the value of that asset. This holds a blessing and a curse for management. The blessing is that the rule gives management some latitude about when an asset value has been impaired. The curse is that once management determines impairment has occurred, it has no latitude and must write down the asset to its fair value. Because of the adverse publicity that restructuring charges have been getting, we may soon see more of the impaired long-lived asset write-downs. Yet from a cash standpoint, the points made earlier regarding non-cash restructuring charges apply here as well for purposes of analysis.

---

18. CODIFICATION OF ACCOUNTING STANDARDS AND PROCEDURES, Statement of Financial Accounting Standard No. 121 (American Inst. of Certified Pub. Accountants 1996).

Inventory Accounting

Another way to test whether the market rewards cash earnings or GAAP earnings is to see empirically what happens when companies switch from FIFO (first in, first out) to LIFO (last in, first out) or vice versa. As noted in chapter 2, assuming that costs are rising, a company can cut its cash tax expense by using LIFO rather than FIFO. The drawback is that by using LIFO, the company reports lower earnings because it is expensing the more recently made or acquired—and hence (at least in most industries) more expensive—inventory, which reduces its earnings. Had the company been calculating expenses based on the premise that it was selling the older, lower cost, FIFO inventory, then its earnings would have been higher.

_____ *Sidebar 22* _____

Explanation of LIFO Reserves

Suppose a company begins year 1 with two television sets, and its year 1 beginning balance sheet is as follows.

Table 63		
Inventory on Balance Sheet Beginning of Year 1		
	LIFO	**FIFO**
Television 1	$100	$100
Television 2	150	150
Inventory	$250	$250

If during year 1 the company buys one more television set for $200, and sells one television set for $250, then at the end of year 1, its balance sheet inventory is as follows.

Table 64			
Inventory on Balance Sheet End of Year 1			
	LIFO		**FIFO**
LIFO replacement cost*	$350	Inventory	$350
LIFO reserve*	(100)		
LIFO inventory	$250		

*Essentially, LIFO replacement cost is the value the inventory would have if the company were using FIFO. (Under SEC rules, reporting companies may, in the alternative, use the actual replacement cost as the LIFO replacement cost number.) The LIFO reserve is fundamentally a plugged number to get from the LIFO replacement cost to the reported LIFO inventory.

Then, in year 2 the company buys one television set for $300, and sells it for $400.

Table 65 Year 2 Income Statement			
	LIFO	**FIFO**	
Sales	$400	$400	Note that tax under
Cost of goods sold	300	150	LIFO is $60 less
Profit before tax	100	250	
Tax @ 40%	40	100	
Profit after tax	$ 60	$150	

Note that under LIFO, the company has lower GAAP earnings but higher cash earnings. Its earnings in economic terms are (1) the earnings of $150 it would have had if it used FIFO plus (2) the $60 of taxes it sheltered by virtue of using LIFO. This sum is the same as its LIFO earnings of $60, plus the year's increase of $150 in its LIFO reserve.

Table 66 LIFO versus FIFO—Balance Sheet and Cash Earnings			
Year 2 Ending Balance Sheet			
	LIFO		**FIFO**
LIFO replacement cost	$500	Inventory	$500
LIFO reserve	(250)		
LIFO inventory	$250		
Year 2 Cash Earnings			
	LIFO		**FIFO**
Profit after tax	$ 60	Profit after tax	$150
Change in LIFO reserve	150		—
Economic earnings	$210		$150

At the end of year 2, the capital includes the following amount of inventory.

Table 67 Year 2 Inventory Amounts			
	LIFO		**FIFO**
LIFO inventory	$250	Inventory	$500
LIFO reserve	250		
Total LIFO inventory	$500		

Another approach is to look at the economic earnings. Note that the difference between the GAAP and cash earnings is $60, just as is the case when cash earnings are calculated. Note also that the capital account is grossed up by the LIFO reserve on the balance sheet, bringing the total inventory to $500, a number that more closely accords with the economic value of the company's assets.

That is, to reflect the economic realities accurately, when calculating return on investment many investors and executives make two adjustments to the GAAP inventory numbers if the company is using LIFO. First, to reflect the value of the company's inventory more accurately, they will add LIFO reserves to the asset base and to the equity of the company when calculating return on assets or return on equity. In addition, when calculating the earnings (that is, the numerator of the return on investment fraction) they will also gross up the earnings by the change (usually an increase) in LIFO reserves during the period in question, in the belief that the increase in LIFO reserves reflects a yet unrealized value created by the company. In the illustration in Table 66, that would mean that when calculating the returns for year 2, the executive or investor analyzing performance would treat the LIFO company's earnings as $210 (that is, the $60 GAAP earnings plus the $150 increase in LIFO reserves) and the asset base as the total LIFO inventory (that is, the net LIFO inventory of $250 plus the LIFO reserves of $250, or the $500 LIFO replacement cost).

Thus there is an opportunity to test whether the market prefers GAAP earnings (in which case it would prefer that issuers use FIFO) or cash earnings (in which case it would prefer that issuers use LIFO). Empirical research has shown that when companies switch from FIFO to LIFO (or vice versa), the price of a share of stock rises or falls to reflect the economic realities rather than the accounting for the issuers' performance. One study reports that companies switching from FIFO to LIFO experienced, on average, a stock price increase of 5% on the date of announcement of the change, and that the amount of change was directly proportional to the present value of the cash taxes to be saved by making the change.[19]

Thus the LIFO-versus-FIFO test seems to support the proposition that when faced with a choice between cash earnings or accrual earnings, the market prefers the former. In effect, the market has struck a silent deal with management. Management has learned to use LIFO to minimize the company's cash taxes and maximize its cash earnings, and the market will recalibrate earnings by adding to earnings the increase in LIFO reserves, as illustrated in Table 66.

Research and Development

At times, an important debate concerning research and development (R&D) costs arises. Under GAAP rules, R&D costs must be expensed as incurred. (The only exception pertains to software R&D, which must be expensed until technological feasibility is established, then capitalized and amortized, although GAAP does not

---

19. Shyam Sunder, *Stock Prices and Risk Related to Accounting Changes in Inventory Valuation*, 50 ACCT. REV. 305–15 (1975); G. BENNETT STEWART, III, QUEST FOR VALUE 24 (1991).

specify the amortization period. Then costs incurred after the product is released to customers are expensed as incurred.) Yet, in most cases, the cost is incurred with the hope of a future gain and, in that sense, an argument is occasionally made that the expenditure is more akin to an investment for the future than a current expense and thus ought to be capitalized.

The proponents of the thesis that R&D costs ought to be capitalized cite the pharmaceutical industry to bolster their case. It is no secret that the pharmaceutical companies generally enjoy high price to earnings multiples, notwithstanding their swoon in 1993–1994, when they lost much of their market value due to the uncertainty about federal health care policy and the apparent possibility of price regulation. The high price/earnings multiples common in the pharmaceutical industry could reflect exceptional growth opportunities, but they could also reflect something much simpler. Looking at the R&D budget of a pharmaceutical company as an investment in the future, the market is, one might argue, capitalizing the cost and amortizing it, probably over a three to five year period. If costs were flat, then capitalizing rather than expensing R&D costs would make no difference. However, because most pharmaceutical companies are growing, and because costs are rising, the R&D costs are rising. Further, R&D costs are a substantial portion of the cost structure of pharmaceutical companies, usually running approximately 10% of revenues. The difference between expensing and capitalizing these costs is not dramatic, but it is enough to explain at least part of the difference between the usual market multiple of about 15 and the usual pharmaceutical company multiple of 17 to 18.

A recent study supports this line of reasoning. A researcher from the University of California and another from the University of Illinois analyzed virtually every major industry in which R&D spending is significant (including chemicals, pharmaceuticals, machinery, computer hardware, electricity, electronics, transportation vehicles, and scientific instruments), and restated the earnings of the companies in each such industry to reflect the capitalization and amortization of R&D costs over the estimated duration of the R&D benefits.[20] (The latter had been found in other studies to vary from chemicals and pharmaceuticals, where the average useful life of R&D is the longest—about 9 years—to scientific instruments, where it is the shortest—about 5 years.) The researchers then ran correlations between (1) GAAP earnings and subsequent stock prices and (2) earnings adjusted to capitalize and amortize R&D expenses and subsequent stock prices. They found a highly statistically significant correlation between the adjusted earnings (that is, R&D capitalized and amortized) and subsequent stock prices.

Furthermore, the proponents of capitalizing R&D argue that by expensing rather than capitalizing the costs, GAAP understates the equity account. Once the adjustment is made to capitalize and amortize R&D, the return on equity in the industry is in much closer alignment with other industries.

The counter, and more traditional, view is that capitalizing R&D is nonsense. After all, if one were to capitalize R&D, why not capitalize all costs, including marketing and overhead? It is a hard line to draw, and a slippery slope, so why start

---

20. Baruch Lev & Theodore Sougiannis, *The Capitalization, Amortization, and Value-Relevance of R&D*, 21 J. Acct. & Econ. 107–38 (1996).

down it? The response is that in contrast to R&D spending, the effect of advertising expenditures is of short duration, usually only 1 to 2 years.[21]

Another wrinkle has crept into R&D accounting in the past few years. When IBM acquired Lotus Development Corporation in 1995 for $3.24 billion, it had to account for the transaction as a purchase inasmuch as it was made for cash. As is typical of software companies, Lotus did not have many tangible assets. To minimize the amount of goodwill on its books, IBM dusted off an accounting rule[22] that permitted IBM, once it acquired Lotus, to treat past R&D costs as an asset. Then it wrote off the asset all at once, taking a one-time charge rather than amortization "hits" to its income statement every year for a much longer period. This is known as a *shadow pooling* because like a pooling, the transaction—although a purchase for accounting purposes—does not create a drag on future GAAP earnings. Now other companies, such as Shiva Corporation[23] are taking a page out of IBM's book when they acquire companies with significant amounts of in-process R&D costs.

Before leaving this point, it is worth noting that the market and the accounting profession have different orientations at times. The accounting profession has historically been—and remains—extremely apprehensive about putting a number on anything that has not been involved in a transaction. Consequently, GAAP financial reports are based on transactions that have occurred and can be measured. GAAP does not purport to deal with values. Further, the accounting profession has understandably become highly skittish about litigation and would rather be conservative, even though a consequence of being conservative is that the financials may not accurately reflect economic reality. This bias is easy to understand if one compares (1) the number of dollars the Big Six firms have paid out in lawsuits in which they were accused of blessing overstated earnings with (2) the sums they have paid in lawsuits in which they were accused of attaching their names to understated earnings.

The market has a different preoccupation, namely value, and would rather be as close to the economic-reality mark as possible than grounded in historic costs and accounting conservatism. When economic reality deviates from accounting convention and conservatism, there is considerable evidence that investors put their cash with the economic realities. To that, accountants say, in effect, "Fine. They do their job, and we'll do ours." Thus, valuing a private company, or a division or other unit of a public company, or understanding how the market is valuing a public company often involves restating the GAAP financials to the extent necessary to capture and reflect the economic realities more accurately.

Deferred Tax Liabilities

As explained in chapter 2, deferred tax liabilities (DTLs) are essentially free capital made available by the government. If the company with DTLs had been keeping its books on a cash basis, there would be no DTL and the equity account would be higher by the amount of the DTL. Because of its virtual permanence (and to reflect

---

21. *Id.* at 112.
22. International Business Machines Corporation, 1995 ANNUAL REPORT.
23. Shiva Corporation, 1994 ANNUAL REPORT.

Table 68
USX Steel Group, 1994*

| | As Reported | Adjustments to | | As Adjusted |
| | | Equity | Net Income | |
		($ million)		
1. Net income	501			
2. Equity	4,302			
3. Return on equity	11.6%			
4. Increase in deferred tax liabilities	403		403	
5. Deferred tax liabilities	1,327	1,327		
6. Adjusted net income				904**
7. Adjusted equity				5,629***
8. Adjusted return on equity				16.1%

*USX Steel Group, 1994 Annual Report.
**Line 1 plus line 4.
***Line 2 plus line 5.

cash realities), many investors consider the DTL to be part of shareholders' equity and, in several ways, they have a point. Not only does a DTL more accurately reflect cash realities, but if the company is growing (as most are, if only because inflation makes the numbers keep looking larger) and investing in new plant and equipment (P&E) to stay in business as old P&E is worn out or grows obsolete, the company is likely to have a permanent DTL. Of course, that is the case only to the extent the company remains a viable going concern and continues to replenish its assets. As long as the company is going strong and appears able to maintain a DTL on an ongoing basis, the bad news for management is that the DTL increases the denominator in the return on equity fraction, but the good news is that investors also make an adjustment to the numerator by adding to earnings the year-to-year change in the DTL. The 1994 results at the USX Steel Group, summarized in Table 68, illustrate the point quite clearly.

Although the topic here is DTLs, it is worth noting that, conversely, increases in deferred tax assets (DTAs) ought to be deducted from GAAP earnings in calculating cash earnings, though DTAs are still rarely material.

Summary of Adjustments to GAAP Earnings

GAAP earnings and cash earnings are often very closely matched, and one is frequently an excellent surrogate for the other. When this is not the case, however, the evidence is strong—though not yet compelling—that over the short term the market prefers cash earnings to accrual earnings.

As a consequence, in valuing a company it is often useful to restate GAAP earnings to reflect cash earnings. Although there are many possible adjustments, and though not every gross-up is important to every company, the most important adjustments are usually (1) to add back any increase in LIFO reserves, (2) to add goodwill amortization expense back to earnings, (3) to add to earnings any non-cash write-offs or restructuring charges, and (4) to add to earnings any increase in DTLs. Just as the annual charges are added to earnings, the total capital account is also grossed up, as described later in this chapter.

There is one non-cash expense, however, namely depreciation, that must be deducted in calculating earnings. To be sure, many analysts will add back depreciation to calculate cash flow. However, if the company is a going concern, then it must replenish its P&E as it becomes worn out or outmoded, or else the company will go out of business. Hence depreciation charges should not be added back in calculating cash earnings. (If you need a refresher about why depreciation is a source of cash, albeit one of many possible sources of cash, please refer to Sidebar 12.) In some years, the company might in fact use the cash flow from depreciation for other purposes (to service debt or buy out a minority shareholder, for example), and rely on raising capital from other sources (such as a sale of equity) to finance new P&E when needed. However, on average over time, the company must use the cash equivalent of depreciation expense to replenish its P&E. Because depreciation is geared to historic costs, as costs rise the depreciation cash flow alone may not be sufficient to replenish the P&E at current costs. Indeed, in periods of high inflation, the insufficiency of depreciation cash flow is a serious problem for P&E intensive companies, as illustrated in Sidebar 23.

_____ *Sidebar 23* _____

Effects of Inflation on Earnings and the Ability to Replenish P&E

Although inflation in the United States has not been a serious problem in the 1990s (indeed there are occasional forecasts of disinflation), inflation tends to increase the cost of most supplies and P&E. Because the depreciation expense is geared to historic costs, it is inadequate to replace P&E at current costs when the old P&E wears out. Because most new inventory costs more to replace than the inventory being sold, cost of sales in many industries is also understated, though this problem is less acute because the inventory is usually not exposed to inflation for as long as the P&E.

The problem hits capital intensive industries especially hard. Bethlehem Steel Corporation's results in 1981, a year in which the country faced double-digit inflation, illustrate the point.

Column 1 summarizes the income statement as reported in accordance with GAAP. Column 2 shows the income statement restated to reflect what the company's expenses would have been if inventory had been purchased or produced at year-end and the company's P&E had been replaced during the year at current costs (with resulting higher depreciation expenses). There are two things to notice.

First, although revenues would have been the same, the cost of goods sold (CGS) and depreciation expenses both would have been higher at current

Table 69
Income Statement Adjusted for Changing Prices

Bethlehem Steel Corporation, 1981*

	(1) As Reported on Historical Cost Basis	(2) Adjusted for Changes in Specific Prices (current costs) ($ million)	(3) Difference
Revenues	7,419	7,419	0
Cost of goods sold	6,324	6,389	65
Depreciation	377	631	254
Selling, general, and administrative expenses	365	365	0
Operating profit	353	34	(319)
Interest	60	60	0
Profit before tax	293	(26)	(319)
Income taxes	82	82	0
Profit after tax	211	(108)	(319)

*Bethlehem Steel Corporation, 1981 Annual Report.

costs, resulting in lower earnings. Bethlehem Steel reported $211 million in net income, as shown in column 1, correctly based on GAAP accounting. However, its real earnings were negative $108 million and its value was being eroded. Further, the company was being put at risk because once its P&E was fully depreciated, it would not have sufficient cash to replace the existing P&E. In theory it could go outside for financing, but the company was already levered, and incurring additional debt under then current circumstances would have been unwise. Any new equity investor would value the company based on the economic realities and offer such a low price for shares as to make an equity offering terribly dilutive. This placed Bethlehem Steel in a serious bind, a position shared by a great many capital intensive companies at the time.

Second, despite the circumstances, the company was being taxed based on illusory earnings. That is, its taxes were the same, $82 million, in each column. The IRC does not reflect the economic realities but rather imposes taxes based on nominal earnings. Thus Bethlehem Steel (as well as a great many companies like it) was facing severe economic losses yet paying out cash taxes to the government, rendering the company less able to finance new P&E. Is it any wonder that our steel industry produces far less steel today than in the 1970s and has been diversifying? The 1986 Tax Reform Act ameliorated this problem to a degree by allowing accelerated depreciation,[24] but if the country ever again experiences double-digit inflation, this problem will return.

---

24. *See* I.R.C. §§ 167, 168 (1986) (provisions pertaining to the modified accelerated cost recovery system).

Although the problem will not be confined to capital intensive companies, it will hit them the hardest, though perhaps not as hard as in the early 1980s due to the change in the tax laws, greater management skill in dealing with inflation, and global alternatives.

Returning to Bethlehem Steel, the only good news from its standpoint was that, although it did badly, its creditors did worse. It had $1 billion in long-term debt, which it could service in ever-cheaper dollars. The decline in the purchasing power of its borrowed funds amounted to $117 million during the year. Although that is not recognized as a source of income under GAAP, the decline in the economic value of the debt liability was a source of value to the company. Indeed, use of debt can be a critical component of a financial strategy for any company anticipating high inflation or operating in a country experiencing double-digit inflation, provided its debt service and repayment is in the local currency. Though a full discussion of the point is beyond the scope of this book, the use of debt to protect against risks faced in foreign environments can be fraught with both dangers and opportunities.

Many loan covenants and definitions are written to measure interest coverage in terms of earnings before interest, taxes, depreciation, and amortization (EBITDA). It is one thing to do this for purposes of definitions and covenants. Yet, if the borrower is really planning to service the debt not only from earnings but also from the depreciation cash flow, then the borrower may be on a going-out-of-business trajectory unless it can find another way to finance new P&E as it becomes needed. In sum, when one is calculating cash earnings, adding back non-cash deductions is fine, with the important exception of depreciation. To reflect the economic realities, depreciation must remain deducted from GAAP earnings to arrive at the best articulation of cash earnings. As noted earlier in this chapter, cash earnings should not be confused with cash flow or free cash flow.

Long-Term or Short-Term Focus?

The conventional wisdom is that investors are focused on the short run. Indeed, anecdotal evidence of analysts being preoccupied with the earnings of the current year, quarter, or even month, is compelling and legion.

Yet that may be noise rather than the thoughtful deliberations of the market leaders. To sort that out, two academic researchers studied the market's reaction to the announcements of major capital spending plans.[25] Specifically, they examined the market's reaction to the announcement of 547 capital spending plans made between 1975 and 1981 by 285 different companies. The announcements were mostly

---

25. John McConnell & Chris Muscarella, *Corporate Capital Expenditure Decisions and the Market Value of Firms*, 14 J. Fin. Econ. 399–422 (1985).

of plans for new plants, but in some cases for new R&D initiatives or investments in other categories of fixed assets.

If the market thinks short term, then one would expect the stock prices to drop in response to the announcements, because in the short run, the investment in the project would adversely impact earnings (due to depreciation and other expenses being incurred before the revenue stream would begin). The researchers found that the market reacted favorably to the announcements and that the share price appreciation was statistically significant. The researchers also found that share prices dropped by a statistically significant amount for companies that announced decreases in capital spending.[26]

That is not to say that the market reacts favorably to every new capital spending plan, for if a new investment seems likely to destroy value, the market will reflect such expected destruction in the current stock price. But if the market believes the new investment will offer salutary returns, it will bid up the stock prices.

Witness Intel Corporation. On October 20, 1995, it announced[27] that it would build an advanced wafer fabrication plant in Ireland (projected to cost $1.5 billion), a flash memory wafer fabrication plant in Israel (projected to cost $1.6 billion), and a computer board factory in Malaysia. Its stock had risen 6.2% in the week before the announcement, a week during which the NASDAQ Composite rose 3.3% and the S&P 500 only 0.7%. During the 10 days after the announcement, the chief investment officer at Oppenheimer & Co. said, "Market psychology is in terrible shape," and, "There's a real psychological problem among portfolio managers . . . and the year's gains are starting to slip away."[28] Intel's stock continued to outperform the NASDAQ Composite and the S&P 500. Thus, even though the market may often be short-sighted, there are instances when it rewards long-range activities.

Net Operating Profit after Tax (NOPAT)

The above discussion describes the major adjustments that may be necessary to convert GAAP earnings to cash earnings. To determine how much a company is really earning by virtue of its operations, two further adjustments are necessary. Once these steps have been taken, one knows what the company's cash earnings from operations would have been had the company been entirely unlevered and paid only cash taxes. Cash earnings calculated in this way are known as the net operating profit after tax (NOPAT).

Unlevering Earnings

The first such adjustment is to unlever the earnings. Financial leverage is very important. In fact, it is so important that one wants to understand it very thoroughly, just as one wants to understand precisely how much value the company is creating with its

---

26. *Id.*
27. Intel Corp., Intel Expands International Manufacturing Sites (Oct. 20, 1995) (press release).
28. David Kansas, *Jittery Investors May Act to Preserve '95 Gains*, WALL ST. J., Oct. 30, 1995, at C-1.

Table 70
Unlevering Earnings

Line		Company X	Company Y	
1	Operating profit	$10,000	$10,000	
2	Interest expense	(0)	(4,000)	
3	Profit before tax	10,000	6,000	
4	Tax (at 40%)	(4,000)	(2,400)	
5	Profit after tax	6,000	3,600	
6	Interest expense	0	4,000	
7	Tax benefit of interest	0	(1,600)	
8	Interest expense after tax	0	2,400	(lines 6 − 7)
9	NOPAT*	6,000	6,000	(lines 5 + 8)

*Net operating profit after tax, which is net income as though the company had no debt.

Note that if Company Y had been unlevered its cash taxes would have been the sum of its own tax of $2,400 (line 4) plus the interest tax shield of $1,600 (line 7), for a total of $4,000.

operations. Accordingly, the value created through operations must be distinguished from the value created through financing. To do so, the NOPAT must first be unlevered.

To unlever the NOPAT, earnings must be restated as though the company had been financed exclusively with equity. Had this been the case, there would have been no interest expense and no interest tax shelter. Taxes would have been higher (due to the absence of the interest deduction), but all the cash earnings would have been available to the equity holders, with the result that the cash earnings available for them would have been greater (by the amount of the interest expense net of the tax shelter). To illustrate, as shown in Table 70, suppose Company X has an operating profit of $10,000 and is unlevered. If the tax rate is 40%, its tax expense will be $4,000 and its NOPAT will be $6,000. Company Y, like Company X, has an operating profit of $10,000, but it is financed with a combination of debt and equity and has an interest expense of $4,000, a pretax profit of $6,000, taxes of $2,400, and profit after tax of $3,600.

There are several things to notice about Table 70. First, Company X has a profit after tax of $6,000 versus only $3,600 for Company Y. Notice also, however, that the providers of capital to Company Y (that is, the lenders plus the shareholders) are able to take $7,600 out of the company ($4,000 interest plus $3,600 profit after tax), whereas the providers of capital to Company X are able to take only $6,000 out of the company. The reason for the difference is that Company Y paid $1,600 less in taxes as a result of the tax shield of the debt. In effect, the $4,000 interest expense cost Company Y $2,400 and the government $1,600.[29] If Company Y had no debt, its pretax profit would—like Company X's—have been $10,000 rather than $6,000. The $4,000 extra pretax profit would have been allocated as $1,600 to higher taxes and $2,400 to higher earnings. The $2,400 higher earnings on top of Company Y's unadjusted profit after tax of $3,600 brings its NOPAT to $6,000, exactly the same as Company X's NOPAT.

---

29. The government gets some of this back when it taxes Company Y's lenders.

The tax shield is a zero-sum game among the company, the providers of capital, and the government, but when viewed exclusively from the perspective of the providers of capital, the tax shield can be a source of value. Indeed it can be an important source; but before we turn to it in greater detail, there are other matters to consider.

Notice that Company X and Company Y have the same NOPAT (line 9 in Table 70). Many find that counterintuitive; but please linger with the thought, for it is highly important. Remember that we are measuring the company's unlevered earnings—simply restating Company Y's cash earnings as if it had no debt (that is, as if it were capitalized just as Company X is capitalized). We are doing this to identify the value of the company's operations, isolating the operations from the company's financing—that is, making Company Y, pro forma, a pure play in its operations. Seen through this lens, it should come as no surprise that Company Y's NOPAT is the same as Company X's NOPAT, inasmuch as they began with the same operating profit.

Reducing Pretax Profit by Cash Taxes Only

In calculating NOPAT, the second adjustment to earnings is to reduce the pretax profit by cash taxes only; that is, to adjust the GAAP tax accruals to the cash realities. This step requires (1) adding to earnings the increase in the DTL account (or reducing earnings by the decrease in the DTL account), (2) subtracting from earnings any increase in the DTA account (or adding to earnings any decrease in the DTA account), and (3) isolating the effects of any interest tax shelter by adding to the tax expense the incremental taxes that would have been paid had the company had no interest deduction. The last step is illustrated in Table 70, where one can observe that Company Y's cash tax, if it were unlevered, would be the sum of its tax bill (line 4) plus the interest tax shield (line 7).

Summary of NOPAT

There are numerous variations on the foregoing description of NOPAT, and so far there is no single, universally accepted method. However, the practice of deriving cash earnings rather than relying on GAAP's definition of earnings is becoming more widespread. The foregoing description of NOPAT is probably the most widely accepted and the most persuasive. In sum, this NOPAT method is calculated by beginning with GAAP earnings and making these adjustments:

1. adding back non-cash expenses (other than depreciation), most notably goodwill amortization, non-cash write-offs or restructuring charges, and increases in DTLs,
2. unlevering the company by adding to earnings any interest expense net of taxes, and
3. adjusting the tax expense not only to isolate any deferred tax, but also to add any tax shield resulting from interest expense; thus the tax expense should be only the cash tax the company would have paid had it been financed exclusively with equity.

An alternative method for calculating NOPAT is to begin with revenues and deduct only cash expenses. This method, known as the *operating method*, also requires that adjustments be made to unlever the company and to deduct only cash taxes calculated as though the company were unlevered. The NOPAT, then, is the amount of cash earnings that would be available to the providers of all the capital if the company were unlevered.

Both methods are illustrated in chapter 11, at Table 98, page 211.

Capital

Total Capital

Total capital is the amount of cash or other consideration that has been invested in the company with the expectation of a return. Total capital includes not only the equity, but also the debt, debentures, preferred stock, and any other securities or instruments that may have been issued by the company. Just as the income statement is adjusted to reflect cash earnings more accurately, capital is also adjusted by adding some gross-ups. Previously we observed that NOPAT includes the year's increases in DTLs, any deductions for goodwill expense, increases in LIFO reserves, increases in bad-debt expense, non-cash write-offs or restructuring charges, and any other non-cash deductions (other than depreciation). Just as the NOPAT is grossed up by such items, reflecting income statement adjustments, the total capital account is grossed up by the balance sheet amounts of these items.

For example, referring to Sidebar 24, the 1997 NOPAT of Amalgamated Industries (a hypothetical company) includes the increase in the LIFO reserves in the amount of $20,000. Correspondingly, the total capital is grossed up by the balance sheet amount of the LIFO reserves of $30,000. Similarly, the 1997 NOPAT includes the $5,000 goodwill expense, and the total capital includes the amount of all the 1997 goodwill expense plus any amounts expensed in previous years. The company's 1997 NOPAT is adjusted upward by the non-cash $30,000 fixed asset write-off, and its total capital is adjusted upward by both the $50,000 1996 fixed asset write-off and the $30,000 1997 write-off.

Sidebar 24

Certain Adjustments to Balance Sheet
to Calculate Total Capital and NOPAT

In addition to any other adjustments, the total capital for Amalgamated Industries will be grossed up by adding (1) its LIFO reserves of $30,000, (2) its goodwill $5,000 amortization plus any goodwill amortization from previous years, and (3) its $50,000 1996 and $30,000 1997 fixed asset write-offs, plus any such write-offs in previous years.

The company's 1997 NOPAT will include upward adjustments for (1) the increase in LIFO reserves of $20,000, (2) the 1997 goodwill expense of $5,000, and (3) the $30,000 fixed asset write-off.

Table 71		
Amalgamated Industries		

	1996	**1997**
Certain balance sheet items		
Inventory replacement cost	$100,000	$130,000
LIFO reserves	10,000	30,000
LIFO inventory	90,000	100,000
Goodwill (net of amortization)	50,000	45,000
Certain income statement items		
Goodwill expense	10,000	5,000
Fixed asset write-offs	50,000	30,000

The most important gross-ups of capital are usually the deferred tax account, the LIFO reserves, the cumulative goodwill previously amortized, and any non-cash restructuring charges or write-offs taken in the previous years.

Return on Capital Invested

Having thus calculated the cash return (the NOPAT) and the total capital (TC), one can calculate the return on capital:

$$\frac{\text{NOPAT}}{\text{TC}} = \text{Return on Total Capital } (r)$$

The return on total capital (r) is equal to the NOPAT divided by the total capital. For example, if NOPAT is $100 and the total capital is $1,000, then r is 10%. As for the total capital, it does not matter whether the cash is invested as equity (as grossed up), debt, or a hybrid security. It expects a return. As for the NOPAT, it also does not matter whether the company elects to pay the earnings attributable to the equity as dividends. What does matter is that the cash earnings are there and available to be paid out.

The return on capital thus calculated is an extremely important number, for it identifies how effectively the company has managed its operations. It is a measure isolated from the effects of leverage. Again, financial leverage is highly important; yet, in measuring value, it is useful to distinguish how much value is created by the company's operations and, separately, how much value is created by its financial leverage. We will return to this point later. First, there is another important matter to consider.

Earning the Cost of Capital

If a company's return on capital is 10% and its aggregate (as opposed to marginal) cost of capital is 12%, is it really creating value? Perhaps the answer is obvious. After all, if you borrow money at 12% and deploy it earning 10%, it would not take long, one would hope, to figure out that you were subsidizing your lenders, your customers, your suppliers, or your workers. Presumably, you would look to get a higher return, cut your cost of capital, or, if you could not do either, exit the business.

Although this seems obvious, one would not know it from reading some management statements. For example, Time Warner's 1991 report to shareholders, noting that four of the company's five businesses set new records, speaks of the company's "strong record of performance" and "outstanding 1991 performance" and achievement, even though the market value of the company's stock dropped by $6 billion on losses of $99 million.[30] Or consider General Motors Corporation, which from 1983 through 1994 generated returns well below its cost of capital. Over the 12 years from 1983 through 1994, the company's return on capital failed to match its cost of capital,[31] and the company's market capitalization rose far less than its cost of equity, despite a strong bull market. One could have bought the stock for $40 a share in 1986 and by 1996 seen it rise to $55, a 37.5% appreciation, during which time the Dow Industrial Average tripled. Yet on February 9, 1988, the chairman's and president's letter accompanying the 1987 annual report described sales exceeding $100 billion, earnings of $3.6 billion, "a strong cash flow, a very strong balance sheet, modernized production facilities, the finest product line in GM's history, and a very strong flow of additional new products."[32] That promise was painfully slow to materialize, although in 1995 the company finally earned its cost of capital.[33] Yet even then, the company's CEO and president, John F. Smith, Jr., acknowledged in 1996 that "we are still not where we need to be."[34]

Investors were figuring out, as you would have, that earning less than your cost of capital is a losing proposition. That requires not only that we know the return on capital, as explained in this chapter, but also the cost of capital, the topic of the next three chapters.

Chapters 7, 8, and 9 pertain to the cost of debt, the cost of equity, and the weighted average cost of equity, respectively. The topics are necessarily rather technical, at least in places. This is particularly true for chapter 8, which concerns the cost of equity. Some readers might wish to skip these chapters and proceed directly to chapter 10.

---

30. Letter to shareholders from Chairman and President of Time Warner (undated) (accompanying Time Warner's 1991 Financial Report).

31. *Stern Stewart Performance 1000*, 8 BANK AM. J. APPLIED CORP. FIN. 107–19 (Winter 1996).

32. GENERAL MOTORS CORPORATION, 1987 ANNUAL REPORT.

33. Irwin Ross, *Stern Stewart Performance 1000*, 9 BANK AM. J. APPLIED CORP. FIN. 115–28 (Winter 1997).

34. GENERAL MOTORS CORPORATION, 1995 ANNUAL REPORT 4 (letter to Stockholders and Friends, dated January 30, 1996).

The Cost of Debt

Chapter

7

A company's weighted average cost of capital is important for two reasons. First, it establishes the level of return on capital that the company must achieve to cover its cost of capital. After all, the whole purpose of a corporate strategy is to manage the owners' capital in a way that gives the owners a favorable return. Second, the weighted average cost of capital establishes the rate at which future earnings will be discounted to determine their present value.

The cost of debt is one of the two components of a company's cost of capital. The cost of capital has been enshrined at most American companies and is a major building block of the economic value added method and of the discounted cash flow method of valuing companies. In this chapter and in chapters 8 and 9, the methods of calculating the cost of debt, the cost of equity, and the weighted average cost of capital, respectively, as well as the concepts behind them, will be explained.

Before getting into the subject, however, a caveat is in order. There is a small but growing opinion that the cost of capital does not matter. The point of view is novel, if not heretical, but is espoused by some leading theoreticians. The proponents of the view would not argue that capital is free. Rather, their arguments are more along the lines that (1) the cost of capital is so hard to measure that the effort is seldom worth the candle, (2) once a company achieves a rate of return that exceeds the consumer price index or some other rather modest threshold, the differences in cost of capital have little impact on a company's value, and (3) to the extent a company adds leverage it loses flexibility, or options to do some things, and that flexibility has value that offsets much of the value of the leverage.

Some companies, whether by design or coincidence, agree with the proponents of the view that capital costs do not matter. For instance, when Philip Morris[1] bought General Foods (for $5.6 billion), it did a thorough analysis of the acquisition, including a study of market share, product lines, cash flow, the multiple being paid, and the way the acquisition would be financed. However, in the final analysis, Philip Morris gave little weight to its cost of capital, considering the acquisition to be strategic. Unfortunately, many companies label initiatives *strategic* when they will not earn

---

1. S.L. Mintz, *Capital Ideas: A Conversation with Hans Storr and Steven Ross*, 12 CFO MAG. 35 (Apr. 1996).

the company's cost of capital but management wants to do them anyway.[2] Although the purchase has worked well for Philip Morris, such acquisitions often do not, for reasons discussed later. Nonetheless, cost of capital is central to the prevailing valuation theory and practice.

Measuring Risk

The beginning point in understanding cost of capital is risk, the fundamental concept being that investors expect to be compensated for bearing risk. The higher the risk, the greater the return the investors expect if they are going to provide capital to the company. Given that an investor can earn a return on Treasury securities with minimal risk of default,[3] he or she will not undertake the risk of buying other debt instruments or equity securities without the expectation of earning a higher rate of return.

It is interesting to observe how interest rates are constructed. There are three types of Treasury securities: bills, notes, and bonds. Treasury bills have maturities up to 1 year, Treasury notes have maturities of 1 to 10 years, and Treasury bonds have maturities of 10 to 30 years. The simplest, the T-bill, is designed to (1) compensate the lender for the expected inflation rate, so the purchasing power of funds lent is returned to the lender (note, however, that the lender will not come out whole if it has to pay a tax on the interest thus "earned"), and (2) pay the lender a real rate of interest for the period of the loan.[4]

Treasury bonds introduce a third element into the equation, namely a longer time horizon. Even assuming there is zero risk of default, investors are exposed for a longer period of time to the risk of volatility in inflation rates. If they buy the bonds and the inflation rate rises, then interest rates will rise and the value of the bonds they hold will drop (to give the buyer a return comparable to that which he or she could earn on a newly issued T-bond). Hence the third component of interest in the T-bond is a term—or maturity—premium.

In the case of corporate debt, a fourth element must be considered, which is the risk that the borrower will be unable to pay the interest on the debt and/or principal as it comes due. Hence, in addition to being compensated for the expected inflation rate, a real rate of interest, and a maturity premium, the lender will want a risk premium to compensate it for the risk in excess of the risk of holding a T-note or T-bond. The premium for risk of default is the incremental interest rate needed to

---

2. In defense of management, at times these initiatives are options. That is, management might commit an affordable level of resources in an attempt to develop a new line of business. If it does not pan out, management can drop it, and if it does pan out, management can commit more resources and build it.

3. Treasury bills are not zero risk. Not only is there some risk that inflation will spike and deprive bill holders of a return, but the two shutdowns of the federal government in late 1995 pointed out the possibility of a default.

4. The formula for capturing the rate of interest, then, is as follows:

$$\text{interest rate} = (1 + \text{expected inflation rate}) \times (1 + \text{real rate of interest})$$

For example, if the expected inflation rate is 5% and the real rate of interest is 2%, then the nominal interest rate charged will be 1.05×1.02, or 1.071, or 7.1%.

induce the lender to lend to the company rather than to buy T-notes or T-bonds, essentially compensating the lender for the credit risk that materializes if the borrower proves unable to service the debt.

Measuring Cost of Debt

The amount that a particular company must pay for long-term debt, being a function not only of then current interest rates but also of other known variables, can be predicted. Moody's, Standard & Poor's, and others rate corporate debt, taking a number of factors into account. Empirically, sheer size of the company is the single most powerful determinant of Moody's ratings and the cost of debt, exceeding even the degree of leverage. This being the case, large companies can often increase their leverage considerably without increasing their borrowing costs very much.

It is striking that for the companies whose revenues exceed approximately $1 billion, adding substantial financial leverage impacts their pretax borrowing rate remarkably little. For instance, after Host Marriott Corporation spun off Marriott International, Inc. in 1993, its financial leverage rose dramatically, because the spun-off unit became essentially debt-free while the former parent unit continued to hold virtually all the debt.[5] Soon after the spin-off, interest rates throughout the economy rose significantly, making it difficult to determine exactly how much the post-spin-off interest rates for Host Marriott rose as a result of the increase in its leverage. The company privately estimates[6] that the incremental pretax cost was no more than half a percent, and that is a reasonable estimate.

When contemplating future projects, a company should measure its cost of debt at its marginal cost of debt—that is, its borrowing rate on incremental debt—and not on its historic interest rates. A good indication of that cost is the yield to maturity on a company's own publicly issued debt.

A company can also determine its marginal cost of debt by asking prospective lenders. If the company is contemplating a material change in the degree of its leverage, it can consult the criteria such as those described above and determine what its cost of debt would be if it were to increase or reduce its financial leverage significantly.

Nontraded Debt

If a company has debt that is not publicly traded, then a reasonable estimate of its borrowing cost is the yield to maturity on the publicly traded bonds of similar companies, or on similar debt securities issued by companies of comparable size, leverage, profitability, and riskiness, albeit not necessarily in the same industry, as explained in chapter 5.

---

5. HOST MARRIOTT CORPORATION, NOTICE OF 1993 ANNUAL MEETING AND PROXY STATEMENT, at 53–72.
6. Telephone discussion with the office of the treasurer, Host Marriott (Apr. 21, 1994).

Target Capital Structure

One often hears executives say that their cost of capital for the next project is determined by whether they plan to finance it with debt or equity. There is a trap inherent in this reasoning. For instance, a company might proceed with project 1, which promises to provide a return of 10%, figuring that it will finance the project with debt costing 6% after tax. Then it proceeds with project 2, which promises to return 9%, because the company plans to finance that with debt costing 7% after tax. Then the company has the opportunity to invest in project 3, which holds the prospect of a 13% return, but management concludes that the company is precluded from embarking on project 3 because the project would need to be financed with equity costing 14%. That is a foolish result, for the company is thereby passing up an investment offering a 13% return, but making investments offering only 9% and 10% returns because of the random fact that it had financed these projects with debt but would have financed the next project with equity. Rather, each project should be considered relative to the company's cost of capital based on its target debt to equity ratio, regardless of whether the particular project will be financed with debt or with equity. That way, on average over time, the company will undertake the best projects.

The reader may have noticed use of the term *target* when referring to the capital structure. Although companies' actual capital structures usually approximate their target capital structures, they do not always do so. Boards of directors should have in mind (and communicate to investors) the target capital structure. This has implications that will be discussed in chapters 9 and following.

The After Tax Cost of Debt

The cost of debt that really matters to companies is the after tax cost, which is the marginal borrowing rate less the tax shield. For example, if the pretax borrowing cost is 10% and the tax rate is 40%, then the borrowing rate is 6%; that is, $10\% (1 - t)$, where t is equal to the tax rate. Further, the cost of debt that usually matters most for a growing company is the cost of borrowing the next dollar of debt. Because the cost of capital usually becomes germane in the context of arranging financing for the next project, it is the cost of the next dollar into the company that is most important.

Reducing Cost of Debt

At times, lawyers can help their borrowing clients reduce their cost of debt by reducing the risk of the debt to the lender. When the circumstances warrant it, the lawyer who can find collateral, ways to secure the lender's security interest, or ways the lender can realize the value of the collateral in the event of default, or who can draft tighter, wiser, or cleaner covenants, can reduce the riskiness of the loan. This ought to reduce the cost of the debt. If the lawyer is counsel to the lender, then the added security might enable his or her client to lower its rates and be more competitive.

The Cost of Equity

Chapter

8

In addition to the cost of debt (chapter 7), the other major cost of capital is the cost of equity. The concept of the cost of equity is one of the most elusive—yet one of the most important, powerful, and intriguing—in the entire area of corporate finance.

Consider a hypothetical entrepreneur who owns all the stock of his or her company, with a value of about $50 million. Needing another $50 million from outside the company to finance its growth, the owner elects to raise equity rather than borrow, apparently wanting to sleep better at night. A few years later he or she sells the company for $200 million. The owner pockets half ($100 million) less taxes, and the new equity investors receive the other half. Had the owner caused the company to borrow, then upon its sale the company could pay off the $50 million in debt and the owner would have netted $150 million pretax ($200 million in sale proceeds, less the $50 million in debt) rather than $100 million.[1] Thus the real cost of equity is not the current dividend the board decides to declare and pay. Rather it is the present value of the expected return to the shareholders, which may be delivered in a variety of ways, most notably (1) the current dividend, if any, (2) all future dividends, (3) funds used to repurchase shares issued by the company, (4) any liquidating dividend, and (5) any cash, stock, or other consideration received from another company in the event the issuer is acquired. In discussing the cost of equity, occasionally all these are together referred to as the dividend. To a lawyer's ear this is an inexact use of the term *dividend*, but this broad definition is commonly used when discussing the cost of equity. You might think of it as the distributions to shareholders in whatever form they are made.

Before delving into the details of calculating the cost of equity, a few more general comments might be helpful. First, think of the cost of equity as the cost of the next dollar of equity to be raised by the issuer. It reflects the minimum return an investor expects to earn on the investment. Thus the cost of equity for the company is the flip side of the expected return to the shareholders buying the shares sold by the company. They are opposite sides of the same coin. Second, the cost of equity for private companies is higher than for publicly held companies, assuming that all other things are equal. The reason is that the shares issued by private companies are less liquid, and liquidity has value because it enables the shareholders to choose when to sell the asset.

---

1. This problem can be solved for the issuer if the new shares are sold for a high enough price; that is, a price reflecting the future returns that are, in fact, earned. The assumption that the earnings can be deployed earning such returns is important.

Let's begin by considering the cost of equity for public companies.[2] At any given level of risk, the investor expects a given level of return. If the investor does not expect to get that level of return from Company A, then he or she will select another investment offering that expected return.

The level of risk tends to vary with the industry and can change over time. A good example of the latter is provided by companies in the power utility industry. By and large, they were, until recently, the least risky companies, for they were essentially assured a rate of return by virtue of their regulated status. However, high inflation hurt them very badly in the late 1970s and early 1980s. Also, technology and a changing regulatory environment are now removing regulatory protection and vastly expanding the geographic scope of competition. Consequently power utilities have become considerably more risky, with a concomitant impact on their cost of equity.

Other industries offer examples of varying levels of risk. For instance, food companies tend to be low on the risk spectrum, for people need to eat, diet vows notwithstanding. The food wholesalers are less risky than the consumer food products companies because, being unbranded, they are less subject to individual tastes. The next least risky companies are those of average risk, which are noncyclical companies (such as medical supply companies) whose products are needed consistently throughout the business cycle. Slightly more risky than average are the cyclical durables companies, such as those producing chemicals, steel, and most notably automobiles. Moving further out on the risk spectrum one next finds the more discretionary cyclicals, such as the airlines, followed closely by the resorts and leisure time companies. The most risky companies are in electronics, software, and other high-technology areas, where rapid technological obsolescence often means that today's winners are tomorrow's losers. Companies within a given industry tend to have about the same risk level, but individual companies can deviate from their industry's patterns.

Finally, an argument can be made that cost of equity is less for retained earnings than for new issues of equity (although the cost of the latter matters the most). This is because the board of directors can usually persuade the owners to leave money in the business, and consequently the expected returns can, arguably, be lower for reinvested retained earnings than for new issues of equity. The reason is that if the retained earnings were paid out as dividends, then all but the tax exempt shareholders would have a tax to pay, and the after tax net would give them less to invest somewhere else. By avoiding—or at least deferring—such tax, the expected return on reinvested earnings can be somewhat lower than the return an investor must expect to buy new issues of equity.

Calculating the Cost of Equity

With that in mind, let's tackle the two major ways of estimating the cost of equity; namely, the dividend growth model and the capital asset pricing model. The former

---

2. As noted in chapter 7, one theory holds that the cost of capital does not matter. If this theory proves accurate, then the cost of equity will not matter either. However, if the company raises new equity and gets a return below the return earned on the preexisting equity, then the preexisting equity shareholders suffer dilution.

focuses on evidence internal to the company, and the latter focuses on market data external to the company. Because that is the order in which they were developed, we will review them in that sequence.

The Dividend Growth Model

Let's begin with an admittedly oversimplified observation and then refine it. Consider a hypothetical company that earns $10.40 per share, pays it out every year as a dividend, and is expected to do so as far into the future as anyone can see, with no growth. It has average risk, and the stock price has been steady at $100. Thus the market is telling us that the company can get $100 in equity in return for an annual dividend of $10.40. One could determine that the expected return to shareholders—that is, the company's cost of equity $(y)^3$ is 10.4%, calculated by dividing the year-end dividend payout to shareholders (D) by the stock price (P).

$$y = \frac{D}{P}$$

Now what would happen if the company suddenly became riskier? It does not matter whether the added risk is caused by a changed regulatory environment, an antitrust action filed against the company, a technological innovation by a competitor, or any one of a myriad of other causes. The incremental risk will drive the stock price down because investors, perceiving more risk, will not hold the stock unless they think they will get a higher return. The clearest way for the return to go up is for the price to drop. That way the buyer of the stock, having paid a lower price, will get a higher rate of return. The converse is also true. If suddenly the company became less risky, then investors would settle for a lower rate of return, which reduces the company's cost of equity. If the cost of equity drops, then the price will rise.

But wait, you say, didn't we establish that the cost of equity is not the dividend? If so, then why is the dividend right in the middle of this equation? Remember that (1) *dividend* is defined broadly for these purposes, (2) this is an oversimplification, and (3) value is a function of the cash return that investors expect. The simple case above presumes that the company will pay a $10.40 dividend—no more, and no less—in perpetuity. Thus, this year's cash dividend is the clear predictor of future cash payments to shareholders.

But now let's complicate the facts slightly to make them more closely resemble the usual situation. Let's suppose the company has a piece of news that prompts the market to expect that the company's cash earnings will grow 5% a year compounded, with no change in riskiness. (Hence the annual dividend will grow from $10.40 to $10.92, then to $11.47, and so on.) In that event, the market does not expect the $10.40 dividend in perpetuity, but rather a slowly increasing dividend. What would you expect to happen to the cost of equity and the stock price (now at $100) if the dividend is $10.40 and about to rise 5% per year compounded? If the risk profile of the company has not changed, then the cost of equity will not change. That being the case, the stock price ought to rise. The formula for predicting the price based on the revised growth expectation is a variation on the formula shown above.

---

3. Cost of equity is also often referred to as R_e or K_e.

The Dividend Growth Formula[4]

$$y = \frac{D}{P} + g$$

g = the expected rate of growth in the dividend (This is a nominal rate, and is not adjusted for inflation.)

Based on the new facts given above:

$$10.4\% = \frac{\$10.40}{P} + 5\%$$

Solving for the new price:

$$P = \$192.59$$

Thus the news of the expected growth will drive the price upward, in this case to about $192.59. By adding growth to the picture, the investors will be getting more for the risk they take. They will bid the price up to get the incremental dividend growth. If the price does not rise upon news of the expected growth, then something else is probably occurring, such as the market discounting heavily the news about the growth, or the market perceiving the risk to have increased. Based on these facts, if the price did not rise upon the news, then the cost of equity must have increased from 10.4% to 15.4%.

$$y = \frac{\$10.40}{\$100} + 5\%$$

$$y = 15.4\%$$

Perhaps summarizing will help: the cost of equity is a function of the perceived risk. Once the investor determines the required rate of return given the degree of risk, the cost of equity can be derived. The cost of equity is the expected rate of return, which essentially results from a process during which each assesses the available alternatives. The price, the dividend and future dividends (broadly defined), and the cost of equity (reflecting the perceived risk) are in a dynamic interrelationship. When a stock is publicly traded, one can deduce the cost of equity by taking the dividend, dividing it by the price, and adding to it the market consensus regarding future growth, as captured by the dividend growth formula set forth above.

Let's consider a company that has no news to report. Regardless of whether it pays a dividend and regardless of whether it is growing, if for reasons external to the company (such as a competitor exiting the business) the perceived risk in owning stock in the company decreases, then—assuming all other things are equal—the expected return can decrease, which in turn means that the company's stock price will rise. Conversely, if the perceived risk rises, then investors will not invest unless

---

4. This formula can also be written as:

$$P = \frac{D}{y - g}$$

where g represents the growth rate of the company, P the stock price, and D the expected annual dividend.

they can get a higher return, which means that the price of the stock must fall, all other things being equal.

In fact, many companies' dividend growth rates are uneven. If the growth rate is expected to be something other than constant, then the formula set forth above must be refined. The following formula is such a refinement, essentially estimating the dividend expected in each future year and discounting each year's dividend by the company's cost of equity.[5]

$$P = \frac{D_0}{1 + y} + \frac{D_1}{\left(1 + y\right)^2} + \frac{D_2}{\left(1 + y\right)^3} + \ldots + \frac{Dn}{\left(1 + y\right)^n}$$

P = stock price

y = cost of equity

D_0 = dividend in current year

D_1 = dividend in next year

D_2 = dividend in following year

D_n = dividend in terminal year

This equation says that if we know the stock price and the expected dividend in future years, then we can solve for y, the cost of equity. Specifically, the formula says that the stock price is equal to the current annual dividend, divided by a discount factor equal to the sum of 1 plus the cost of equity, plus the expected dividend in the next year divided by a discount factor that is the sum of 1 plus the cost of equity squared, plus the expected dividend in the following year divided by the cube of 1 plus the cost of equity, and so on through as many years as one can project, at which point, in year n, the dividend is expected to level off and be constant thereafter. The formula is then used to solve for y, the cost of equity.

This set of equations, as well as the concept captured by them, is known as the *dividend growth model.* It tends to work well for companies enjoying steady dividends and slow growth, such as utilities and other companies in mature businesses that do not grow more than about 5% per year. If a company is expected to go through multiple stages of growth, then the model can be adapted to those facts. For instance, if a company is expected to go through four years of 20% annual growth before stabilizing at 5% annual growth, the model still states that the price of the stock is equal to the discounted present value of all future dividends.[6] In the

---

5. MICHAEL C. EHRHARDT, THE SEARCH FOR VALUE 35–51 (1994); *see also* BRADFORD CORNELL, CORPORATE VALUATION 196–97 (1993).

6. The formula for this is as follows, based on the text's example of 4 years of 20% growth, followed by a long period of stability at 5% growth.

$$P = \sum_{t=1}^{4} \frac{D_1}{(1 + y)^1} + \sum_{t=5}^{\infty} \frac{D_4(1 + g)^{t-4}}{(1 + y)^1}$$

t = time period
D_1 = first year's dividend
D_4 = year 4 dividend

You do not need to know this formula. What you might want to remember is that if the growth rate can be reasonably predicted, there is a formula that can be used to derive the cost of equity even if the expected growth rate is uneven. *See* EHRHARDT, *supra* note 5, at 43.

case of rapidly growing (typically younger) companies, which are likely to see their growth rates taper off, it is necessary to either (1) make specific dividend forecasts for each future year until reaching the year at which the growth can be expected to stabilize and become constant, as explained in chapter 11, or (2) value the company as an option, as discussed later.

In general, however, the dividend growth model is difficult to apply to companies with unpredictable, or rapid, growth. For example, in its heyday, Reebok International, Ltd. was growing 300% a year,[7] but its cost of equity was far below that level.

The Capital Asset Pricing Model

Because the dividend growth model is effective at estimating the cost of equity only for slow-growth companies, and is quite poor at estimating the cost of equity for more volatile or rapidly growing companies, academic researchers, in the 1970s, developed the capital asset pricing model (CAPM) (rhymes with "tap them").

CAPM is based on some very explicit assumptions,[8] which have prompted considerable criticism, mostly from practitioners who encounter problems the theorists have ignored or assumed away. For instance, CAPM makes not only the same assumption as the discounted cash flow (DCF) model that all that is known or even knowable by investors is incorporated into the price of the stock—that is, that the market is perfectly efficient—but also that there are no taxes or transaction costs associated with buying, holding, or selling securities. Such assumptions prompt many practitioners to say, in effect, "Okay, Jules Verne, come back when you have something real," to which theoreticians respond by saying that empirical tests show the CAPM is, in fact, about right, if not always exact; that it is better than any other measure yet developed; and that, like most innovations, it can and will be improved upon.[9]

This chapter summarizes the key elements of this sometimes complex topic, in terms understandable to those who have little background in theoretical finance and who are more interested in the major concepts than in the mathematical details. If you find yourself in a situation requiring you to master the details, you will then need to study them. Here we will focus on the architecture, not the plumbing.

---

7. Reebok's sales were $13 million in 1983, $66 million in 1984, $307 million in 1985, and $919 million in 1986. Net income over this period grew from $0.6 million to $132 million. *See* REEBOK INTERNATIONAL, LTD., 1987 ANNUAL REPORT 1.

8. CAPM makes eight explicit assumptions:
   (1) The investor's objective is to maximize the utility of terminal wealth.
   (2) Investors make choices on the basis of risk and return. Return is measured by the mean returns expected from a portfolio of assets; risk is measured by the variance of these portfolio returns.
   (3) Investors have homogeneous expectations of risk and return.
   (4) Investors have identical time horizons.
   (5) Information is freely available to investors.
   (6) There is a risk-free asset, and investors can borrow and lend at the risk-free rate.
   (7) There are no taxes, transaction costs, or other market imperfections.
   (8) Total asset quantity is fixed, and all assets are marketable and divisible.

9. *See* DIANA R. HARRINGTON, MODERN PORTFOLIO THEORY, THE CAPITAL ASSET PRICING MODEL & ARBITRAGE PRICING THEORY: A USER'S GUIDE (1987) (includes excellent discussion of CAPM and its strengths and weaknesses).

Table 72
Possible Outcomes of Two Independent Investments

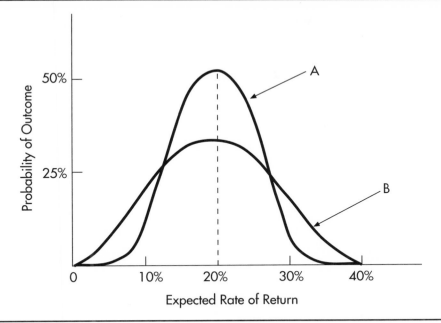

Pricing stocks is a matter of measuring risk and return—that is, the upside potential and the downside danger. As for the latter, we need a measure or estimate of how wrong our forecasts might be. One measure of forecast uncertainty is breadth of the range of possible returns. CAPM is premised on the idea that changes will occur and that such changes cannot be forecasted. It measures a company's sensitivity, both upside and downside, to future changes in macro-level factors such as inflation, and also measures the uncertainty in an investment by examining the range of possible outcomes, or returns, on it. There are two specific measures of such range or breadth. One is the variance in outcomes, which is the squared deviation of the expected returns from the mean forecasted return.[10] The second, and more widely used, measure is the square root of the variance, which is known as the standard deviation.

To illustrate, consider shares issued by two companies, A and B, as illustrated in Table 72. Shares of Company B are riskier than shares of Company A, because the range of forecasted returns from B is broader than the range of expected returns from A. The measure used for this is the standard deviation of expected returns. In this example, two-thirds of the time the returns expected from Company A fall between 15% and 25%, whereas two-thirds of the time the expected returns from Company B fall between 12% and 28%, making B a more volatile and riskier security.

---

10. *Id.*

However, CAPM measures the riskiness of a security not in isolation, but rather—because investors have other alternatives—by comparing its volatility relative to the volatility of the market as a whole. It then measures the cost of equity for a particular company in three steps. Investors buying equity of a particular company expect a return that will (1) compensate them for the risk-free rate, plus (2) provide a premium for holding an equity investment rather than a risk-free investment, plus (3) provide a premium (or discount) for investing in a security that is riskier (or less risky) than the market as a whole. These three components of the cost of equity are addressed in turn below.

Risk-Free Rate

CAPM assumes that a zero risk investment exists, although virtually every investment is exposed to inflation risk. Models have been developed that use short sales to offset returns to create a zero risk equilibrium, but ordinarily the Treasury bond rate is used as a proxy for the zero risk investment. Scholarly debate continues regarding whether the T-bill rate or the T-bond rate ought to be used as the surrogate for the risk-free rate. Proponents of the former argue that the T-bill rate is less risky and is thus preferable. Proponents of the latter argue that the T-bond rate ought to be used because its duration corresponds more closely with the expected holding period of most equity holders. The latter position is, on balance, more persuasive and has the upper hand in the debate.

Premium for Holding Equity Investment

Investors also expect a premium for investing in equities rather than zero risk investments. Although CAPM seeks to estimate future returns, in practice it uses historical results to calculate this premium. Equities have generally paid a rate of return well in excess of risk-free rates, as explained in Sidebar 25. From 1926 through 1995, stocks returned an average of 10.54%, counting both dividends and stock price appreciation, using arithmetic compounding.[11] Over that same period, Treasury bonds paid an average of approximately 6% less. Consequently, the market has come to expect a premium for holding equity securities, and that premium has averaged approximately 6%.[12]

---

11. Ibbotson Associates, Stocks, Bonds, Bills and Inflation 1996 Yearbook.

12. The historic returns on equities are no more than an average. In some years, the Standard & Poor's 500 composite stock price index did much better than 10.54%, and in some years it did far worse. (Its best year since 1925 was 1933, when it returned 54%, and its worst year since 1925 was 1931, when it returned a negative 43%.) If one can take a longer time horizon, there is less volatility. Looking at $10,000 invested over any ten-year period beginning in 1926 and running through 1992 (57 decade-long periods), the best such period (1948–58) generated a 20.1% compound annual return, and the worst decade (1928–38) generated a negative 0.9% compound annual return. Indeed the investor who bought into the market in 1929 had to wait until 1954 to see his or her investment return to its original nominal value and longer to recoup its real value. Clearly these returns are far more volatile than the returns on Treasury bills, and the investor has historically been compensated accordingly, although not necessarily in the short run—earning the risk premium may require patience. One should also bear in mind that these returns are averages of the prices of stocks of a large number of companies, and they are free of brokerage commissions and taxes.

_____ **Sidebar 25** _____

Rates of Return after Adjusting for Taxes and Inflation

The astute investor recognizes that inflation is not the only adversary, for unless the investor is tax exempt, after paying taxes on the interest and suffering inflation erosion of the net, his or her return may be negative.

Two researchers studied[13] the returns on $1 invested from year-end 1925 to year-end 1993 in the Standard & Poor's composite stock index, compared with another $1 invested in T-bills over the same period. Making reasonable assumptions about the investor's tax rate as the rates changed over the 68 years, the researchers found that the first $1 had appreciated to $800.08, and the second to $10.82. The difference was due to compounding: the stocks (including dividends and capital gains) compounded at 10.33% (using geometric compounding), whereas T-bills compounded only at 3.69%. Over the span of 68 years, this spread of 6.64%, compounded annually, resulted in a 74-fold difference in nominal wealth.

Table 73
Nominal Compound Growth Rates

	Year-End 1925	1993	Nominal Compound Growth Rate
T-bills	$1	$10.82	3.69%
Standard & Poor's Index*	$1	$800.08	10.33%

*Including dividend reinvestment

However, when adjusted for taxes and transaction costs, the returns were by no means as good.

Table 74
Compound Growth Rates after Taxes and Transaction Costs

	Year-End 1925	1993	Nominal Compound Growth Rate*
T-bills	$1	$3.99	2.06%
Standard & Poor's Index**	$1	$157.72	7.73%

*Net of taxes and transaction costs
**Including dividend reinvestment

_____

13. Laurence B. Siegel & David Montgomery, *Stocks, Bonds and Bills after Taxes and Inflation*, J. Portfolio Mgmt., Winter 1995, at 17–25.

And when inflation is factored in, the results became dramatically different.

	Year-End 1925	1993	Real Compound Growth Rate*
Table 75			
Compound Growth Rates after Taxes, Transaction Costs, and Inflation			
T-bills	$1	$0.49	(1.04%)
Standard and Poor's Index**	$1	$19.39	4.46%

*Net of taxes and transaction costs, and inflation
**Including dividend reinvestment

In May 1996, the U.S. Treasury Department announced plans to issue bonds indexed to inflation. Some observers commented that this would make purchasers of such bonds indifferent to the inflation rate. However, compare two alternatives. In the first, the bonds pay 3% above an inflation rate of 4%, and in the second, the bonds pay 3% above an inflation rate of 12%.

Table 76
Returns on Inflation-Indexed Bonds

	Inflation Rate	
	4%	**12%**
Premium	3%	3%
Nominal return before tax	7%	15%
Tax rate	39.6%	39.6%
Tax	2.8%	5.9%
Nominal return after tax	4.2%	9.1%
Inflation rate	4%	12%
Real rate of return	0.2%	(2.9%)

Thus, the tax paying investor who buys the bonds ought not be indifferent to the inflation rate.

The real rates of return are also sensitive to the tax rate. For instance, if the investor were in the maximum individual tax bracket and that rate were increased to 48%, the real return would be as follows.

Table 77

Returns on Inflation-Adjusted Bonds at 48% Tax Rate

	Inflation Rate	
	4%	**12%**
Premium	3%	3%
Nominal return before tax	7%	15%
Tax rate	48%	48%
Tax	3.4%	7.2%
Nominal return after tax	3.6%	7.8%
Inflation rate	7%	15%
Real rate of return	(3.4%)	(7.2%)

Thus, the holder of the bonds does increasingly badly as the inflation rate rises and as the tax rate rises.

The tax exempt investor can be indifferent not only to the tax rate, but also to the inflation rate (assuming it is measured accurately), as illustrated by the following comparison.

Table 78

Returns on Inflation-Adjusted Bonds for Tax-Exempt Investor

	Inflation Rate	
	4%	**12%**
Premium	3%	3%
Nominal return	7%	15%
Inflation rate	4%	12%
Net return	3%	3%

Sidebar 26

Arithmetic versus Geometric Rates of Compounding

If the methodology for calculating return on investment over time used arithmetic averaging (that is, all the increases from one year to the next were simply added up and divided by the number of years being considered), then the average return on equities from 1926 through 1995 would be higher (approximately 12.32%) than if returns were compounded geometrically (10.54%). To understand the difference between geometric and arithmetic compounding, consider an investment of $1,000 in a company. In year 1 the stock price plummets by 50%, and the $1,000 falls to a value of $500 for a return of minus 50%. In year 2, however, the $1,000 value is restored, for a would-be return of 100%. If one were to calculate returns by using an arithmetic average, the average return would be (100% − 50%)/2, or 50%/2 = 25%. By contrast, the formula for the geometric average rate of return is the following equation, in which one solves for g, the geometric rate of return.

$$\$1,000 \ (1 + g)^2 = \$1,000$$

The exponent is the number of years or other period over which the return is being calculated.

Hence the geometric rate of return in the example above is zero; after all, the $1,000 is, after two years, worth only $1,000, representing a zero return. Scholarly debate exists concerning which is more appropriate—the arithmetic method or geometric method of calculating previous compound growth rates. The issue is not trivial, for a variation of even 2%, when compounded over several decades, makes an enormous difference. A recent study concludes that a weighted average of the two methods is preferable.[14]

Premium for Investing in Risky Securities

Recently it has been observed that over the long run, the risks in stocks are less than the risks of holding bonds. Looking at every 20-year holding period from 1802 to 1992, the worst real return for stocks was an annual average of 1.2% and the best was an annual average of 12.6%. By contrast, the returns for holding long-term bonds ranged from minus 3.1% to 8.85.%[15] In light of this experience, one could argue that there is no need for an equity risk premium. That is, if one's investment time horizon is 20 years or more, history indicates that equities may indeed be less risky than bonds or even bills. If the equity risk premium is negligible, then the cost of equity is less than it is generally believed to be. In that event, future cash flows to equity holders would be discounted less and equity valuations would increase. Glassman and Hassett[16] found that the March 1998 Dow Jones Industrial Average of 8800 was consistent with an equity risk premium of 3%.

---

14. Daniel C. Indro & Wayne Y. Lee, *Biases in Arithmetic and Geometric Averages as Estimates of Long-Run Expected Returns and Risk Premia*, 26 FIN. MGMT. 81–90 (Winter 1997).

15. James K. Glassman & Kevin A. Hassett, *Are Stocks Overvalued? Not a Chance*, WALL ST. J., Mar. 30, 1998, at A-18. Glassman and Hassett base some of their analysis on work by Jeremy J. Siegel of the University of Pennsylvania, notably his book *Stocks for the Long Run.*

16. *Id.*

Keep in mind, however, that by using the U.S. equity market to estimate the riskiness of equity holdings, one could fall into a survivorship bias. At the turn of the century, there were six major stock markets—in the United States, England, Russia, Germany, Argentina, and Japan—all roughly the same size. By midway through the twentieth century, investors in all but two of those markets saw the value of their holdings substantially, if not entirely, destroyed. By measuring the returns only in a successful market, one risks overstating the expected returns.

To measure the riskiness of the stock of a particular company, in practice CAPM usually begins with the often criticized premise that the best available measure of future risk is the historic volatility of the stock price relative to the volatility of the market as a whole.[17] If the volatility of the stock has been equal to that of the market as a whole, then its *beta* is 1.0. If the volatility of the stock has been greater than that of the market as a whole, then its beta is more than 1.0. If the stock's volatility is less than that of the market as a whole, then its beta is less than zero. Sidebar 27 provides some particulars about the forecast of beta.

_____ *Sidebar 27* _____

Calculation of Beta

The most challenging, but purest, way to measure a company's beta is to estimate its future stock price volatility relative to the market; after all, the objective is to estimate future risk. In practice, however, the historic volatilities are usually used. Either way, there are several steps in measuring volatility. First, CAPM users must choose how to determine the return on the average asset. Although the Standard & Poor's 500 is often used, some argue that the entire market ought to serve as the reference index. There is also scholarly debate about whether—when historic volatility is used—the measurements of volatility ought to be taken daily, weekly, or monthly, and whether they ought to be taken over a relatively short and recent period of time or over a longer period, such as five years. It can be worth calculating the cost of equity by differing methods (such as daily for a month, versus monthly for 5 years) and then using an average of the costs thus calculated.

Suppose, for example, that the measurements are taken monthly for five years, providing 60 points of comparison between the market and the stock under review.

_____

17. Also, for instance, recent research (still in process) has been finding that the ratio of the book value of a company's common equity to the market value of its common equity correlates closely with stock market returns. A low book value relative to market value usually means that the market value is high, because the market is sanguine about the company's prospects, and vice versa. One might intuitively suspect that if the market has bid up a company's stock price, then the investor is at greater risk. However, by and large, the companies with low book to market ratios tend to be persistently strong performers, and those with high book to market ratios tend to be persistently poor earners. Consequently, the low book to market ratio companies tend to have a lower cost of equity. As this research develops further, it might displace the other methods of estimating the cost of equity, including CAPM. *See, e.g.*, Eugene F. Fama & Kenneth R. French, *The Cross-Section of Expected Stock Returns*, 47 J. Fin. 427–65 (June 1992).

Table 79
Calculating the Volatility of a Company's Stock Price Relative to the Market, Step 1

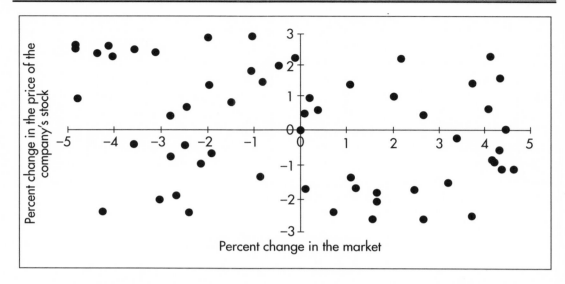

As depicted in Table 79, at each measurement time one would calculate the percentage change in the price of the company's stock and the percentage change in the market index. For example, if at the first measurement time the market had risen 2% and the company's stock price 1%, one would plot a point at that point. If at the second measurement time the market had declined 3% and the company's stock had declined 2%, one would plot a point at that point.

Eventually there would be 60 points, as shown in Table 79. The extreme scattering of points in Table 79 indicates a low correlation between the stock price and the market, which in turn indicates a low level of reliability of the stock's beta as a measure of risk, as further discussed below. A computer would then regress the points to a straight line, as shown in Table 80. (*Regress* means finding the line that, in comparison with all other possible lines, has in the aggregate the shortest total squared distance to all the points.)

The slope of the line can then be read. If, for example, the line slopes up at exactly 45 degrees, indicating that for every 1% change in the market there is a 1% rise in the price of the company's stock, then the company's stock has a beta of 1.0. If the slope of the line is such that every time the market goes up 1% the company's stock goes up 2% (and every time the market drops 1% the company's stock price drops 2%), then the beta is 2.0. If every time the market goes up 1% the company's stock price goes up 0.5% (and every time the market drops 1% the company's stock price drops 0.5%), then the beta is

Table 80
Calculating the Volatility of a Company's Stock Price Relative to the Market, Step 2

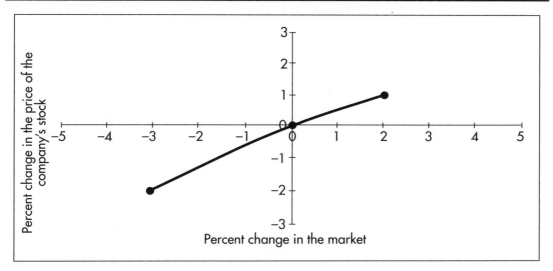

0.5. It is possible to have negative betas. This means that the stock price of the company moves opposite to the movement of the market—if the market is up, the stock price goes down, and vice versa. Mining stocks, most notably gold stocks, are the best example of this, for gold prices generally rise in periods of high inflation and uncertainty, which are just the conditions that usually drive the market downward, and vice versa. A zero beta is also possible, but rare. It connotes a stock price movement that is totally uncorrelated with the market.

Once the beta for a company's stocks has been calculated or found (you can look them up in a library by checking Value Line or various other publications, although these are almost always based on historic stock volatilities), CAPM uses the beta to complete the task of measuring the cost of equity. It does so by applying the following formula.

$$y = R_f + B(R_m - R_f)$$

Here is the translation: the cost of equity (which, you may recall, equates to the return an equity investor must expect to receive if he or she is to buy the stock for a given price) is equal to the risk-free rate (that is, the Treasury bond rate of approximately 4.6%) plus beta (that is, the particular company's risk index relative to the market) times the market risk premium (that is, the spread of approximately 6% between what the market has, on average, returned and the Treasury bond rate).

If, for example, a company's beta is 1.5, then its cost of equity would be calculated as follows.

$$y = 4.6\% + 1.5\,(10.5\% - 4.6\%)$$

$$y = 4.6\% + 1.5\,(5.9\%)$$

$$y = 4.6\% + 8.85\%$$

$$y = 13.45\%$$

By contrast, if the company's stock is less volatile and has a beta of only 0.5, then its cost of equity would be calculated as follows.

$$y = 4.6\% + 0.5\,(10.5\% - 4.6\%)$$

$$y = 4.6\% + 0.5\,(5.9\%)$$

$$y = 4.6\% + 2.95\%$$

$$y = 7.55\%$$

Thus the difference between a beta of 1.5 and a beta of 0.5 is the difference between a cost of equity of 13.45% and a cost of equity of 7.55%. Let's look at what that might mean in terms of a stock price. Suppose a company is growing its revenues and dividends at 6% a year and is expected to continue doing so. Suppose also that it is paying a dividend this year of $1 per share to its equity holders. Conceptually, at least, the stock price can be determined as follows for the company whose beta is 1.5 (thus indicating that a prospective equity investor will invest if he or she can get a return of approximately 13.45%).

$$13.45\% = \frac{\$1.00}{P} + 6\%$$

$$7.45\% = \frac{\$1.00}{P}$$

$$P = \frac{\$1.00}{.0745}$$

$$P = \$13.42$$

By contrast, if the company's beta is only 0.5 (indicating that the prospective equity investor will invest if a return of about 7.55% can be expected), then its stock price will be $64.52.

$$7.55\% = \frac{\$1.00}{P} + 6\%$$

$$1.55\% = \frac{\$1.00}{P}$$

$$P = \frac{\$1.00}{1.55\%}$$

$$P = \$64.52$$

Notice the application of the dividend growth model, despite the use of CAPM. Notice also, however, that the dividend growth model was used only after determining the cost of equity by using CAPM, and only to determine the price of the stock once the cost of equity had been determined. As this illustrates, CAPM can be used only to estimate the cost of equity, whereas the dividend growth model can be used to estimate the cost of equity or to determine a stock price. As a word of caution, the dividend growth model is best applied to mature companies, the growth of which is likely to be constant.

Apart from the explicit assumptions, there are three problems with beta. First, if historic rather than forecast stock price volatilities are used, then if a company is widely watched and actively traded, the beta is probably a much more reliable gauge of volatility than if the company is not. If a stock is thinly traded and not well known, then the beta is a much more dubious measure. An indication of the latter is when the plotted check points (on a graph such as the one in Table 79) are widely diffused rather than tightly clustered. The statistical measure of this is r^2, which indicates whether the check points are widely diffused (as in Table 79) or tightly clustered. A low r^2 indicates that the beta might be the result of statistical randomness, and that the beta is less reliable than if the r^2 is high. A high r^2 suggests a tight and consistent pattern to the stock's volatility and hence greater reliability.

Second, when the beta calculation is based on historic trading data, as it usually is, it ignores forthcoming changes. Usually that is unavoidable; however, in some cases it can be dangerous. For instance, in 1983, the world knew that as part of the settlement of its antitrust case with the federal government, AT&T was about to be broken up and become a very different company. To use historic performance to measure future risk in such cases can be unwise if the market has not had a chance to react to the news during the period in which beta is measured.

Third, when the beta calculation is based exclusively on historic data, beta looks to the future only by looking in the rearview mirror. It is one thing for the market to do so in assessing a company's riskiness, but another thing for management to rely on beta in measuring the risk of future projects. Boards of directors and management have much more information and knowledge about the company's future prospects than does the market. Consequently, for management to look to the market to ascertain the company's risk accords too much deference to the market.

For example, Archer Daniels Midland Company, the Decatur, Illinois-based processor of wholesale foodstuffs, derived approximately 40% of its 1995 total profit of $746 million from corn sweeteners, a sugar substitute used in colas and other foods and beverages. The world price for sugar was about half the domestic price of $0.223 per pound, but federal import restrictions were keeping foreign sugar out. Therefore, companies used corn sweeteners instead, which cost about $0.12 per pound. If the import quotas were eliminated or significantly liberalized, then Archer Daniels Midland's corn sweetener earnings, and its overall corporate earnings, would have been materially and adversely impacted. Yet the risk of this would not have been apparent in a review of the company's historic, even if then recent, stock price volatility. The beta was running about 0.95, indicating slightly below average riskiness and a cost of equity of about 10.2%. But if federal sugar import quotas had been about to disappear or diminish, that riskiness would rise substantially, and/or future cash flow would decline. The 1996 market price of Archer Daniels Midland's stock probably reflected these risks. However, if management had reason to expect a reduction in trade protection, it ought to have used its judgment rather than historic stock price volatility to measure future risk. That is, management ought to have a more accurate read of the risk it faces than does the market. This would be even more important if the risks were not discernible to the public, unlike a change in import quotas.

Whether the cost of equity is measured by CAPM or not, it is risk related. Consequently, the lawyer who can help his or her client diminish its risk has created value by reducing the client's cost of capital. Ways to reduce risk include locking supply channels, getting tighter or more enforceable noncompete or nondisclosure agreements, and securing good patents or Food and Drug Administration licenses.

Preferred Stock

It is difficult to generalize about the cost of preferred stock because the particulars of preferred share contracts vary considerably. In the plain vanilla case, in which the preferred stock pays a fixed dividend and is outstanding in perpetuity, the cost is a simple application of the dividend growth model, but without the growth. The cost is merely the dividend divided by the market price of the stock. Because the dividend on the preferred stock is not tax deductible, the pretax and after tax costs of the preferred are the same. If the preferred stock is not publicly traded, however, the price per share may be difficult to determine. In that case, one must look at the yield on comparable preferred shares. It is not necessary that the companies issuing the securities be comparable, only that the preferred shares be of comparable risk.

If the preferred stock is convertible at the option of the holder, then it can be valued as a package consisting of two parts, the nonconvertible preferred and a warrant. The former can be valued as described above. The warrant is essentially an option and can be valued as such, as described in Sidebar 28.

_____ *Sidebar 28* _____

Valuing Options

Suppose your client has an option to buy shares of a company at any time over the next 5 years at $115 per share. At present the stock is trading at $100, but that does not mean the option is worthless because if, for example, the stock price rises to $125 per share, the options would be worth $10 per share. To be sure, if the stock price falls, stays the same, or rises but not above $115 per share, then the options will expire worthless. But the possibility of the stock price rising above $115 gives the option value until the option expires.

The value is a function of five variables, each quite logical when considered by itself. First, the more volatile the underlying stock, the greater the potential for a dramatic upside move and hence the greater the value. Second, an advantage to holding the option rather than owning the underlying asset is that the option holder can use the freed-up capital to invest in a different asset. The higher the current interest rates, the higher the opportunity cost, and the higher the value of the option.

Third and fourth, the relationship between the price of the underlying stock and the exercise price of the option both impact the value of the option. The further the exercise price of the option is below the price of the stock, the more value the option has. Conversely, the higher the exercise price of the option is above the price of the underlying stock, the less value the option has.

Finally, the longer the time until the option expires, the more value it has. That is fairly intuitive; after all, time is on the side of the option holder.[18]

There are some projects within companies, and indeed some entire companies, that can be better valued as options than by the discounted cash flow or economic value added methods. Companies that are not yet generating earnings or value are akin to options that are out of the money. Their value lies in the possibility that in the future, they will generate substantial returns and be in the money. The length of time they can stay in the game without running out of capital and human resources, the extent of their success if it occurs, and the level of opportunity costs all impact the value of the stock of such companies.

The Black-Scholes formula in footnote 18 does not work for valuing projects as options because the formula requires a stock price, and projects within companies have no stock price. The formulas for valuing internal projects as options are still being developed.

Convertible Securities

Estimating the cost of convertible debt is extremely complex. If a convertible bond may at certain points be converted by the holder, at his or her option, for a specified number of shares, then the conversion feature is like an option and has value for the holder and a cost for the issuer.

For instance, assume that on May 1, 1998, a company has outstanding a convertible bond maturing on November 1, 2009; that it pays a coupon of 8% and is convertible, at any time until maturity, into 10 shares of the issuer's stock; and that on May 1, 1998, the bond was trading at 95. That being the case, its yield to maturity as of May 1, 1998, was 8.696%.

If the bond were not convertible, the contractual coupon payment would be its cost. However, if it is convertible, then its cost is equal to the issuer's cost of equity. If the cost of equity were, say, 12%, then the bond yield of 8.696% and the equity cost

---

18. The above comes together in the following formula:

$$P = S \times N(d_1) - E \times N(d_2)e^{-rt}$$

where:

d_1	=	$[1n(S/E) + (r + \sigma^2/2)t]/\sigma\sqrt{t}$
d_2	=	$[1n(S/E) + (r - \sigma^2/2)t]/\sigma\sqrt{t}$
P	=	Price of the option
S	=	Price of the underlying stock
E	=	Exercise price of the option
t	=	Time remaining before expiration (in years)
r	=	Continuously compounded risk-free rate of interest on a security that matures at the time the option expires
σ	=	Standard deviation of continously compounded returns on the stock
N(d)	=	Probability that a deviation of less than d will occur in a normal distribution with a mean of zero and a standard deviation of 1

Happily, there are computer programs available that solve the equation for you, should your memory ever lapse and you can no longer recall this equation.

of 12% place bounds on the cost of the convertible debt. But where within that range is the real cost?

The convertible bond can be priced as a debt instrument plus a warrant, or option to convert. The pricing of interest rate derivative securities cannot be done using the Black-Scholes model for a number of reasons, not the least of which being that the model makes assumptions that are incompatible with the pricing of such securities. Thus more esoteric formulas, beyond the scope of this book, are used.

The pricing of convertible debt can also be complicated by a call provision. The call has a value, and that value diminishes the value of the bond. Bond holders will take the call provision into account when they buy the bond, and will require compensation in the form of higher interest rates.

The Weighted Average Cost of Capital

Now that you know all you (hopefully) ever wanted to know about the cost of debt and the cost of equity, it is time to explain how to calculate a company's weighted average cost of capital.

As noted at the beginning of chapter 7, a school of thought is emerging that contends the cost of capital does not matter much. Indeed, it is entirely possible that research will find a strong correlation between stock prices and some measure of financial performance that is unrelated to the cost of capital. Based on valuation methodology used at this time, however, cost of capital is considered to be extremely important, for several reasons. First, as you will see later, it is used as the discount rate to bring projected future cash earnings to their present values. Second, it is used to test whether the company is earning its cost of capital on existing projects. Third, it defines the hurdle rate for proposed new projects. Think of the cost of capital as the investor's opportunity cost at the company's level of risk. It is the return an investor can expect to receive by investing in another company of comparable risk.

Given the cost of debt and cost of equity, the cost of capital that matters most to the company is its weighted average cost of capital (c^*). Once one knows the company's cost of debt and cost of equity, then the weighted average cost of capital is not difficult to compute. To illustrate, if the company's after tax cost of debt is 6% (for example, 10% pretax less a 40% tax shield) and its cost of equity is 12%, and if each constitutes half the company's total capital, then the weighted average cost of capital is calculated as shown in Table 81.

	After Tax Cost	$\times$	**Percent of Total Capital**	=	**Weighted Cost**
Table 81					
Calculating the Weighted Average Cost of Capital					
Debt	6%	$\times$	50%	=	3%
Equity	12%	$\times$	50%	=	<u>6%</u>
				c^* =	9%

Ninety percent of the time, the above is all you want or need to know. Sometimes, though, it is useful to know a little more. Referring to the above example, in
which the weighted cost of capital is 9%, you might ask whether the company can
reduce its cost of capital by borrowing more, buying in stock, and substituting debt
for equity. Could a company shift its debt to 75% of total capital and cut its c^* from
9% to 7.5%, as follows?

	After Tax Cost	×	Percent of Total Capital	=	Weighted Cost
Table 82					
The Weighted Average Cost of Capital Formula: Dynamic Cost of Capital					
Debt	6%	×	75%	=	4.5%
Equity	12%	×	25%	=	3.0%
				$c^* =$	7.5%

The answer to your question is yes and no. Yes, you are moving in the right
direction, but no, 7.5% is not quite precise. The reason is because as the company
increases its leverage, the risk to which the equity is exposed rises and the shareholders expect a higher return, which means the dilution will rise for the existing
shareholders, which in turn means a higher cost of equity for the company. In short,
as the leverage rises, the cost of equity rises. It is a dynamic relationship.

In fact, we can predict how much the added leverage will cause the cost of
equity to rise. But first, we need a bit more background. The cost of equity is a function of two factors: (1) the business risk of the company's operations in the absence
of leverage, and (2) the added risk resulting from any financial leverage. Each are
addressed in turn.

The Unlevered Cost of Capital (c)

If a company has no leverage at all, then its cost of equity (y) is the company's unlevered cost of capital (c). The unlevered cost of capital is important because it reflects
the risk inherent in the company's operations only, untainted and uninfluenced by
any financial leverage. The unlevered cost of capital, as you will see, plays an important role in valuing a company's operations. Even if the company has financial leverage, it still has an unlevered cost of capital (c), which is not to be confused with c^*,
its weighted average cost of capital. We know that c^* is a function of (1) the company's unlevered cost of capital, which reflects solely the risk of the operations, and
(2) the effects of financial leverage. Hence:

$$c^* = c[1 - t(\text{debt}/\text{total capital})]$$

If, for example, c is equal to 11.25%, the tax rate (t) is 40%, and debt constitutes 50% of the total capital, then:

$$c* = 11.25\% \, [1 - (.40 \times 50\%)]$$
$$c* = 11.25 \, [(1 - .20)]$$
$$c* = 11.25 \times 80\%$$
$$c* = 9\%$$

Inasmuch as we normally begin by knowing $c*$ rather than c, however, we are more likely to use the formula to solve for c. In the above illustration, if we had known that $c*$ was 9% but did not know c, then we could find c as follows.

$$c^* = c\big[1 - (.40 \times .50)\big]$$
$$.09 = c(1 - .20)$$
$$.09 = c \times .80$$
$$c = \frac{.09}{.08}$$
$$c = 11.25\%$$

This is important because if we want to calculate pro forma what the cost of equity would be if the financial leverage were increased or decreased, we must first find c. Then we would reason that investors would expect a return on their equity to compensate them not only for the risk of the company's operations, which c does, but also for the incremental risk resulting from the financial leverage.

The Financial Risk Premium

A company's cost of equity is equal to its unlevered cost of capital plus a financial risk premium (FRP). The FRP is the incremental return the equity investors will expect to compensate them for the added risk visited upon the company by its financial leverage. It can be calculated by using the following equation (b is the pretax borrowing rate).

$$\text{FRP} = (1 - t)(c - b)\frac{\text{debt}}{\text{equity}}$$

This equation says that the FRP is a function of three variables. Although the formula is normally written in the sequence in which it appears above, the reverse order captures the logic better. First, as the debt to equity ratio rises, the financial risk of the equity also rises, due to the added risk of insolvency. The equation captures that in the debt/equity portion, as further described in Sidebar 29. Second, as the borrowing rate converges on the unlevered cost of capital, the portion of the risk born by the shareholders declines. Finally, the same is true as the tax rate rises—the government subsidizes the cost of the debt.

_____ **Sidebar 29** _____

Book Values versus Market Values

Ready for a tough question? In calculating the debt to total capital or debt to equity ratios, should one use the book value or market value of the debt and the equity? Most commentators, analysts, and economists assume there is a single correct answer. Others believe the answer is that it depends. Before you conclude that this is a mealymouthed compromise, consider the following.

The critical issue is what the capital will cost at the margins; that is, what the company would have to pay for equity if it were to do an equity financing. Thus the cost ought to be a function of the marketplace, not what generally accepted accounting principles (GAAP) recorded as the proceeds of the company's previous offerings, which may have been many years earlier.

The difference may not be trivial, as illustrated by Coca-Cola Company. As shown below, calculated on a book basis in accordance with GAAP, the company's debt constitutes 42%, and its equity 58%, of its total capital.[1] But because the company's stock is trading at such a high multiple of book value, on a market basis its capital is 98% equity and 2% debt.

Table 83
Coca-Cola Company's Leverage

December 31, 1996

	Book Value ($ million)		Market Value ($ million)	
Debt	4,513	(42%)	4,513	(2%)
Equity	6,156	(59%)	178,514	(98%)
Total	10,669	(100%)	183,027	(100%)

Notice first that the enormous spread between the book and market values of the equity means that over the years Coca-Cola has done a great job of creating value for its owners. Notice also that the selling shareholder benefits from the expectation of high future value creation, and that the buyer will get a good return only if this occurs. And notice finally that the high market premium for the stock means that, with equity being a very high percentage of total capital, the weighted average cost of capital is higher than if the com-

_____

1. COCA-COLA COMPANY, 1996 ANNUAL REPORT.

pany were more leveraged. Ironic, is it not, that the company's very success has driven up its cost of capital? Think carefully about the implication of that. Isn't the market telling Coca-Cola that it ought to finance its next project with debt rather than equity? After all, in financing new projects, it is the incremental cost of capital that matters. And for purposes of that calculation, using market values makes the most sense.

There is one potentially important refinement on the above analysis: whichever method one uses, when calculating the cost of equity the company's target capital structure ought to be used. Often there is no difference between the current and target capital structures. However, if there is reason to believe the issuer will become more leveraged in the future, for example, then the equity investor ought to require a higher return than would otherwise be the case.

But for purposes of evaluating management, does it make sense to measure returns based on the market value of the capital they are working with? Is it fair to tell Coca-Cola's management that it will not be evaluated on the basis of its return on the $5 billion of equity it was given to work with, but rather, on the $178 billion value the market places on the equity? Usually not, because the latter number captures the expected value creation for all future years, not just the current year. The market's perception of the company's ability to generate future value and hence the stock price can, though, be influenced by the very top executives' words and actions. Therefore, it may make sense to gear a significant portion of such executives' compensation packages to stock prices, such as by using stock options.

Once one has calculated c, one can then calculate the new FRP with the higher leverage, and then use the new y to calculate the new weighted average cost of capital.

$$y = c + FRP$$

As noted above, the calculation of c, the unlevered cost of capital, is as follows:

$$c^* = c[1 - t(\text{debt}/\text{total capital})]$$

$$9\% = c[1 - (.40 \times .50)]$$

$$9\% = c[1 - .20]$$

$$c = .09$$

$$.80$$

$$c = 11.25\%$$

Now let's calculate the new FRP based on the debt level rising to 75% of total capital, at a borrowing rate of 10%.

$$FRP = (1 - t)(c - b)\frac{\text{debt}}{\text{equity}}$$

$$FRP = (1 - .40)(.1125 - .10)\frac{.75}{.25}$$

$$FRP = (.60)(.0125)(3)$$

$$FRP = .0225$$

$$FRP = 2.25\%$$

Note that the FRP rose as the leverage rose. In our earlier example, when the debt to total capital ratio was 50:50, the cost of equity was 12%, connoting a 0.75% FRP.

Although rather unusual, there are situations in which the cost of equity should not rise with added leverage. This occurs when a change in interest rates (and hence a change in the company's costs) will almost certainly be accompanied by a change in revenues that is equal in direction and amount. To illustrate, consider a bank that has designed its capital structure in such a way that any change in interest rates, whether up or down, has an identical impact on the bank's revenues and its costs. In that case, greater use of financial leverage does not alter the cost of equity, because due to the constant spread between revenues and costs, there is no change in the amount of risk.

Calculating the New, Pro Forma, Cost of Equity and Cost of Capital

By increasing its leverage the company increased its FRP and, correspondingly, its cost of equity. That is, because the cost of equity is equal to the unlevered cost of capital (c) plus the FRP, we can find the new cost of equity in the more levered company by summing the unlevered cost of capital and the FRP. When the unlevered cost of capital is 11.25% and the FRP is 2.25%, the cost of equity has risen to 13.5%.

$$y = c + FRP$$

$$y = 11.25\% + 2.25\%$$

$$y = 13.5\%$$

Thus, by increasing its leverage from 50% to 75%, the company has increased its cost of equity from 12% to 13.5%. In addition, the added leverage will increase the borrowing cost. As noted in chapter 7, one could estimate the amount of such increase remarkably accurately by referring to the empirical research and seeing what happened as companies of comparable size increased their leverage by like amounts. Bearing in mind the tax shield, and depending upon the size of the company and other factors impacting the sensitivity of the company's borrowing cost to its leverage, the effect of raising the leverage from 50% to 75% would be to raise the after tax borrowing cost from 6% to approximately 6.4%.

Even though the added leverage caused the cost of equity and the cost of debt to rise, the weighted average cost of capital declined, as shown in Table 84. The reason is that the tax shield covered a larger portion of the capital cost. That is, the tax

Table 84

Adding Leverage Can Lower the Weighted Average Cost of Capital

	After Tax Cost	×	Percent of Total Capital	=	Weighted Cost
Debt	6.4%	×	.75	=	4.8%
Equity	13.5%	×	.25	=	3.375%
				$c^* =$	8.175%

benefit of the debt rose and more than offset the incremental returns expected by the lenders and equity investors as a result of the added risk of the debt financing. The value of leverage is solely in the tax shield. In a tax-free environment, the weighted borrowing rate and cost of equity would net out to c—it would be a matter of merely swapping risk between them.

The Weighted Average Cost of Capital Revisited

Companies have several costs of capital. The unlevered cost of capital is the cost of equity if the company had no debt. As such, it is the return an equity investor would expect to receive if he or she were to buy stock in the unlevered company. The company's after tax cost of debt is its borrowing cost less the tax shield; that is, $b(1 - t)$. The company's cost of equity (y) rises from c when the company is unlevered, to c plus the financial risk premium to compensate equity investors for the incremental risk imposed by the leverage. Finally, the cost of capital that matters most is the weighted average cost of capital (c^*). Notice that c^* tends to decline initially as leverage rises. Then later it bows up again slightly as leverage rises, reflecting that the premiums charged by lenders and shareholders begin to offset the advantages of the tax shield.

The upshot of this is that companies typically come out ahead if they reduce their cost of capital by using financial leverage, at least up to a point, which will vary from one company to another. The target debt to total capital ratio is usually best at the low point in the c^* curve. However, this is not always the case. As explained in chapter 4, some companies have so much business risk that they would be unwise to compound the risk by taking on financial leverage, especially if they have high operating leverage. Thus some companies, despite the theoretical advantages of driving their cost of capital down by borrowing, would be ill-advised to do so because their business risk (especially if compounded by high operating leverage) is simply too high to add the discretionary risk of high financial leverage. Not only start-ups, but also other companies that cannot be confident of meeting their break-even points, would be generally ill-advised to assume more than very modest financial leverage. In addition, some companies may find the value of financial flexibility to exceed the benefits of incremental leverage.

Having said that, there are highly successful and intelligent individuals who have done very well leveraging risky businesses. For example, although the chemical industry is known for its high operating leverage, the owners of Cain Chemical leveraged it some 40 to 1^2 when they formed it in 1987 from a half dozen intermediate petrochemical facilities and related pipelines along the Texas Gulf Coast (as discussed in chapter 13). Fortunately they were in a position to absorb the loss in the event that business went badly. Happily it did not. Commodity chemical prices rebounded, and the investors did very well, for the operating and financial leverage each worked to the owners' advantage. Yet still, when the business risk is high, one ought not undertake high financial leverage unless one is prepared to suffer a loss of the entire investment.

By this time you might be sensing, if you did not already, that inherent in the value of a company are at least two factors, the value of the business operations unlevered, and the value of the tax shield resulting from borrowing. These can be measured and managed separately, as explained in the next chapter.

---

2. Michael C. Jensen and Brian Barry, *Gordon Cain (A)*, HBS Case Services N9-391-112, Harvard Business School, Boston, Massachusetts, 1990, at 6.

Valuing the Company

As noted in chapter 6, one way to value equity is to project the company's future earnings available to shareholders and discount such earnings to present dollars, using the cost of equity as the discount rate. This requires projecting not only the income statement but also the balance sheet, to take account of additional borrowings or equity dilution needed to finance the contemplated growth.

At times there are advantages to using a more detailed method for valuing a company or business, and such methods are explained in this chapter and in chapter 11. The advantages are twofold. First, these methods lend themselves to a clearer analysis of the value added by leverage versus the value added by operations. Second, the economic value added model in particular enables its user to monitor value creation from year to year, which has substantial advantages for resource allocation and compensation purposes. Before getting further into the particulars, it bears noting that the real flywheel of value creation is doing a good job with operations. If that is done, the rest tends to be easy; if it is not, then the rest is difficult and the company is more likely to need a magician or miracle worker than financial analysis.

A company's value has three major components: the value of current operations, of leverage, and of growth. Although they can be lumped together, it can be helpful, at least for conceptual purposes, to unbundle the value into its component parts.

The Value of the Current Operations

The first major component of a company's value is the value of current operations on an unlevered basis. This valuation assumes that the company will continue to produce its net operating profit after tax (NOPAT) at present levels in perpetuity, that it will make no new investments other than to use all its depreciation to replace existing plant and equipment (P&E), that all NOPAT will be paid out as earned in dividends to shareholders, that the balance sheet will not change, and that the income statement will be the same from one year to the next.

Seen in this light, the valuation of the company's current operations—producing the same, constant level NOPAT each year—is much like the valuation of an annuity or a very long-term bond, as it is simply the NOPAT divided by the cost of capital. Here, because we are valuing the company unlevered, the cost of capital is the unlevered cost of capital (c).

$$\frac{\text{NOPAT}}{c} = \text{value of current operations}$$

Consider Company X, the NOPAT of which is \$24,000, and which has an unlevered cost of capital of 12%.

$$\frac{\$24,000}{.12} = \$200,000$$

Thus the value of Company X's operations is \$200,000. This is the value of Company X's current operations were it financed exclusively with equity. The \$24,000 annual dividend is akin to interest on a 12% bond of unlimited duration, albeit with a higher rate of return than a bond issued by the same company would pay, reflecting the equity risk.

Value of Leverage

We noticed earlier (Table 70, page 141) that financial leverage can increase the total amount of cash available to the providers of capital, by virtue of the interest tax shield. Consider Company X and Company Y, which are identical in all respects except that Company Y has substituted debt for some of its equity, as illustrated in Table 85. Each company began a few years ago with \$100,000 of invested capital. Because of Company X's success, the value of its equity has risen to \$200,000. Company Y formerly financed exactly as Company X, but it borrowed \$100,000 to buy in half its equity and now has \$100,000 of equity and \$100,000 of debt at a 10% borrowing rate.

Company X's shareholders can be paid \$24,000 from this year's earnings. By contrast, Company Y's shareholders and lenders could receive \$28,000 from the company (\$18,000 in profit plus \$10,000 in interest). Clearly the \$4,000 advantage to Company Y is the direct result of the tax shield provided by the interest expense, and the tax shield has value. The value of the leverage is solely in the tax shield. In the absence of taxes, the borrowing cost and the cost of equity would net out to the unlevered cost of capital, as it would just be a matter of swapping risk between them.

There are two ways to calculate the value of the tax shield, and they provide exactly the same result. One way is to divide the tax savings by the pretax borrowing rate. Based on Company Y's tax savings (ts) of \$4,000 and borrowing rate of 10%, the value of the tax shield (assuming no change over time in the company's debt level, borrowing costs, or tax rates) is as follows.

$$\frac{ts}{b} = \text{value of leverage}$$

$$\frac{\$4,000}{10\%} = \$40,000^{[1]}$$

---

1. Query whether this value, at least for many companies, might be of lower risk than the value of operations.

Table 85
Calculation of NOPAT

	Company X	Company Y
Operating profit	$40,000	$40,000
Interest expense	0	10,000
Profit before tax	40,000	30,000
Tax at 40%	(16,000)	(12,000)
Profit after tax	24,000	18,000
Interest expense	0	10,000
Tax benefit of interest expense	(0)	(4,000)
Interest expense after tax	0	6,000
NOPAT	24,000	24,000

The other way to calculate the value of the tax shield is by multiplying the tax rate by the amount of debt. Given Company Y's tax rate (t) of 40%, and based on its total debt (D) of $100,000, the value is calculated as follows.

$$tD = \text{value of leverage}$$

$$40\% \times \$100,000 = \$40,000$$

Putting these two components of value together, Company Y now has $200,000 in value by virtue of its operations and $40,000 of value of leverage, for a total value of $240,000.

Consider what has happened as a result of the leverage. Company X began with $100,000 in invested equity (that is, book value), and it caused that equity to have a value of $200,000 (that is, real economic value, which is likely to be reflected in the marketplace). By contrast, by substituting cheaper debt for equity and sheltering some earnings, the value of Company Y's total capital rose to $240,000. From the standpoint of Company Y's equity holders, several important things have been made to happen. First, they received $100,000 in cash when the company borrowed and used the proceeds to buy in half their shares. Second, by virtue of the tax shield, the value of the company rose by $40,000, from $200,000 to $240,000. The value of their equity became $140,000 (that is, the total value of $240,000 less debt of $100,000). Thus, after the company borrowed and bought half its outstanding shares, the equity holders had (1) $100,000 (less any federal, state, and local taxes) in proceeds of the stock buyback plus (2) shares worth $140,000, for a total of $240,000.[2]

Because Company X did not refinance, the holders of its stock have 1,000 shares having a total value of $200,000, and each share is worth $200. By contrast, after Company Y bought in half its shares, its shareholders held only 500 shares. Yet, because the value of the equity was $140,000, the value of each share had risen to $280 ($140,000 in equity value divided by 500 shares), an appreciation of 40%.

---

2. Keep in mind, however, that financial flexibility has value as well as a cost. It is the value of choices—such as seizing a new business opportunity—and it can be valued as an option or series of options.

Table 86
Value of Company, Debt, and Equity

Total value = Value of equity + value of debt

Total value	$240,000
Value of debt	100,000
Value of equity	140,000

Table 87
Impact of Leverage on Earnings per Share and Price/Earnings Ratio

	Company X	Company Y	Difference
Equity value	$200,000	$140,000	
Number of shares outstanding	1,000	500	
Value per share	$200	$280	40%
Earnings	$24,000	$18,000	($6,000)
Earnings per share	$24	$36	50%
Price/earnings ratio	8.33	7.78	(10.7%)

However, note what happens to Company Y's price/earnings ratio (P/E). Because of the interest expense, Company Y's profit after tax (PAT) is $18,000, but, because now there are only 500 rather than 1,000 shares outstanding, the earnings per share (EPS) have risen to $36, which is 50% higher than Company X's $24 per share. The EPS rose faster than the P/E, and the reason is important.

The reason lies in the fact that the yield on the stock is equal to the inverse of the P/E; that is, 1 divided by the P/E. As leverage rises, the yield on the stock will rise to reflect the added risk because investors, perceiving incremental risk, will drive down the price of the stock to a point where the expected return compensates them for the added risk of the now more highly leveraged company. Hence, as the yield rises, its inverse—the P/E—falls, reflecting that although the earnings are rising, investors will pay less of a premium for the stock because of the added risk inherent in the leverage that caused the EPS to rise.

Note, however, as illustrated in Table 88, that as a company substitutes debt for equity, its value and the value per share of its equity both rise. This increase is measurable, and constitutes the value of leverage.

As Table 88 further illustrates, the leverage drives down the weighted average cost of capital, which indeed is the very source of the value of the leverage. The company can continue this process and buy in more shares. For instance, as shown in Table 88, if the company were to borrow another $56,000 and buy in another 200 shares at $280 each, then in the following year, if the financial performance remains the same, a total of $30,552 could be paid out from earnings to investors ($16,380 in interest plus $14,172 in dividends). The EPS would rise to $47.24 (that is, $14,172 in earnings divided by the 300 shares outstanding), and the value per share would rise to $354.67, calculated as shown in Table 89.

Table 88
Impact of Leverage on Earnings per Share and the Price/Earnings Ratio

	No Debt	$100,000 Debt	$156,000 Debt	$226,934 Debt
Net operating profit	$40,000	$40,000	$40,000	$40,000
Interest (10% on $100,000)	0	10,000		
(10.5% on $156,000)			16,380	
(11.0% on $226,934)				$24,963
Pretax profit	$40,000	$30,000	$23,620	$15,037
Tax 40%	16,000	12,000	9,448	6,015
Net PAT	$24,000	$18,000	$14,172	$9,022
NOPAT	$24,000	$24,000	$24,000	$24,000
Cash for investors	$24,000	$28,000	$30,552	$33,985
Number of shares outstanding	1,000	500	300	100
EPS	$24.00	$36.00	$47.24	$90.22
Value of company	$200,000	$240,000	$262,400	$290,774
Value of equity	$200,000	$140,000	$106,400	$63,840
Value per share	$200.00	$280.00	$354.67	$638.40
P/E	8.33	7.78	7.51	7.08
Yield (that is, P/E)	12%	12.86%	13.3%	14.1%
Financial risk premium	0	0.86%	1.3%	2.1%
c^* (weighted average cost of capital)	12%	10.0%	9.1%	8.3%
c (unlevered cost of capital)	12%	12%	12%	12%

This process can continue until the point at which the added risk of the leverage drives up the borrowing rates and the cost of equity more rapidly than it drives up the tax savings. Adding leverage however, must be conducted with careful judgment, for incremental leverage, though mathematically elegant and enticing, can be hazardous. Yet, in the right hands and under the right circumstances, it can be highly valuable. Like an accelerator on a car, its use can be effective, but it requires knowledge of the traffic and road conditions and a skilled and prudent driver who uses it correctly in light of all the circumstances.

One reason why some managements do not use more leverage when they could do so is risk aversion. This is fine for owner-managed companies, but for other companies it can create a tension between managers and the shareholders. The former tend to have their careers (their biggest assets) in the company; the latter are more diversified and able to carry the risk of having the company leverage more.

However, another factor is sometimes at work. When companies increase their leverage, they lose some flexibility, especially if the loan agreements carry restrictive covenants. With more leverage the company may not have the liquidity to pursue opportunities that may be or become available to it, and such options might have value. The counter to that is that if the opportunities are good ones, the company

Table 89

Value of Company When $156,000 in Debt Is Substituted for Equity

$$\text{Value of operations} = \frac{\text{NOPAT}}{c}$$

$$\frac{\$24,000}{12\%} = \$200,000$$

$$\frac{\text{tax savings}}{\text{borrowing rate}} = \text{Value of leverage}$$

$$\frac{\$16,000 - \$9,448}{10.5\%} = \frac{\$6,552}{10.5\%} = \$62,400$$

Value of operations	$200,000
Value of leverage	+62,400
Value of company	262,400
Value of debt	−156,000
Value of equity	106,400
Number of shares outstanding	300
Value per share	$354.67

could issue stock or borrow money to provide the financing. In some cases, the window of opportunity might open and close before the necessary capital can be raised. Thus shelf registrations might be particularly valuable for companies that are already leveraged but might want to move quickly.

For example, Philip Morris, with some $15 billion in long-term debt and $14 billion in equity based on book value,[3] or some $64 billion based on market value, could leverage more. If it were to go from a strong A to a weak A debt rating by borrowing more, the cost would be about 20 basis points, which alone might not be a sufficient deterrent. However, the company would lose flexibility. That flexibility costs Philip Morris several hundred million dollars a year, on a net income of about $5 billion, but may have that much value, depending upon the opportunities that are, or might become, available to the company.

Value of Growth

So far we have described two components of corporate value, namely the value of existing operations in perpetuity and the value of financial leverage. However, most companies grow, and growth can significantly impact value. Note that growth alone does not necessarily mean a company is creating new value. In fact, even if EPS is rising, a company may be destroying, rather than building, value.

---

3. PHILIP MORRIS COMPANIES, INC., 1996 ANNUAL REPORT.

You may not find that idea intuitive, but do not reject it out of hand; rather, keep it in mind as we proceed.

The value of the future of the company can be captured in the following formula. The letter I represents the average amount of incremental capital that will be deployed in each of the future years, r is the return on capital, T presents the number of years in which growth is expected, and the denominator is a measure for discounting the future values added to the present value (c^* is the weighted average cost of capital).

$$\text{future value added} = \frac{I(r - c^*)T}{c^* (1 + c^*)}$$

This formula[4] is offered more for conceptual purposes than for practical ones, as it is very difficult to apply in practice. However, it captures and presents some very useful concepts. First, the value of a company's future prospects depends in part on the amount of capital that can be deployed earning a positive spread between return and cost of capital. Second, the greater the spread between the company's return on capital and cost of capital, the more value the company will create. Third, the longer the company can keep doing the foregoing, the more value it has. Finally, the higher a company's cost of capital, the more steeply its future value creations will be discounted.

Notice also that there are no assurances that the spread between the return and the cost of capital will be positive. It can be negative, and, when it is negative, value is being destroyed. More specifically, in connection with future plans, if the market believes management will put more capital to work earning a negative spread between return and cost of capital, the market will reflect that expected value destruction. Indeed when a stock is being hammered by the market, it is often because the market foresees future value destruction.

Although the above formula for future value creation (destruction) is useful conceptually, actual projections, a topic discussed below, are much more useful in practice for measuring corporate or business value. Before turning to projections, however, two refinements are worth noting.

Refinements on Value Estimation

Substantial Cash and Cash Equivalents

Some companies have an enormous portion of their assets invested in cash equivalents. As of the end of its 1996 fiscal year, Microsoft Corporation, for example, had $6.94 billion in cash, amounting to 69% of its total assets, as explained in chapter 2, page 32. One can presume that either the board was seeking to avoid the tax consequences of a dividend payment or that Microsoft was planning, or at least keeping its powder dry for, a major acquisition (or a series of minor ones), or another corporate initiative.

If one were to place a value on Microsoft, a clean way to do it would be to treat the cash investments separately from the software business, value each of them, and

---

4. This formula is analogous, but not identical, to the terminal value concept described in the text.

then combine the values. That can be done rather simply by (1) deducting the company's after tax interest earnings on the cash from NOPAT and deducting the cash from the total capital, and (2) valuing the software business without the cash and then adding the cash to the value of the software business, with the total being the value of the company. A refinement is that the company needs some cash to be in business, and one would want to include such amount in the total capital needed in the software business. The appropriate amount of cash would be determined by estimating how much the company needs, over a span of two to four weeks, to meet the payroll and make other necessary payments to vendors and taxing authorities.

Were Microsoft to pay out its cash as a dividend or use it to repurchase stock, the company would have a different financial profile, and it would be more risky; for the cash, which serves as financial ballast, would be gone, at least to the extent of the dividends or amount of funds used in the stock repurchase. This added risk would be reflected in the company's cost of capital, which would then be geared solely to the risk of being in the software business on a stand-alone basis.

Nonrecurring Cash Revenues (Expenses)

Another matter occasionally requiring special attention is nonrecurring revenue or expenses. Usually it is best to distinguish the value of the operations from the value (positive or negative) of the nonrecurring items. For example, if the company has settled a significant lawsuit and is required to make cash payments over the next several years, then the company can be valued without expensing these payments. The present value of the expected litigation-related payments ought to be deducted from the value of the company thus calculated. Similarly, if the company has, for example, contracted to sell an asset for a price significantly above the company's cost basis for such asset, then it is usually best to value the company without reference to such gain, and then add the value of the gain to the value of the company without it.

On rare occasions it is advisable to use a different discount rate for the extraordinary item than is used for the cash flow from the company's normal operations. This occurs when the extraordinary item is significant and has a different risk profile than the company's operations. However, even then, calculating a different discount rate ordinarily makes little difference because the extraordinary revenue or expense is usually received or paid within a year or two. Because the discounting occurs over such a short period, the result is that even differences of several points in discount rates usually have negligible impact on value.

Measuring Future Cash Generation

Often the most difficult way to determine a company's value is by projecting its revenues, expenses, and cash earnings; discounting that cash stream to present dollars; and then allocating the cash stream to the respective classes of security. Yet the method can also be the most accurate, if one has a reasonable basis for making the projections. The method subsumes all three components of value, namely the value of current operations, the value of any financial leverage, and the value of any future growth. The value of the interest tax shield, if any, is captured in the calculation indirectly, for it serves to reduce the weighted average cost of capital below the unlevered cost of capital. This, in turn, decreases the discount rate, which in turn increases the value.

There are three difficult steps in making a useful set of projections. The accuracy of the valuation by this method hinges upon carefully formulating all three. First, the projections themselves must be reasonably accurate. Second, a reliable terminal value must be developed. Third, the correct discount rate must be used. These three topics will be addressed in turn. If the company has multiple sectors, groups, divisions, or other units, each unit ought to be evaluated separately and then combined, giving credit for any financial or other synergies and deducting any headquarters overhead that the company incurs.

The Projections

When it comes down to the crunch, the value of a company turns on the amount and timing of cash the company will earn for the providers of capital. It is not necessary that the company in fact make the cash payments to the owners, only that it earn the cash and have the ability to pay it out to owners. In fact, across the U.S. economy, the vast majority of all capital stays in the company, as the investors—through the boards of directors—elect to reinvest the vast majority of the cash earnings.

Just as cash earnings drive value, perceptions of value determine prices of securities. The fact that stocks are bought and sold reflects different perceptions of value. Some analysts base their perceptions on painstakingly thorough attempts to quantify expected revenues, expenses, cash flow, terminal values, and discount rates. Other investors base their perceptions on a great deal of intuition and little attempt at quantified precision. Just as the genius of good management lies in taking capital and generating returns in excess of the cost of capital, the genius of good investing is to forecast accurately how well the company will do. Each is forward looking and hence each is fraught with uncertainty much of the time.

When there is an effort to quantify, projections begin with revenue forecasts. Good projections of sales require a familiarity with the industry in which the company competes, the strength of the company relative to its competitors, the strength and scope of its product line, its technological position (if technology is important to it), expected prices, unit volume (often a function of the company's cost and price position relative to its competitors), the company's historic sales growth rates, the quality of management (both generally and relative to competitors), and other salient information.

Usually the revenue projections are one of the most important, if not the most important, determinant of value, and it is worth developing these projections very carefully. The projections ought to be done in nominal dollars—that is, without an effort to squeeze inflation out of them. Discounting for inflation is handled through the discount rate.

The rate of inflation built into the revenue projections ought to be the same as the rate of inflation inherent in the discount rate. As noted in chapter 7, page 148, and chapter 8, page 158, the weighted average cost of debt and the cost of equity are each based in part upon the Treasury bill rate, which has an expected inflation rate built into it. One can do the projections initially in real dollars and then increase them by the presumed inflation rate built into the T-bill rate used in estimating the cost of capital.

The level of difficulty in projecting revenues varies considerably from one company to another. At one extreme, power utilities (at least historically) and apartment houses in stable neighborhoods have such a predictable and steady customer base, revenue, expense, and earnings history that differences among appraisers ought not vary by more than a modest amount. At the other extreme, a start-up company's revenues and expenses can be so difficult to project that two appraisers, each working in good faith, can arrive at values differing by orders of magnitude. One author found a case involving the valuation of a proposed instant sign franchising company, in which the business valuation experts on the two sides agreed on the valuation method to be used and agreed on the discount rate but differed by 2500% concerning the value of the company, mainly because of differences in their projections of the company's sales.[5]

Differing perceptions of value need not kill a contemplated acquisition, offering, or buyout, but they often do so. Rather, creative executives and counsel can develop ways to structure transactions (such as creating special classes of securities) that tie each party's financial rewards to the accuracy of the party's forecasts.

In addition to forecasting revenues, one must also forecast expenses. Some can be forecast by linking them to a percentage of revenues, and some are best forecast on their own.

The projections ought to include not only the income statement but also the balance sheet and the cash flow statement. In addition, it is advisable to convert the income statement to cash earnings, and to convert the balance sheet to capture all the capital invested, as explained in chapter 6. Each of these components of the financials must be interrelated so that, for example, if prices drop and unit volume and expenses do not change, then revenues drop; gross margins, operating margins, and pretax margins drop; taxes drop; PAT drops; the cash account drops; and borrowings might rise, which will increase interest expense, which in turn will reduce taxes and earnings, which in turn will reduce NOPAT and impact the total capital, which in turn will impact the return on total capital and the value of the company. The projections must capture all the interrelationships so that the full impact of a change in any variable is correctly measured.

It is important to project the balance sheet and, derivatively, the total capital account, carefully, especially in three major respects. First, any new capital needed from outside sources, whether debt or equity, ought to be built into the projections. For example, through fiscal 1995, Wal-Mart Stores, Inc., grew at least 21% per year (and in the 1970s and 1980s, often twice that), but over that period consistently reinvested approximately 88% of its earnings.[6] This builds the equity account. In addition, Wal-Mart borrowed more money to help finance its growth,[7] for if it did had not done so, then its leverage would decline, with corresponding impact on its rate of return. Some companies must finance their growth with new issues of equity, and the terms on which that is done can significantly impact the return to existing shareholders. Without attempting to describe here all the possibilities, the capital structure ought to be projected carefully, keeping in mind that it usually should change as the company goes through different stages.

---

5. Bradford Cornell, Corporate Valuation 125 (1993).
6. Wal-Mart Stores, Inc., 1995 Annual Report.
7. *Id.*

Second, the balance sheet projections ought to reflect investment in new P&E, as needed to implement the qualitative elements of the company's strategy. Third, any necessary changes in working capital must be reflected in the projections.

The projections ought to be done for as many years into the future as one can see with reasonable clarity. There is no standard number of years that one ought to project. If the company and its industry are very stable, then it may well be feasible to project some 20 years into the future. Traditionally the power utilities have fit that description, although now a better example is an apartment complex in an upscale neighborhood with a stable rent roll, a preponderance of long-term leases, and nothing adverse and new looming on the horizon. Indeed, in cases such as utilities and apartment complexes, it is important to try to project out for as many years as the expense of depreciating the company's assets will be borne by the company or its owners. By contrast, many of the companies in Silicon Valley are in businesses in which the technology changes rapidly; thus projections beyond two years are so speculative that they are only marginally reliable, at best. Unless such companies are valued as options, which is often advisable, it is useful to project out as far as one can because years not specifically projected are folded into and subsumed by the terminal value, and the simplifying assumptions used to project the terminal, or continuing, value are often less accurate than specific cash flow forecasts.

Terminal Value

After projecting out for as many years as is feasible, the valuation process focuses on a terminal value. The concept behind the terminal value is that at some point in the future the inexorable forces of competition set in and the company, even if it has been growing at extraordinary rates or earning extraordinary returns, stabilizes at equilibrium in its competitive environment. At that equilibrium point, the company's returns are usually expected to be at, or close to, the returns in the economy.

The terminal value can be highly important. In a study published in 1990, researchers from McKinsey & Company, Inc., reported that terminal values accounted for 56% of the total value of tobacco companies, 81% of the total value of sporting goods companies, 100% of the total value of skin care companies, and 125% of the total value of high-tech companies.[8] Indeed, when the terminal value constitutes more than 100% of the present value of the company, it is because in the nearer term the company will be earning substandard returns (and perhaps even incurring losses) before reaching the years of value creation. In general, the more rapidly a company is growing, the higher the proportion of the terminal value in relation to the total value.

Selecting a terminal year can be difficult. It ought to be far enough into the future that the company is growing at a steady and sustainable rate. Its need for new investment should be down to a point where its cash flow is sufficient to finance the growth without a requirement for new equity, although reinvested earnings might justify new debt without increasing the financial leverage. Further, the company's costs should have stabilized relative to its revenues, and its margins should be fairly constant. If the company has multiple business lines or divisions that are expected to reach their terminal dates in different years, then each ought to

---

8. Tom Copeland et al., Valuation: Measuring and Managing the Value of Companies 208 (1990).

be valued separately to accommodate their differences, and then combined in determining the company's overall value.

The year that one chooses as the terminal year ought to be a normal year rather than an aberrational one. To some extent, this problem is solved by using cash earnings rather than earnings calculated under generally accepted accounting principles (GAAP). For example, a bank's earnings might be atypically low as a result of writing off bad loans, and using NOPAT rather than GAAP will automatically correct for this. Yet the terminal year still might be at the top or bottom of a business cycle, and using NOPAT does not always solve the problem. Many industries—including the steel, chemical, and auto industries—are cyclical, and using a terminal year at the top or bottom of the cycle is likely to be misleading. One way to minimize the risk of a bad mistake is to compare the growth rate and DuPont Formula ratios inherent in the projections (described in chapter 4) for the terminal year with the normalized growth rate (described in chapter 5) and corresponding DuPont Formula ratios. If the terminal year numbers are much different from the latter, then one ought to consider carefully whether the terminal year numbers ought to be modified.

If projected NOPAT over the next five years is to grow at varying rates and the pattern is such that the terminal year appears to be atypical, there are several statistical adjustments that might be made. First, one could simply use the average of the five years' earnings in calculating the terminal value. However, because a simple average often gives undue weight to the earlier years, it can be better to calculate a weighted average of the five years, using a technique such as the sum-of-the-years'-digits method, to weight the more recent years more heavily. Another technique is to normalize the earnings. This can be done by regressing the cash earnings to what they would have been had they been growing at a steady pace rather than bouncing around. These techniques are explained in chapter 5.

Once the terminal year has been selected and the cash earnings for that year have been estimated, it becomes possible to estimate the continuing value of the company as of that year. As noted above, the concept is that the company's business has stabilized at that point and will continue as is, growing revenues and cash earnings at a modest but constant rate in perpetuity.

The Constant Cash Flow Growth Model

The first method for determining the terminal value of the firm is the constant cash flow growth model. This model assumes that at a certain point in the future the company's operations reach an equilibrium state, which the company then maintains in perpetuity. The value of the company's free cash flow of the terminal year is calculated and then discounted to the present.

Free cash flow is not quite the same as NOPAT. Although there is some ambiguity in the term, free cash flow is usually defined as NOPAT plus depreciation and amortization (or often, simply earnings) less (1) increases in working capital and (2) increases in fixed assets. (In case you need a reminder, NOPAT, explained in detail in chapter 6, is the company's cash earnings on an unlevered basis, and *net* means net of depreciation, which is deducted.)

There is some debate about whether depreciation ought to be added to NOPAT in determining free cash flow. Clearly it is a source of cash. However, the cash is needed to replenish P&E as necessary, with the result that cash flow from depreciation cannot be taken out of a going concern on a regular basis. Yet this is taken into account by deducting the new investment in P&E in calculating the free cash flow. Hence it is appropriate for these purposes to add depreciation to earnings in calculating free cash flow. Alternatively, depreciation can be excluded from the calculation of NOPAT and netted out of the increase in fixed assets in calculating free cash flow. Sidebar 30 illustrates this point.

_____ *Sidebar 30* _____

Alternative Methods of Handling Depreciation in Calculating Free Cash Flow

In scenario A, the cash flow from depreciation is added to NOPAT to calculate cash flow from operations. The new investment includes the portion financed with the cash flow from depreciation.

In scenario B, the cash flow from depreciation is not added to NOPAT to calculate cash flow from operations. The new investment does not include the portion financed with cash flow from depreciation.

Whichever method is used, the free cash flow is the same.

Table 90 Free Cash Flow under Alternative Methods		
	A	**B**
NOPAT	$1000	$1000
Deprecation	100	—
Cash flow from operations	1100	1000
Less new investment	500	400
Less new working capital	200	200
Free cash flow	$400	$400

Once the free cash flow in the terminal year has been determined, one is in a position to calculate the continuing value, at least if the weighted average cost of capital and the expected growth rate in perpetuity are known. The formula holds that the terminal value is equal to the free cash flow in the terminal year, divided by the net of c^* less the expected growth rate.

$$\text{continuing value} = \frac{\text{expected free cash flow in terminal year}}{(c^* - \text{growth rate})}$$

For example, if the free cash flow expected in the terminal year is $10 million, the weighted average cost of capital is 10%, and the expected nominal growth rate in perpetuity is 5%, then the continuing value is calculated as follows.

$$\text{continuing value} = \frac{\$10 \text{ million}}{(10\% - 5\%)}$$

$$\text{continuing value} = \$200 \text{ million}$$

This continuing value is then discounted to present dollars in calculating the company's value.

In estimating a growth rate, a common mistake is to assume an unrealistically rapid rate of growth. After adjusting for inflation (that is, in real terms), the growth of the U.S. economy has averaged 2% to 3%, reflecting the 1% average growth rate in the population plus increases in the living standard. Consider that if a company grows more rapidly than the economy's real rate of growth plus the inflation rate, and if it does so in perpetuity, then at some point, its value will be infinite, and eventually its revenues will constitute almost the entire economy. To be sure, it would be a very long time before that happened, but the point remains that one should be quite skeptical of assumed real growth rates in excess of about 2%. Thus if the expected inflation rate is 3.5%, one ought to be leery of assumed nominal growth rates much in excess of 5.5%. One of the most common pitfalls is to assume too high a growth rate in the terminal year.

It can be useful to separate the expected nominal growth rate into its two component parts, namely the expected real growth rate and the expected inflation rate, to force a disciplined analysis of each. If that is done, then the expected nominal growth rate in perpetuity is as follows.

$$((1 + \text{expected real growth rate}) \times (1 + \text{expected inflation rate})) - 1$$

Implicit in the foregoing is that it is best to project NOPAT growth in the terminal year in nominal rather than real terms because the discount rate will capture and adjust for inflation. To use the real growth rate would double count the discount and unduly penalize the company. Having said that, some appraisers find it useful to project the expected rate of growth in the terminal year in real terms and then augment that amount by the expected inflation rate, as described above. That is, by distinguishing the real rate of growth from the inflation rate, the appraiser can make sure the assumption about inflation in the NOPAT growth rate and the discount rate are consistent.

The Value Driver Formula

The second method of determining the terminal value is the value driver formula or model. This formula is based on four variables.

First, the value driver model projects NOPAT out to the terminal year. The rate at which the present NOPAT will grow in reaching the terminal NOPAT is highly important and must be consistent with the prior years' performance and rate of reinvestment to support the growth. The higher the rate at which the NOPAT will grow in perpetuity, the greater the terminal value of the firm.

A second critical variable in using the value driver model is the rate of return on investment (r) in perpetuity. Clearly the higher the rate of return on newly invested capital, the greater the continuing value will be. The inexorable forces of competition in a market economy are such that rates of return in perpetuity much in excess of economy-wide norms are reason for skepticism.

Third, the model forces its user to assume a growth rate in perpetuity. The comments above pertaining to the constant cash flow growth model apply as well to the value driver model. Finally, the fourth variable is the firm's cost of capital.

These factors are captured with the following formula.

$$\frac{\text{NOPAT}\left(1 - \dfrac{g}{r}\right)}{c^* - g} = \text{continuing value}$$

NOPAT = expected normalized unlevered cash profit after tax

g = expected nominal rate of growth in NOPAT when the company is normalized, in perpetuity

r = expected rate of return on new investment at equilibrium

c^* = weighted average cost of capital

To illustrate, if the terminal year NOPAT is $1,000, the expected nominal growth rate 5%, the rate of return 11%, and the weighted average cost of capital 9%, then the continuing value is as follows.

$$\frac{\text{NOPAT}\left(1 - \dfrac{g}{r}\right)}{c^* - g} = \text{continuing value}$$

$$\frac{1,000\left(1 - \dfrac{.05}{.11}\right)}{(.09 - .05)} = \$13,636.35$$

The continuing value thus calculated must then be discounted to present dollars. If the terminal year is 7 years in the future, indicating a present value factor of 0.547 (the result of discounting at the cost of capital for 7 years), then the present value of the continuing value is $13,636.35 multiplied by 0.547, or $7,459.55. Notice that the continuing value of the terminal NOPAT rises as (1) the projected NOPAT rises, (2) the growth rate rises, (3) the rate of return rises, and (4) the cost of capital falls.

Seemingly minor differences in assumptions can drive major differences in the continuing value. To illustrate, in the foregoing example, were we to assume an 6% rather than a 5% growth rate in perpetuity, the expected continuing value would rise from $13,636.35 to $15,151.50, a 10% increase in the expected continuing value. Particularly because continuing value is often a major portion of the total estimated value of a company, it is highly important to be very careful when making the estimates used in deriving the terminal value.

There is another wrinkle in the value driver model. In equilibrium the company will incur depreciation expenses and will make investments in new P&E and working capital, and the model assumes that the depreciation will be sufficient to finance the new investment in P&E. The problem is that, due to inflation, the cash flow from depreciation is not likely to be sufficient to replace the P&E as it becomes fully depreciated. Therefore the company may need more new capital from outside the company to finance new P&E. After the new capital has been raised, NOPAT will be earned on a larger capital base; consequently the raising of this added capital will reduce the rate of return on invested capital below what it would have been had the new investment not been needed. The same phenomenon is at work in connection with working capital, although the impact is unlikely to be as great because the working capital normally turns over more rapidly than P&E, with the result that inflation works its effect on working capital for a shorter period than it does on P&E. As a consequence, one must be very careful in applying the value driver model in practice, and build into the model a calculation of the amount of new capital needed to finance the incremental (that is, not covered by depreciation) P&E and working capital and to reduce the company's rate of return on invested capital accordingly, before using the above formula. If we lived in an inflation-free world, the value driver model and the constant cash flow growth model would give the same continuing value.

The Convergence Formula

Occasionally one sees continuing value calculated on the basis of another assumption, namely that in many industries, over time, competition becomes so intense that the return on investment is driven down to the cost of capital. (There is no shortage of industries in which the return on new capital has been driven below the cost of capital and remains there until shakeout occurs, and the remaining companies begin once again to earn their cost of capital, although they might not earn much more. The airline industry provides one example, although we are still waiting for the shakeout to be extensive enough for the remaining firms, on average, to earn their cost of capital.)

The convergence model begins with the value driver formula (CV = continuing value).

$$CV = \frac{NOPAT\left(1 - \frac{g}{r}\right)}{(c^* - g)}$$

The model then assumes that the return on capital converges on, or by the terminal year equals, the cost of capital. This being the case, one can substitute c^* for r and restate the formula.

$$CV = \frac{NOPAT\left(1 - \frac{g}{c^*}\right)}{(c^* - g)}$$

Multiplying the right side of the formula by c^*/c^* gives

$$CV = \frac{\left[NOPAT\left(1 - \frac{g}{c^*}\right)\right]c^*}{(c^* - g)c^*}$$

which simplifies to

$$CV = \frac{NOPAT(c^* - g)}{c^*(c^* - g)}$$

which simplifies to

$$CV = \frac{NOPAT}{c^*}$$

Note that this convergence formula does not assume there will be zero growth. If it did make that assumption, it would be flawed in the case of most companies, for even if those companies are to have no real growth on an indefinite basis, they usually at least keep up with inflation. Rather, the convergence formula has assumed a growth rate, but the algebra has canceled it out of the formula by assuming that the return on incrementally invested capital will equal (that is, will have converged on) the company's cost of capital, and thus that the incremental investment will create no new value.

The convergence formula is more likely to understate than overstate the continuing value. This is because the formula assumes that as of the terminal year, the company's return on capital has declined to the cost of capital. This may well happen over time, as the returns on new investments (earning lower returns and eventually earning only the cost of capital) constitute an ever-larger portion of the company's total capital. However, this convergence usually does not happen by the terminal year.

The Aggressive Formula

It is not uncommon to see another formula used in calculating the terminal value. The formula assumes that earnings growth will decline to, and stabilize at, the inflation rate. Although that assumption is conservative, and tends by itself to understate the continuing value, another assumption is made, namely that the earnings ought to be discounted at the real (that is, inflation adjusted) cost of capital less the growth rate (which is assumed to be the inflation rate). This results in the following formula.

$$CV = \frac{\text{NOPAT}}{(c^* - g)}$$

By assuming that earnings will grow in nominal terms but then discounting them only in real terms, the formula tends to overstate value. This problem is compounded by a second implicit assumption, namely that earnings will grow at the inflation rate with no new investment. However, the depreciation will over time prove inadequate to finance new P&E. Hence new P&E will be required, but its cost is assumed not to rise with inflation. The assumption that the company will get a growing return without having to finance any new investment means that the presumed return on capital approaches infinity. This discrepancy drives down the $(c^* - g)$ part of the formula, which in turn drives up the continuing value. Because the continuing value is thus pumped up, this is known as the *aggressive* formula, which is almost certain to be flawed.

The Liquidation Value Method

One ought not complete a terminal valuation of a company without at least considering its value on liquidation. The realizable market value of each category of assets (net of transportation costs, commissions, and any other transaction related costs) can be estimated and the value of the liabilities can be estimated. The net, of course, is the value of the equity. If the providers of capital include not only equity holders but also other categories of capital, such as secured and unsecured lenders and preferred stock holders, then the respective categories of capital providers may have conflicting opinions about whether the company ought to be liquidated, as illustrated during the bankruptcy proceedings in New York involving Eastern Airlines in the early 1990s. From the equity holders' perspective, the liquidation value ought to be determined and set a floor on the value of the company. Because most companies have greater value as going concerns than on a liquidation basis, this method usually does not provide the most useful valuation of the company.[9]

Selecting the Discount Rate

The third task in valuing a company based on its future cash earnings is to select the rate used to discount the future earnings to their present value. The reason that determining an appropriate discount rate is so difficult is that it must correctly reflect the operating and financial risk of the company, and quantifying risk is one of the most difficult tasks in the realm of corporate finance. Yet, you will be pleased to know that you have done this work already if you read chapters 7, 8, and 9, for the discount rate is the rate of return that the providers of capital must expect to receive to provide an adequate incentive not to deploy their capital elsewhere. In that sense the discount rate reflects the opportunity cost to the providers of capital.

Note that the term *providers of capital* is used rather than equity holders, because the discount rate reflects the weighted average cost of capital rather than solely the cost of equity. The reason for this is that the risk to which providers of capital are exposed includes (1) the risks inherent in the company's operations and (2) the added risk of financial leverage, if the company has debt. By using the company's weighted average cost of capital as the discount rate, each of these sources of risk is captured. Furthermore, we are valuing the company, not merely the equity. Hence the cost of all the company's capital must be used.

Valuing the Company as an Option

Companies can value projects like options. For example, if a company owns a right to explore for oil or gas below a certain parcel of land, that right is essentially an option to explore for oil and gas. If the company proceeds to explore, it might find oil and gas, or it might not. If it does, then the find will have value, depending upon the size of the find. The present value can be estimated by quantifying the probability of a find, the likely size of the reserve, the cost of extracting the oil and gas, the price of oil and gas at the time the field is developed, the amount of any royalties, tax rates, and the discount rate. Some companies have many projects, each of which can be valued and added to the value of operations and tax shield to derive a value for the company.

Some companies in the early stages are like projects. They may develop value, and they might not. Their value, if any, can be estimated, much like estimating the value of an undeveloped oil and gas field or mine. Owning a share of stock in such

---

9. *In re* Eastern Airlines, Inc., No. 89-B-10449 (Bankr. S.D.N.Y. Mar. 9, 1989).

a company is in that sense akin to buying an option. If the software start-up succeeds, how big will the success be? What is the likelihood of success? How long will it last? You get the idea. The method for valuing options is set forth in chapter 8, Sidebar 28, pages 168–169.

Summary

Once the projected financial performance of the company, the terminal value, and the discount rate have been estimated, they can be combined to estimate the value of the company. This is illustrated in chapter 11, Tables 95–101 (Random Industries). Indeed, chapter 11 uses the building blocks set forth in this chapter to explain two important methods of valuing companies.

The Discounted Cash Flow Method and Economic Value Added Method[1]

Chapter

11

At present the two most widely used methods of valuation are the discounted cash flow method and the economic value added method, both of which are illustrated in this chapter. Finance is a dynamic field—even as this book goes to press, research is being conducted that may improve upon these methods before many more years elapse. Future research may show that total return to shareholders (TRS) correlates more closely with one or more financial measures other than discounted cash flow or economic value added.

The economic value added method has emerged as the leading challenger to the discounted cash flow method of valuing companies or businesses. It was developed by the New York consulting firm Stern Stewart & Company,[2] and has been adopted as of late 1996 by approximately 250 companies,[3] including AT&T, Coca-Cola Company (which has seen its stock rise more than tenfold since adopting the economic value added method in the early 1980s), Quaker Oats Company (which was outperforming Standard & Poor's 500 Index until it made its ill-fated acquisition of Snapple), Eli Lilly, Transamerica, Georgia-Pacific Corporation, Olin Corporation, Deere & Company, Boise Cascade Corporation, and Merrill Lynch (with special adjustments to the cost of capital calculations to reflect the high leverage of a financial institution).

Other methods of valuing companies are appearing. Among those, the most notable is the cash flow return on investment (CFROI) measure developed and espoused by the Boston Consulting Group, and adopted by Procter & Gamble Company and some 100 other companies as of late 1996.[4] To no small extent, the competition among the various emerging measures represents a competition for consulting business, and such competition tends to magnify minor differences in the measures. To determine cash earnings relative to the capital or assets under management, each method makes adjustments to earnings under generally accepted accounting principles (GAAP).

Economic value added and CFROI are claimed by their respective proponents to correlate more closely with TRS than any other measure. As noted elsewhere, TRS

---

1. The acronym for *economic value added* is a registered trademark of Stern Stewart & Company, in the United States.

2. G. BENNETT STEWART, III, THE QUEST FOR VALUE (1991).

3. Randy Myers, *Metric Wars: Marketing Battles Erupt as Stern Stewart and Rivals Seek Your Hearts, Minds, & Dollars,* 12 CFO MAG. 41–50 (Oct. 1996).

4. *Id.* at 42, 49.

Table 91
Economic Value Added/Shareholder Value

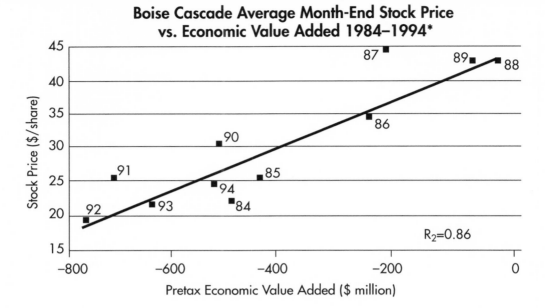

Boise Cascade Average Month-End Stock Price vs. Economic Value Added 1984–1994*

*Report of Boise Cascade Corporation security analyst meeting, October 24, 1995

is the stock price appreciation plus any dividends, usually measured on an annual-ized basis.[5] No study has yet proven which financial measure correlates most closely with enhanced shareholder value across all companies. The most unbiased study on the subject was a 1996 report from the University of Washington, which concluded that the economic value added method correlates no more closely with shareholder value than earnings.[6] The issue is highly important; certainly more studies will be done, their methodologies will later be challenged, and then more studies will be done. In the meantime, without waiting for a definitive answer for all companies, any single company can conduct its own study to determine which financial variable empirically correlates most closely with its own stock price.

---

5. Calculating TRS can be tricky if a company has had a share repurchase program during the period under management. If shares have been purchased at prices below the ending price, TRS is over-stated unless an adjustment is made. Accordingly, the economic value added method measures the market value (MV) of a company's outstanding shares less its book equity to determine the market value added (MVA). The higher the MVA, the more value management has added to the invested cap-ital. If shares have been repurchased, the sums expended in the buyback are deducted from both the MV and from the book equity, with the result that the buyback will have had no impact on the MVA.

6. Myers, *supra* note 3, at 41, 44.

Boise Cascade Corporation, for example, is persuaded that economic value added is the financial measure that drives the company's stock price, reporting a very high 0.86 correlation, as shown in Table 91.[7]

Because the economic value added method has been adopted by a significant number of companies (and in some estimates more than twice as many companies as any other measure), it merits explanation. Many other valuation techniques are based on similar cash-return-on-cash-invested methodologies. Therefore, if you understand the economic value added method, you will be well equipped to understand the various other methods as you come across them. Before turning to it, however, an explanation of the discounted cash flow method is in order, for it is the chronological and intellectual forerunner of the economic value added method.

Discounted Cash Flow Method

The discounted cash flow method essentially projects the future performance of the company and then discounts the cash flows to present dollars to estimate their present value. Bear in mind that definitions of cash flow are not universally agreed upon, and there are several ways to calculate it. Essentially, the major alternatives are (1) to discount the future cash flow to equity, in which case the correct discount rate is the cost of equity, and (2) to discount the future cash flow to all the capital (that is, to the debt plus equity), in which case the correct discount rate is the weighted average cost of capital. The former is often referred to as residual cash flow, the latter as free cash flow.

Residual Cash Flow Method

The residual cash flow method involves projecting into the future the company's cash earnings for each year (or other suitable time period), including the terminal year. To do this, one estimates future revenue, expenses (including depreciation), interest, and cash taxes. To the net, one then (1) adds back the depreciation and other non-cash expenses, (2) deducts (adds) any increases (decreases) in property plant and equipment (PP&E), other long-lived assets (LLAs), and working capital, and (3) adds any new debt (or subtracts any repayments of debt). The net is a residual cash flow that is available to the equity holders (unless loan covenants provide otherwise). This residual cash flow is then discounted to present dollars by using the company's cost of equity.

Free Cash Flow Method

The free cash flow method involves calculating the present value of the enterprise (that is, the value of the debt plus the equity, both calculated for these purposes on a book value, not market value, basis) and then deducting the debt to determine the

---

7. Boise Cascade Corp., Report of Boise Cascade Security Analyst Meeting, Oct. 24, 1995.

present value of the equity. This method makes the same projections just described, excluding any cash flows associated with interest or debt levels. The resulting cash flows for each year are then discounted to present dollars at a discount rate equal to the company's weighted average cost of capital. The value of the debt can then be deducted to determine the net present value of the equity.

For any given period, the calculations are as follows.[8]

Table 92
Cash Flow Calculations

Residual Cash Flow to Equity	**Free Cash Flow to the Enterprise**
Revenues	Revenues
− Expenses	− Expenses (except interest)
− Depreciation	− Depreciation
− Interest	<u>− Cash taxes</u>
<u>− Cash taxes</u>	Cash earnings
Cash earnings	+/− Depreciation
+/− Depreciation	+/− New working capital
+/− New debt	+/− <u>New PP&E and other LLAs</u>
+/− New working capital	Free cash flow
+/− <u>New PP&E and other LLAs</u>	
Residual cash flow	

Table 93
Alternative Method of Calculating Free Cash Flow

Free cash flow
    Revenues
    − Cash expenses (other than depreciation and interest)
    <u>− Cash taxes*</u>
    Cash earnings
    +/− New working capital
    +/− <u>New PP&E and other LLAs</u> (net of depreciation)
    Free cash flow

$$\frac{\text{Free cash flow}}{c^*} = \text{Company value}$$

    Company value
    <u>− Debt</u>
    Equity value

*See footnote 8 below for a discussion of cash taxes.

8. One of the factors in Table 92 is cash taxes. As described in chapter 6, cash taxes reflect two adjustments to the tax displayed on the GAAP financial statements. First, taxes are calculated as though the company had no debt and hence no interest tax shield. Second, one deducts only the tax paid in cash; thus, for instance, any increase in deferred tax liability is deducted from the accrued tax in calculating the cash tax.

If one is estimating the equity value, the discount rate ought to be the company's cost of equity. If one is estimating the value of the debt plus the equity, then the discount rate ought to be the company's weighted average cost of capital.

If there is no growth expected, one could make the calculation more directly by dividing the residual cash flow by the cost of equity to estimate the equity value, or by dividing the free cash flow by the weighted average cost of capital to estimate the value of the debt and equity.

Table 94
Calculation of Value if No Growth Is Expected

$$\frac{\text{Residual cash flow}}{y} = \text{Equity value}$$

$$\frac{\text{Free cash flow}}{c^*} = \text{Company value}$$

$$\begin{array}{l} \text{Company value} \\ \underline{- \text{ Debt}} \\ \text{Equity value} \end{array}$$

NOPAT Method

A third method is to calculate the company's cash earnings (net of depreciation; that is, without adding back depreciation) on an unlevered basis (which, as you may recall from chapter 6, is the company's net operating profit after tax, or NOPAT). From the NOPAT one then deducts any increase—or adds any decrease—in PP&E (net of depreciation), other LLAs, and working capital. This method is used and illustrated in Table 101, page 214. In Table 101, line 148 (column 1), for example, you can see for 1998 the projected unlevered cash earnings of $105, less the new investment of $79 (which includes increases in working capital, PP&E net of depreciation, and other LLAs). The NOPAT less the new investment thus defined is the 1998 free cash flow of $26 (at line 148, column 3), which is then brought to a present value of $25 (line 148, columns 4 and 5). The present value of all future free cash flow of $1,236 (line 154, column 5) to capital, plus any cash not needed to support the operations and thus not included in the valuation, less the present debt of $350, gives at line 157 the present value of the equity of $1,055.

Refinements on Use of Methods

There are two refinements worth noting in connection with the use of these methods. First, the changes in working capital built into the analysis ought to include only operating working capital. Even though GAAP includes all current assets in its definition of working capital, for present purposes the current assets ought not include any excess cash or other assets not needed to run the business, and the current liabilities ought to include only those liabilities that arise in operating the business (such as accrued liabilities and accounts payable). Even though under GAAP certain liabilities (such as current portions of long-term debt and currently payable deferred tax liabilities) are, strictly speaking, current liabilities, in this context we are looking only for those current liabilities that arise from operations. Such other liabilities must be taken into account in valuing the particular company, but they are independent of the inherent value of the operations.

Second, and more difficult, one ought to distinguish between capital expenditures needed to maintain the business on an "as is" basis, and those used to grow or expand the business. Ideally, in calculating the residual cash flow and free cash flow numbers, one ought to deduct only the investment in PP&E needed to maintain the business. Expenditures needed to maintain the existing business are not discretionary. By contrast, investment of cash to finance growth could have been paid out to the owners or used for other purposes without eroding the strength of the existing operations.

For instance, consider two companies, each of which generates cash earnings of $100 and reinvests the full $100. One company needs to reinvest $50 to maintain that level of cash earnings for another year, and the other company needs to invest only $10 to do so. The former company has a free cash flow of $50 (that is, $100 in cash earnings less the $50 spent for new PP&E needed to maintain the existing level of operations), whereas the second company has a free cash flow of $90 (that is, $100 in cash earnings less the $10 spent for new PP&E needed to maintain the existing level of operations). Notice that the second company has more value for its owners, for they can take out $90 per year and still have the same business, whereas the owners of the first company can take out only $50 per year if they want to maintain the enterprise.

Now let's assume that the first company reinvests not only $50 of its cash earnings, but the remaining $50 as well, and even goes as far as to borrow another $25 and sell another $25 in stock, the proceeds of which are used to invest in growth opportunities. In this event the company has generated cash earnings of $100 but has invested $150 ($50 to maintain its existing operations and $100 to pursue a growth opportunity). The result is a negative cash flow of $50. Although the cash flow is negative, the move is a wise one if the investment of $100 in growth opportunities promises to have a net present value in excess of $100. If the net present value is less than $100, then the investment is unwise.

If the financials reveal a negative residual or free cash flow, and if the reason is that the company is investing more than its cash earnings, then one must assess whether the growth opportunities the company is pursuing are wise. If so, as has been the case over the years at General Electric Company, Johnson & Johnson, and many other companies, including many start-ups, then the negative residual or free cash flow is desirable. On the other hand, if the investments are in projects that will not earn the cost of capital, then they are destined to diminish the value of the company. In short, one of the real challenges in finance is to determine which companies with negative cash flows are destroying value and which are creating value.

Sometimes the residual or free cash flows are negative simply because cash earnings are negative, which is often indicative of the company having serious business problems. After all, unsuccessful companies usually have negative or poor earnings. Yet even negative cash earnings are not always proof that the company is unsuccessful. There are times, such as during a start-up phase or the downturn in a business cycle, that promising companies have negative cash earnings as well as negative residual or free cash flows.

Finally, it can be very difficult to determine which portion of the capital investment in new PP&E is to maintain the existing business and which portion is to expand it. Most textbooks and practitioners make the major assumption that the cash flow from depreciation must be reinvested to maintain the present operations, and that investment above that level is to fund growth. As noted in chapter 4, that assumption can be problematic, especially in an inflationary environment, because the historic costs, to which depreciation is linked, may be less than the actual current cost of replacing rolling stock, machinery, or other PP&E needed to maintain current levels of activity. On the other hand, some equipment—such as electronic equipment—is declining in cost, with the result that at times the depreciation may be more than adequate to replace obsolete assets. (However, this is difficult to measure because for a variety of reasons, such as technological improvements, one might not replace old equipment with precisely the same equipment.) The same phenomenon occurs when a hotel refurbishes, as the expenditures for new furniture, fixtures, and equipment are typically less than the construction costs. In short, determining the portion of the new investment being used to finance growth can be very difficult. In most cases using the depreciation number is about right, although, on average, it falls a bit short of enabling the company to maintain its existing level of operations.

Some of the best and most accurate cash flow determinations (and valuations) are done by those inside the companies rather than by outsiders. This is because insiders have better access to information, such as how much of the company's investment is needed to maintain existing operations rather than to grow the company. Outsiders are often left making estimates and assumptions.

Of course, when using comparables in doing valuations, one is usually an outsider and thus necessarily must rely on estimates and assumptions about matters such as cash flow refinements and discount rates. In such instances, it is usually best to use a few financial measures (such as cash flow; earnings before interest and taxes, or EBIT; earnings before interest, taxes, depreciation, and amortization, or EBITDA; and profit after tax, or PAT) as the basis of comparison, make the comparison with four or five comparables in each case, and at least look at the averages. To be sure, the insider can do projections far more reliably than the outsider, although even the insider is sometimes well-advised to look at comparables, if only as a cross-check or a flag for when the projections might be unduly optimistic or pessimistic or at variance with the stock market's expectations. After all, the market is making its own assessment of each public company's future performance, including cash flow performance.

The Economic Value Added Method

The basic concept underlying the economic value added method[9] is that a company is not adding value unless it earns a rate of return on capital (measured for these purposes on a book, not market, basis) in excess of its cost of capital. If it is earning an excess, then the more capital with which it is doing so, the more value it is creating.

---

9. STEWART, *supra* note 2, at 320–349 (includes more details on the economic value added model).

Unless a company earns a return on its book value capital that is equal to or in excess of the cost of that capital, it is destroying value for its shareholders.

More specifically, calculating the economic value added involves three variables: the company's return on capital (r), its weighted average cost of capital (c^*), and the amount of total capital (TC) with which it is working. The economic value added is the return on the total capital, usually calculated on a book basis, less the cost of that capital. For instance, if a company earns a return of 15% on capital of $1,000, and if the cost of that capital is 10%, then the company is earning a positive spread of 5% on the $1,000, and the economic value added is 5% of $1,000, or $50. Conversely, if the company's cost of capital is 10% and it earns only 5%, then the company has destroyed $50 in value. After all, the investor could have earned a 10% return somewhere else with comparable risk.

The return on capital is NOPAT divided by the total capital, as explained in chapter 6 and stated in the following formula.

$$\frac{\text{NOPAT}}{\text{TC}} = r$$

Thus we have a way to measure the value created in any given year:

$$\begin{array}{r} \text{total capital} \times \text{return on total capital} \\ - \underline{\text{total capital} \times \text{weighted average cost of capital}} \\ \text{economic value added during the year} \end{array}$$

Using abbreviations, one can restate this as follows.

$$(\text{TC} \times r) - (\text{TC} \times c^*) = \text{economic value added}$$

And one can reduce the formula to the following.

$$\text{TC}\,(r - c^*) = \text{economic value added}$$

For any given period, this captures the value added by both the then current operations and by the leverage, if any.

Of course the value of a company is not merely the amount of value it creates in any single year, but rather, in that year and all future years. Thus, the present value is the combined value of the current year's value added, plus the next year's value added discounted to the present, plus the following year's value added discounted to the present, and so forth, including the terminal value discounted to present dollars. The value of all future years' value creations is a function of (1) how many more years the company can keep growing and earning a return on its incremental capital that exceeds the cost of such incremental capital, (2) how much the return on capital exceeds the cost of capital, (3) how much capital the company can deploy that earns a return in excess of the cost of capital, and (4) the discount rate.

Consider two companies, identical in all respects, including identical income statements and balance sheets, identical amounts of leverage, and identically attractive returns on investment. One company, however, provides its owners with every reason to believe that it will grow about 30% a year for several years to come, whereas the other company gives every reason to believe that it will not grow at all. Thus the companies are identical in terms of the value of their current operations and the value of their leverage, but very different in terms of their future prospects. Part of the value of the first company is its ability to deploy new capital in ways that will generate a return in excess of its cost of capital.

The economic value added for each year for which there are specific projections, plus the economic value added in the terminal year, can be calculated and discounted to present dollars. To this sum, one adds the value of any marketable securities the company may have above and beyond the amount of cash needed in connection with its operations, as illustrated by Microsoft Corporation, discussed in chapter 2. This sum constitutes the economic, or financial, value of all the capital of the company. To calculate the value of the equity, one deducts from the total the value of the debt obligations, and the net is the value of the equity.

An Example: Random Industries, Inc.

Tables 95–102 (pages 208–215) illustrate this process for Random Industries, Inc., a hypothetical company that is an amalgam of numerous real companies. Tables 95, 96, and 97 set forth Random's projected income statement, balance sheet, and cash flow statement for five years into the future. Tables 98 and 99 set forth calculations of NOPAT and total capital, which have been derived from Tables 95 and 96, respectively. You might notice that NOPAT has been derived using two different methods. As explained in chapter 6, the financial method begins with the PAT (Table 98, line 66), adds back the non-cash expenses (lines 67–71) other than depreciation, and adjusts the taxes to reflect only the tax that Random would have paid in cash had it been unlevered. The result is NOPAT (line 77). The other method calculates NOPAT on an operating basis, beginning with the revenues (line 78) and deducting only the cash expenses (lines 79–81) and depreciation (line 82), deducting no interest expense and deducting only the amount of taxes Random would have paid in cash (line 90, which is derived in lines 92–97) had it been unlevered. It does not matter which method of calculating NOPAT is used. Both methods reach exactly the same result of $105 in 1998, as you can see by comparing lines 77 and 91 in Table 98. The former merely works from the bottom of the income statement to the top, and the latter begins at the top and works its way down. Often it is advisable to calculate NOPAT by both methods, to have a cross-check on one's accuracy of calculations. The NOPAT calculated by both methods ought to remain equal as one varies the projection assumptions and runs a sensitivity analysis, as discussed later.

Like NOPAT, the total capital is calculated in two distinct ways, as shown in Table 99 (page 212). The financial method uses the liability side of the balance sheet and totals all the invested capital, including all the adjustments and gross-ups as described in chapter 6. Table 99 includes a capitalization of research and development (R&D) expenses in the event you want to see how that works, although, as noted in chapter 6, there is a school of thought that advises against doing so. The operating method uses the asset side of the balance sheet, with much the same adjustments and gross-ups, and then deducts the non-interest-bearing liabilities; that is, those liabilities not financed with capital on which investors expect a return. The method one uses should not matter, for they yield exactly the same result, as you can see by comparing lines 110 and 129. As is the case with calculating NOPAT, it is often advisable to calculate the total capital by both methods as a way of cross-checking one's accuracy.

Table 100 (page 213) sets forth the calculation of Random's return on capital, cost of capital, and economic value added for each year for which there are projections, including the terminal year.

Table 95
Random Industries

Income Statement	1998	1999	2000	2001	2002	2003
1 Sales	1,029	1,111	1,200	1,296	1,399	1,469
2 Cost of goods sold	617	666	720	777	840	882
3 Gross profit	411	444	480	518	560	588
4 MG&A	206	222	240	259	280	294
5 Depreciation	26	29	32	35	38	42
6 R&D	31	33	36	39	42	44
7 Goodwill amortization	6	5	5	5	5	4
8 Amortization of other assets	4	4	4	4	4	4
9 Operating profit	139	151	163	176	191	200
10 Interest expense	32	32	32	32	32	32
11 Pretax profit	106	119	131	144	159	167
12 Tax of 40%	43	48	52	58	63	67
13 Profit after tax (PAT)	64	71	78	86	95	100

DCF Method versus Economic Value Added Method

The payoff for doing the above calculations occurs in Tables 101 and 102. Table 101 sets forth the valuation of Random based on the DCF method. The DCF method, like the economic value added method, calculates the cash earnings. But then the two methods diverge. The DCF method deducts from NOPAT (for example, $105 in 1998, at line 148, column 1) any increase in working capital and fixed assets (net of depreciation expense) (for example, $79 in 1998, at line 148, column 2) to arrive at the free cash flow (for example, $26 in 1998, at line 148, column 3). The free cash flow is the cash that can be distributed to the investors after all new investments have been financed. Notice that in the terminal year the depreciation is presumed to offset (exactly) any new investments in plant and equipment (P&E), and that there is no need for new working capital because the company is no longer growing. (As noted in chapter 6, this presumption is dubious due to inflation.) The free cash flow for each year and the terminal year are then discounted back to present dollars, and the total is the net present value ($1,236 at line 154) of the company's capital. To this sum should be added any cash and marketable securities not needed in the business (line 155) and thus not used in valuing the business. From the total one can deduct the interest bearing obligations (line 156) to arrive at the value of the equity (line 157). The price or value per share (line 159) can be calculated by dividing the value of the equity by the number of shares currently outstanding (line 158).

The economic value added method is a bit different from the DCF method. It tracks the economic value added for each of the projected years and the terminal year (Table 102, column 5) and then discounts the amounts to present dollars (Table 102, column 7). When this is added to the present capital (line 166) and the excess cash (line 168), the sum is the present value of all the company's capital (line 169). As is true with the DCF method, to determine the value of the equity alone (line 171) one deducts the value of the debt (line 170) from the value of the total capital. One

Table 96
Random Industries

Assets	1998	1999	2000	2001	2002	2003
14 Cash	200	200	200	200	200	200
15 Accounts receivable	254	274	296	319	345	362
16 Less doubtful accounts	(13)	(14)	(15)	(16)	(17)	(18)
17 Net accounts receivable	241	260	281	304	328	344
18 Inventory replacement cost	309	333	360	389	420	441
19 Less LIFO reserves	(31)	(33)	(36)	(39)	(42)	(44)
20 LIFO inventory	278	300	324	350	378	397
21 Total current assets	719	760	805	853	906	941
22 P&E	364	391	419	451	486	525
23 Less accumulated depreciation	106	118	132	147	163	182
24 Net P&E	259	272	288	304	323	343
25 Goodwill	17	15	15	15	14	13
26 Less accumulated amortization	12	10	10	10	10	9
27 Net goodwill	5	5	5	5	4	4
28 Other assets	13	11	13	13	12	11
29 Less accumulated amortization	10	7	8	9	8	7
30 Net other assets	3	4	5	4	4	4
31 Total assets	985	1,042	1,103	1,166	1,236	1,292
Liabilities						
32 Short-term debt	150	150	150	150	150	150
33 Accounts payable	154	167	180	194	210	220
34 Accrued expenses	21	22	24	26	28	29
35 Total current liabilities	325	339	354	370	388	400
36 Deferred taxes	51	59	66	74	82	91
37 Long-term debt	100	100	100	100	100	100
38 Subordinated debt with warrants	100	100	100	100	100	100
39 Equity	409	444	482	522	566	601
40 Total liabilities and equity	985	1,042	1,103	1,166	1,236	1,292

can then compute the value per share (line 173) by dividing the value of the equity by the number of shares outstanding (line 172).

Terminal Value

One advantage the economic value added method has over the DCF method is that the terminal value is almost always a higher portion of total value when the DCF method is used than when the economic value added method is used. The reason for this is that DCF is calculated net of new investment in P&E and also net of new investment in working capital. Under the DCF method, this often pushes the positive cash flow and hence the expected value creation out toward the terminal date. This can be seen by comparing Random's terminal value as calculated under the DCF method

Table 97
Random Industries

Cash Flow Statement	1998	1999	2000	2001	2002	2003
41 Profit after tax	64	71	78	86	95	100
42 Depreciation	26	29	32	35	38	42
43 New deferred tax	7	7	8	8	8	9
44 Goodwill amortization	6	5	5	5	5	4
45 Amortization—other	4	4	4	4	4	4
46 New accounts receivable	(19)	(20)	(22)	(24)	(26)	(17)
47 New doubtful accounts	1	1	1	1	1	1
48 New inventory	(23)	(25)	(27)	(29)	(31)	(21)
49 New LIFO reserves	2	2	3	3	3	2
50 New accounts payable	11	12	13	14	16	10
51 New accrued expenses	2	2	2	2	2	1
52 Net cash flow from operations	82	89	97	106	116	136
53 New short-term debt	0	0	0	0	0	0
54 New long-term debt	0	0	0	0	0	0
55 New sale of equity	0	0	0	0	0	0
56 Dividends paid	(4)	(36)	(40)	(47)	(51)	(65)
57 Net cash from financing	(4)	(36)	(40)	(47)	(51)	(65)
58 New P&E	39	43	47	52	57	62
59 Add to goodwill	5	5	5	5	4	4
60 Add to other assets	3	5	5	3	4	4
61 Net cash from investing	47	53	57	60	65	70
62 Net new cash	31	0	(0)	0	0	0
63 Beginning cash	169	200	200	200	200	200
64 Ending cash	200	200	200	200	200	200
65 Unused STD capacity	53	69	87	106	126	140

($1,000, in Table 101, line 153, column 5) with the terminal value calculated under the economic value added method ($233, in Table 102, line 165, column 7). The more rapidly the company is growing, the more accentuated the problem of having the preponderance of the value in the terminal value.

By contrast, the economic value added method tracks the value creation from year to year because new investment and new working capital are not deducted from NOPAT and do not impact the return on capital for that reason. Such investments do, however, impact the return on capital for a different reason, namely that under the economic value added method the investments increase the amount of capital with which the company is working, which in turn impacts the return on capital and the value creation. Thus an advantage of the economic value added method is that any error in estimating the terminal value is very unlikely to have as substantial an effect on the terminal value as does an error in estimating the terminal value using the DCF method. In other words, as Random Industries illustrates, the economic value added method places less emphasis on the terminal value, thereby diminishing the risk of error.

Table 98
Random Industries

NOPAT—Financing Method	1998	1999	2000	2001	2002	2003
66 PAT	64	71	78	86	95	100
67 Goodwill amortization	6	5	5	5	5	4
68 Increase (decrease) in LIFO reserves	2	2	3	3	3	2
69 Increase (decrease) in doubtful accounts	1	1	1	1	1	1
70 Credit R&D expense	31	33	36	39	42	44
71 Less R&D amortization	(25)	(28)	(31)	(33)	(36)	(39)
72 Plus increased deferred taxes	7	7	8	8	8	9
73 Adjusted income available to common	85	93	100	109	118	121
74 Interest expense	32	32	32	32	32	32
75 Tax benefit of interest	13	13	13	13	13	13
76 Interest expense after tax	19	19	19	19	19	19
77 Net operating profit after tax	105	112	119	128	137	141

NOPAT—Operating Method	1998	1999	2000	2001	2002	2003
78 Sales	1,029	1,111	1,200	1,296	1,399	1,469
79 Cost of goods sold	617	666	720	777	840	882
80 Operating profit	411	444	480	518	560	588
81 MG&A	206	222	240	259	280	294
82 Depreciation	26	29	32	35	38	42
83 Amortization of R&D	25	28	31	33	36	39
84 Amortization of other assets	4	4	4	4	4	4
85 Operating profit	150	162	173	187	201	209
86 Increase (decrease) in NIBCLs						
87 Increase in LIFO reserves	2	2	3	3	3	2
88 Increase in doubtful accounts	1	1	1	1	1	1
89 Adjusted net operating profit before tax	153	165	177	191	206	212
90 Less cash operating taxes	(48)	(53)	(58)	(63)	(68)	(71)
91 NOPAT	105	112	119	128	137	141
92 Provision for taxes	43	48	52	58	63	67
93 Less increase in deferred taxes	(7)	(7)	(8)	(8)	(8)	(9)
94 Plus tax savings of interest (line 97)	13	13	13	13	13	13
95 Cash operating taxes	48	53	58	63	68	71
96 Interest expense	32	32	32	32	32	32
97 Tax benefit of interest expense	13	13	13	13	13	13

Furthermore, the economic value added method enables shareholders, the board, and management to monitor value creation or destruction as it is occurring. To illustrate, compare Table 101, line 148, column 3, with Table 102, line 160, column 5. The former shows Random's cash flow for 1998. For many companies the cash flow expected one year out is negative, rendering it an almost useless measure of value.

Table 99						
Random Industries						

Capital—Financing Method	1998	1999	2000	2001	2002	2003
98 Short-term debt	150	150	150	150	150	150
99 Long-term debt	100	100	100	100	100	100
100 Subordinated debt	100	100	100	100	100	100
101 Total debt	350	350	350	350	350	350
102 Doubtful account reserve	13	14	15	16	17	18
103 Plus previously amortized goodwill	12	10	10	10	10	9
104 Plus previously amortized other assets	10	7	8	9	8	7
105 Plus LIFO reserves	31	33	36	39	42	44
106 Capitalized R&D	45	51	56	61	67	73
107 Deferred taxes	51	59	66	74	82	91
108 Equity	409	444	482	522	566	601
109 Adjusted equity	571	617	673	732	793	843
110 Total capital	921	967	1,023	1,082	1,143	1,193
111 Debt/total capital	38%	36%	34%	32%	31%	29%

Capital—Operating Method	1998	1999	2000	2001	2002	2003
112 Cash	200	200	200	200	200	200
113 Accounts receivable	241	260	281	304	328	344
114 Doubtful account reserve	13	14	15	16	17	18
115 Inventory	278	300	324	350	378	397
116 LIFO reserves	31	33	36	39	42	44
117 Total current assets	762	807	856	908	965	1,003
118 Accounts payable	154	167	180	194	210	220
119 Accrued expenses	21	22	24	26	28	29
120 Total NIBCLs	175	189	204	220	238	250
121 Net working capital	587	618	652	688	727	753
122 Net P&E	259	272	288	304	323	343
123 Goodwill	5	5	5	5	4	4
124 Previously amortized goodwill	12	10	10	10	10	9
125 Capitalized R&D	45	51	56	61	67	73
126 Other assets	3	4	5	4	4	4
127 Previously amortized other assets	10	7	8	9	8	7
128 Total fixed assets	334	349	372	394	416	440
129 Total capital	921	967	1,023	1,082	1,143	1,193

Even for Random, the free cash flow expected in 1998, although positive at $26, is virtually meaningless because it can be controlled by investing more or less in the business. To be sure, one could instead measure performance by NOPAT, but that would ignore the amount and cost of capital, neither of which should be ignored. By contrast, the economic value added method provides rather prompt feedback about how the company is doing without the result being influenced significantly by the level of

Table 100 Random Industries						
Financial Measures	**1998**	**1999**	**2000**	**2001**	**2002**	**2003**
130 NOPAT	105	112	119	128	137	141
131 Beginning capital	842	921	967	1,023	1,082	1,143
132 Return on beginning capital (r)	12.45%	12.16%	12.34%	12.51%	12.70%	12.31%
Cost of Capital	**1998**	**1999**	**2000**	**2001**	**2002**	**2003**
133 STD interest rate	7.5%	7.5%	7.5%	7.5%	7.5%	7.5%
134 Pretax borrowing cost	9.2%	9.2%	9.2%	9.2%	9.2%	9.2%
135 Tax rate (t)	40 %	40 %	40 %	40 %	40 %	40 %
136 After tax interest cost	5.5%	5.5%	5.5%	5.5%	5.5%	5.5%
137 Debt ÷ total capital	38.0%	36.2%	34.2%	32.4%	30.6%	29.3%
138 Beta	1.0	1.0	1.0	1.0	1.0	1.0
139 Unlevered cost of capital (c)	10.7%	10.7%	10.7%	10.7%	10.7%	10.7%
140 Cost of equity (y)	11.2%	11.2%	11.2%	11.1%	11.1%	11.1%
141 Equity ÷ total capital	62.0%	63.8%	65.8%	67.6%	69.4%	70.7%
142 Weighted cost of debt	2.1%	2.0%	1.9%	1.8%	1.7%	1.6%
143 Weighted cost of equity	7.0%	7.2%	7.3%	7.5%	7.7%	7.8%
144 Cost of capital (c*)	9.1%	9.2%	9.2%	9.3%	9.4%	9.4%
Economic Value Added						
145 Return on capital × total capital	105	112	119	128	137	141
146 Cost of capital × total capital	76	84	89	95	102	108
147 Economic value added (EVA)	28	28	30	33	36	33

new investment. In 1997 one can measure the current value added and project the 1998 value added. Within a year one will know whether the company is on course.

The terminal value by either method can be brought to present value in either of two ways. One way is simply to apply the present value factor to the terminal year's cash flow (in the case of the DCF method) or economic value added in the terminal year (in the case of the economic value added method). An alternative method is to multiply the DCF or economic value added in the terminal year by a present value factor calculated by a three-step process. The first step is to determine the value of $1 per year in perpetuity beginning in the terminal year. That value is determined by dividing $1 by the company's weighted average cost of capital (c*). For example, if a company's c* is 10%, then each $1 of cash flow or economic value added has a value, as of the terminal year, of $10. The second step is to discount the value of that $10 to the present. If the appropriate discount rate is 10% and the number of years the value is being discounted is 10, then the discount factor is 0.349, and the present value of $10 in perpetuity beginning in the terminal year is $10 × 0.349, or $3.49. The third step is to multiply the terminal year DCF or economic value added by the discount factor. For example, if the terminal year DCF or economic value added were $1,000, and the present value factor 3.49, then the present value of

Table 101
Random Industries
Discounted Cash Flow Valuation

	Year	1 NOPAT*	2 New Investment (I)	3 Free Cash Flow	4 PV Factor*	5 PV of FCF
148	1998	105	79	26	0.958	25
149	1999	112	46	66	0.877	58
150	2000	119	56	63	0.803	51
151	2001	128	58	70	0.735	51
152	2002	137	61	76	0.672	51
153	Residual value	141	0	141	7.111**	1,000
154	Intrinsic operating value					1,236
155	Plus cash					169
156	Less total debt					350
157	Intrinsic equity value					1,055
158	Number of shares outstanding					100
159	Value/share					10.55

Discount rate of c (mid-year)
**Present value of $1.00 in perpetuity beginning in 2003:
1. $1.00 in 1998 is discounted to $0.67 in 2003
2. $0.67 ÷ c* (9.4%) is 7.111

having $1,000 per year in perpetuity beginning in 10 years would be $3,490 (that is, $1,000 × 3.49 = $3,490). Thus the value today of receiving $1,000 a year in perpetuity beginning in 10 years is $3,490, assuming a 10% discount rate.

Value Creation

Returning to the economic value added system, there are several ways in which companies can create value.

First, they can increase the return on capital. There are two ways to do this: increase NOPAT, or earn the same or greater NOPAT with less capital. (Note that this releases capital that the owners can use, albeit net of any taxes on the distribution, to earn a return somewhere else.) This is analogous to the DuPont Formula discussed in chapter 4, where we saw that companies could improve their return on assets by increasing their margins or their asset turnover (by increasing sales or by reducing their assets).

Second, companies can drive down the weighted average cost of capital when that is appropriate. This requires (1) convincing investors that they have overestimated the risk, (2) investing in less risky, value creating, projects, or (3) moving toward a capital structure that is more heavily weighted toward debt than is

Table 102

Random Industries
Economic Value Added Valuation

		1	2	3	4	5	6	7
	Year	Return on Beginning Capital (r)	Cost of Capital (c*)	Performance Spread (r−c*)	Beginning Capital	EVA*	PV Factor**	PV of EVA
160	1998	12.45%	9.07%	3.38%	842	28	0.958	27
161	1999	12.16%	9.15%	3.00%	921	28	0.877	24
162	2000	12.34%	9.24%	3.10%	967	30	0.803	24
163	2001	12.51%	9.32%	3.19%	1,023	33	0.735	24
164	2002	12.70%	9.39%	3.31%	1,082	36	0.672	24
165	2003 and beyond	12.31%	9.44%	2.87%	1,143	33	7.111***	233
166	Plus 1997 total capital							879
167	Intrinsic operating value							1,236
168	Plus cash							169
169	Value of total capital							1,405
170	Less total debt							350
171	Intrinsic equity value							1,055
172	Number of shares outstanding							100
173	Value/share							10.55

*Col. 3 × col. 4

**Discount rate of c* (mid-year)

***Present value of $1.00 in perpetuity beginning in 2003:

1. $1.00 in 1998 is discounted to $0.67 in 2002

2. $0.67 ÷ c* (9.4%) is 7.111

215

presently the case. As noted in chapter 4, there are some companies for which such added leverage makes sense and some for which it would be unwise.

Third, companies can deploy more capital on new projects that earn a return in excess of the cost of capital. Indeed, part of the present value of some companies is the ability to do just this, as illustrated by Wal-Mart Stores, Inc., at least through its fiscal 1997. An important source of the market's perception of Wal-Mart's corporate value has been the company's ability to expand from its present base of some 2,000 Wal-Mart locations, 500 Sam's Club locations, and nearly 200 Supercenters by finding new locations, whether in the United States or in foreign countries, and opening and operating such locations to earn a return in excess of the company's cost of capital. The major investment banks and other professional investors are watching closely for evidence that will indicate whether Wal-Mart will be able to roll out its formula, or an adaptation of it, overseas. The fact that Wal-Mart's stock price dropped from early 1994 until early 1996 indicated that the market had previously overestimated Wal-Mart's ability to grow although its stock's rapid price appreciation in early 1998 indicated that investors had become much more sanguine about Wal-Mart's prospects. Yet, over the span of two decades, by committing more capital to new locations, Wal-Mart created enormous value.

Fourth, if the company has a history of committing capital to projects that earn a return less than the company's cost of capital, then merely ceasing such conduct will, at least on a relative basis, create value. More will be said about this point below.

An Example: Wal-Mart Stores, Inc.

Through fiscal 1997, Wal-Mart has done a brilliant job of creating value by earning positive spreads between its returns on capital and its cost of capital, although during the prior decade the spread had been slowly declining. This has been due to a number of factors:

1. The company picked the best locations first and now must add new stores in places offering returns that, while still positive, provide less of a premium above the cost of capital.
2. Competitors such as Target Stores, Inc. (a division of Minneapolis-based Dayton Hudson Corporation) and even Sears, Roebuck & Company have had the time to study and emulate Wal-Mart's practices, offering stiffer competition than they did previously and than did the "Mom and Pop" stores with which Wal-Mart traditionally competed.
3. To sustain a high growth rate, Wal-Mart has needed to move into urban locations (that are more competitive and that have higher cost structures than the rural areas in which it operated historically), and overseas (where competition, customer tastes, and other factors are different). Whereas it used to be able to grow 35% to 40% per year by adding new locations in rural areas, the best of those locations have been chosen, forcing Wal-Mart into urban areas such as Chicago, Los Angeles, and the outskirts of New York, where land and labor costs are higher and competition stiffer, and into overseas markets such as China and Argentina where Wal-Mart's returns to date have been lower.
4. Wal-Mart's absolute growth has been rising every year. However, as the company grows, it is harder and harder to sustain the same relative growth

rates. Whereas from 1984 to 1985 the company grew at an annual rate of 32% by increasing its revenues by $2 billion, from 1996 to 1997 it would have needed to increase its revenues by $30 billion to achieve the same percentage growth rate. As it was, from 1996 to 1997 its revenues grew by $11 billion. That one year's growth alone almost would have placed Wal-Mart in the Fortune 100, but it was not enough to sustain the earlier percentage growth rates.

That is not to say that Wal-Mart is not continuing to create new value, for it has, at least through fiscal 1997. The picture for Wal-Mart in fiscal 1996 was unusual and interesting. Its net income rose by only $59 million on an incremental equity investment of $2 billion,[10] indicating only a 3% return on equity at the margins. However, if one gives the company credit for the $302 million increase in deferred tax liabilities and the goodwill amortization of approximately $104 million, both of which are equity equivalents, the total cash generated for its owners on the incremental $2 billion of equity invested was $465 million, a handsome return of some 23% at the margins, and well in excess of the company's cost of equity. The company is monitoring its performance very closely to make sure it does not commit capital to projects (mostly foreign) that do not earn the cost of capital. At this time, the jury is still out concerning whether its foreign (at least non-Canadian) ventures will succeed.

The following graph illustrates a pattern of deploying capital in a way that earns returns declining to a point where they approach the cost of capital.

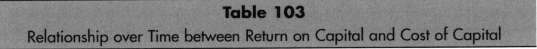

Table 103
Relationship over Time between Return on Capital and Cost of Capital

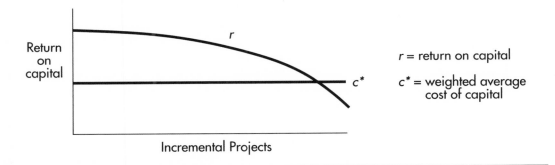

Return on capital

r

c*

r = return on capital

c* = weighted average cost of capital

Incremental Projects

One of these years, Wal-Mart, like any growth company, will reach a point where it can no longer find projects that will earn a return in excess of its cost of capital. What it can and should do at that point will be discussed later. Suffice it here to say that although it is clearly becoming much more difficult, part of Wal-Mart's strength has been its ability to deploy new capital where it can earn returns in excess of its cost of capital, and part of that skill is accurately projecting the returns that will be earned on new investment.

10. Wal-Mart Stores, Inc., 1996 Annual Report.

Value Erosion

The opposite can also happen. Many companies invest new capital and earn on it a return less than its cost. This diminishes the value of capital, and it happens somewhere every day of the week, not because people are bad or stupid but often because they are unaware of what they are doing. Part of the problem is that the destruction of value can be masked by rising earnings. The reason a company's value might be eroding, even though earnings are rising, is that the measure ignores the cost of capital in general and the cost of equity in particular. If, for example, the earnings rose, but the amount of equity deployed rose by more, then the company is doing less well. Moreover, the fact that earnings rose does not mean much if in the prior year the company fell even shorter of earning its cost of equity, as the following example illustrates.

Table 104			
Why an Increase in Earnings per Share Is Not Proof of Value Creation			
	Year 1	**Year 2**	**Difference**
Earnings	$ 2 million	$ 2.5 million	25%
Earnings per share	$ 1.00	$ 1.25	25%
Equity	$20 million	$22.5 million	13.5%
Return on equity	10%	11%	10%
Cost of equity	12%	12%	0

In the above example, earnings per share and returns on equity are all up, but the company still has not earned its cost of equity, and value erosion is occurring.

In addition to a great deal of value destruction taking place because management is unaware that it is not earning the company's cost of capital, there is a second reason why value destruction occurs. Companies often misforecast their performance. Many CEOs, both within the company and in their communications with Wall Street and shareholders, express confidence that earnings will improve. They compound the problem by putting new capital to work earning returns that fail to meet the cost of capital, thereby destroying value and leaving shareholders with stock worth even less than if the company had simply stuck with the mediocre or bad hand with which it began.

To illustrate, one publicly held company, a producer of soft drinks, said in its annual report that was released in the spring of 1995 and that covered the company's fiscal year ending January, 1995, "We expect a year of dramatic growth and financial progress. . . . My confidence in the future of the company has never been higher."[11] Yet for the year ended January 27, 1996, the company reported a loss of $29 million,[12]

---

11. Cott Corporation, 1995 Annual Report.
12. Cott Corporation, 1996 Annual Report.

Standard & Poor's downgraded its already speculative debt, and its stock price, which had hit $38 per share in 1993, fell from some $11 per share at the time the above words were written to $9 per share in May of 1996, a drop of approximately 20% over a period in which the Standard & Poor's 500 Index rose approximately 35%.

In short, if a company continues to deploy new capital earning less than its cost of capital, it is diminishing the value of its capital, and its stock price will sooner or later (probably sooner) reflect that. Indeed one of the keys to the success of the hostile takeovers of the 1980s was that many of the targets had been wasting shareholder value with repeated, unsuccessful new investments. By merely taking the company over and turning off the spigot, the raiders created (relative to what management had been doing), or at least preserved, value. It is not hard to understand why shareholders embraced many of these takeovers as a way to cure the risk of ongoing investments that dissipated value. Part of the skill of good management is to forecast future performance accurately and deploy (or not deploy) capital accordingly. Good projections and sensitivity analysis, if done well, can be enormously valuable in this respect.

Sensitivity Analysis

One of the advantages of a comprehensive spreadsheet, such as that for Random in Tables 95–102, is the opportunity it offers to ask "what if" questions. If the computer model has been set up correctly, one can alter different variables and see how much each change impacts the value of the company. One can use the spreadsheet to determine how much the value would differ if, for example, the rate of sales growth over the next five years decreased from 10% to 9%, gross margins rose from 60% to 61%, interest rates rose by 1.5%, tax rates rose, debt was substituted for equity, accounts receivable increased from 50 to 60 days, or any other change occurred. Any component of the projected income statement or balance sheet can be altered and the impact on value determined. Note that if Random Industries were a public company, a keen observer could decipher, through "reverse engineering," what the market must be expecting in terms of growth rates, margins, and other determinants of value. The inference will not be precise, for there are multiple variables that drive the value, but it can be instructive.

To illustrate, Random Industries could contemplate the effects of a change in its revenues. There will be a ripple effect in other financial items, such as the cost of sales, operating profit, taxes, PAT, receivables, capital requirements, interest expenses, cost of capital, and return on capital. Each such change (and the changes caused by those changes) must be handled correctly by the model, resulting in changes in the income statement, balance sheet, cash flow statement, NOPAT, total capital, and valuation. In Random's case, a change in revenues in Table 95 would impact all the other financial statements, including the value per share in Tables 101 and 102. One can add to the model a sensitivity grid, as follows.

Table 105	
Sensitivity Analysis: Impact of Revenue Change on Random's Value per Share	
Increases in Revenues	**Value per Share of Random Industries**
5%	$ 6.32 down 40.1%
9%	$ 9.58 down 9.2%
10%	$10.55 —
11%	$11.58 up 9.8%
15%	$16.62 up 57.5%

It is possible to build the model so the impact of changes in multiple variables—such as sales growth rates, the cost of debt, and tax rates—can be tested simultaneously. Though that can be helpful, it is often more useful to test the impact of changes in any particular variable one at a time, so one can identify, and focus attention on, the variables that have the greatest impact on value. For instance, in Random's case, though a decrease in revenues from 10% to 9% diminishes the value of the equity from $1,055 to $959, or 9.1%, an increase in the depreciation schedule (although probably much easier to achieve) from 10 to 20 years increases the value of the equity from $1,055 to $1,075, or only 2.3%, and a 1% increase in borrowing costs reduces the value of the equity from $1,055 to $1,025, or only 2.8%.

Sensitivity analysis, correctly done, provides an excellent method for identifying the factors that drive the value of the company. It can tell management where to focus its efforts. For example, the projections might tell management that value is very highly sensitive to minor changes in revenue levels and minimally sensitive to major improvement in inventory turnover (or in some cases, vice versa). Hopefully, management has control of the value drivers, such as inventory levels or credit policy, or at least can influence factors at the margins, such as sales levels. When management cannot control the critical determinants of value (such as petroleum prices, if the company is in the plastics industry, or interest rates), the projections can at least alert management to the importance of the variable.

Even if a company cannot control a critical determinant, it may be able to develop ways to control the impact of such variables on the company. For example, it could use long-term supply contracts to lock in costs, which might be wise to the extent the company has a contract under which it is obligated to supply a customer. A company that should have done this but did not is Westinghouse, the diversified company based in Pittsburgh. While seeking to sell the construction of nuclear power plants, Westinghouse offered and agreed to supply its customers, the utilities, with uranium at fixed and modest prices on a long-term basis when they signed the construction contracts. Unfortunately the price of uranium later rose dramatically, and Westinghouse was stuck having to buy dear and sell cheap, a problem it could have skirted by obtaining long-term supply contracts at costs at or below the prices at which it was obligated to sell.[13] (But, a

---

13. Vasil Pappas, *Westinghouse Bid to Settle Uranium Suits Out of Court Faces Consumer Opposition*, WALL ST. J., Apr. 8, 1977, at 10.

word of caution: if the buyer is in a regulated industry, the regulatory authority might have the power to void long-term contracts, such as long-term take or pay contracts, leaving the vendor that relied on the contract in a bad position.)

As Westinghouse learned, not only is management sometimes unable to control a critical variable, sometimes it cannot even predict it. Although no one knows what interest rates will be next year, they can be a critical determinant of the financial performance of many companies, such as savings and loan institutions. Good projections can tell management the level of its exposure to changes in interest rates, and help it decide whether it should use swaps or derivatives to manage the duration and rates of the company's borrowings.

Columbia Gas, the natural gas pipeline now based in Virginia, did the same thing.[14] Subscribing to the conventional wisdom of the time that natural gas prices could only rise, and fearful of shortages, Columbia Gas signed long-term take or pay contracts with natural gas suppliers (which committed it to purchase gas at prices that turned out to be high), believing that it could resell the gas in the spot market for much higher prices. When natural gas prices tumbled in the early 1980s and early 1990s, Columbia was stuck paying high prices under its take or pay contracts with natural gas companies, even though it could not resell except at much lower prices. The result for the company was bankruptcy.[15]

By identifying and quantifying the variables to which value is most sensitive, management can best focus its efforts. The first task is to identify all the factors that might impact the value of the company, without trying to prejudge their likelihood or salience. These include economy-wide phenomena (such as higher tax rates or lower interest rates), factors unique to the industry (such as price cuts or technological innovations by key competitors), and factors unique to the company (such as union wage increases or longer collection cycles). As illustrated in Table 106 (on page 222), this exercise can help management position the company to maximize its value creation and minimize its exposure to risks it does not want to take.

Variables *A* through *K* represent all the factors management has identified that might impact corporate value. Clearly *B* is the potential development it ought to watch and manage most carefully, followed by *A*, *D*, and *H*.

This determination is made by plotting each of these factors against two variables, as illustrated in Table 106. First, the likelihood of each occurring (whether or not management can control or predict precisely the likelihood of occurrence) is assessed as best one can. Second, the factor's salience or impact upon value is assessed. (A good set of projections can be very useful in this exercise.) The resulting display indicates to management where it might best focus its attention, or at least indicates which phenomena will have the greatest impact on value. Here again, this methodology is no substitute for good qualitative judgment. However, it can be a powerful and useful supplement to other more qualitative techniques of management and decision making. The projections ought not be used as an altar to which one must bow deeply, but rather as a potentially valuable resource to be used in conjunction with good management judgment derived from intelligence, information, and experience. When used correctly,

---

14. Suein L. Hwang, *Columbia Gas, Subsidiary, File for Chapter 11*, WALL ST. J., Aug. 1, 1991, at A-3.
15. *In re* Columbia Gas Systems, Inc., 136 B.R. 930 (Bankr. D. Del. 1992); *see also In re* Columbia Gas Systems, Inc., 997 F.2d 1039 (3d Cir. 1993).

Table 106
Identifying Which Variables to Manage

Likelihood of Occurring

Impact on Company Value		Low	Medium	High
	High	C	D	B A
	Medium	J	I G	H
	Low	E	K	F

good quantitative analysis becomes a way to elevate the level of discussion and minimize the risk of bad mistakes, not a way to make up for an absence of wisdom.

If it has developed a good model, good management can use it to develop a very precise estimate of the value of the company. It can also be used by investors and prospective investors in making investment decisions. Indeed, it is because different investors read reality differently, and have different expectations about what the future holds, that stocks are bought and sold. If all investors thought the same thing, there would be far fewer trades (although some would still occur because individuals' needs for liquidity change, even if their perception of a company's risk or return does not).

One might ask how this fits with the disclosure requirements of the federal and state securities laws. To date, materiality has been measured in terms of earnings and occasionally with reference to assets. As the state of the art and the level of practice for measuring value improves, as it rapidly is, it is entirely possible that the regulatory and judicial practice will evolve, perhaps rapidly, toward assessing materiality in terms of impact on value. Hence, the lawyer with responsibility for disclosure might soon want to assess the impact of a development on the company in terms of value, not merely GAAP earnings. Referring to Table 106, if prospective development *F* were to occur, it would merit less attention and disclosure than development *H*, for example. Whether the impact is measured based on earnings or value, the ability to do a good sensitivity analysis would be very helpful to the executive or counsel making or defending disclosure decisions. Under the Private Securities Litigation Reform Act of 1995, issuers providing forward looking statements cannot be held liable in private actions for projections and other predictions of future performance, as long as the statements are accompanied by a "meaningful cautionary statement" or the defendant did not commit actual fraud. Being able to demonstrate that the company's statement was based on a model the issuer used to make projections of earnings and value (for internal use) and to formulate strategy ought to carry the defense of any disclosure-related action a long way.

Using Forecasting Tools to Meet Varying Needs of Parties

There is another subtle, but at times highly potent, lesson in the above. There may be numerous categories of capital providers, including equity holders, secured lenders, warrant holders, and others. The categories are limited only by the imagination of counsel, their clients, and, to a lesser degree, state corporate laws. The critical point is that each category of capital provider may be sensitive to different variables, or different degrees of change in the same variables.

Lenders and Equity Holders

For example, assume that a company has one equity holder and one lender. Assume further that if the company runs a certain risk successfully, the equity holder gets a 10 to 1 return on investment in two years, and nothing otherwise. By contrast, the lender has a ceiling on its return. If the risk turns out badly, both the equity holder and the lender lose all or most of their capital. In such a situation, the two parties may have diametrically opposed views of the advisability of running the risk. Inasmuch as equity holders control the board, unless the lender uses its loan covenants (whether financial or nonfinancial) to prohibit the company from running certain kinds of risks, then once the ink is dry on the loan agreement the lender may lose much, if not all, of its influence.

Similarly, good and credible projections give the providers of capital comfort in connection with the company's prospects. For instance, if Random Industries were negotiating with lenders, and if the lenders were concerned about the possibility of operating expenses rising, Random executives could turn to the model and say, in effect, "Okay, let's see what happens if we let our operating expenses rise. How high would they have to go before the loan would be at risk?" As shown in Table 107, Random's operating expenses could rise from 20% of revenues to 30% of revenues and still not impair the ability of the company to service the subordinated debentures or the long-term debt.

Table 107
Impact of Changes in Random's Operating Expense on Lender's Safety*

	Operating Expenses as a Percent of Revenues					
	15%	20%	30%	33%	35%	36%
Long-term lender	9%	9%	9%	9%	0	0
Subordinated debenture holders	12%	12%	12%	9%	0	0
Shareholders	28%	20%	9%	0	0	0
Warrant holders	196%	0	0	0	0	0

*The cells show the return on capital.

As Table 107 indicates, the long-term creditor is whole until the operating expenses rise above 33% of revenues, at which time capital begins to erode. The subordinated debt holder is safe only until the operating expenses rise above 30% of revenues, and the equity holders begin to see the value of their holdings erode once the operating expenses rise at all above the current level of 15%.

Management could also use its forecasting tools in another way in connection with lenders. In the simple case, if the company has net worth and interest coverage covenants with lenders and can project that the former will get tight but the latter will be easy to meet, it might take the initiative and offer to agree to a tighter interest coverage covenant in return for some loosening of the net worth covenant.

Buyers

A good set of forecasting tools, and the ability to translate those into corporate values, can also be highly useful in an acquisition, helping the buyer assess the value of the prospective acquiree (1) on a stand-alone "as is" basis and (2) under the prospective buyer's ownership. By arming itself with this information, the buyer can minimize the risk of paying too much. Suppose, for example, that Random Industries is in negotiations to buy Target Corporation, a hypothetical publicly held company (not the retailer owned by Dayton Hudson) with no earnings to date but with an enormous natural gas find that will come on stream in a few years. Target's stock is trading at $88.62 per share, which Random's management believes is about right given its expectations regarding natural gas prices and discount rates, and based on all the available information regarding the size of the find.

However, Random's management believes that by virtue of operating synergies it will be able to reduce general and administrative expenses by about 20% below Target's present levels. On that basis, it believes it can bid up to $97.51 per share for Target. If it is right, then any net of $97.51 less the price paid will inure to the benefit of Random. If Random is planning to make the proposal in terms of a stock-for-stock deal, and if Random shares are trading at $10.55 per share, then Random should be willing to pay up to 9.24 shares of its stock for each share of Target (that is, 9.24 shares of Random times $10.55 per share equals $97.51). If there are 10 million shares of Target outstanding, that implies a $975 million value of Target.

Thus the total capital Random would deploy to complete the acquisition would be $975 million (including transaction expenses). Given Random's cost of capital of approximately 9.2%, this means that unless Target generates a return of 9.2% (or $92 million) per year, Random will have destroyed value. To be sure, even if Target's returns in the first year do not cover Random's cost of capital, over the long term they might, and the market is likely to reflect the long-term expectations as well as the current performance.

The larger point remains that the likely impact of the acquisition on the value of the acquiror can be measured. For instance, if Random were to commit $975 million to the purchase of Target, it could measure and monitor the value of Target on an ongoing basis. If after the acquisition natural gas prices were to rise such that Target's value rose to $1.5 billion, this would reflect a value creation for Random shareholders of $525 million. Assuming that after the acquisition there were 192.4 million shares of Random outstanding, this would represent an accretion of $2.73 per share for Random's owners, increasing the value per share from $10.55 to $13.28, a 26% increase. One could, of course, measure the impact of other scenarios as well, such as a drop in

Table 108	
Acquisition of Target by Random	
Market price per share of Target stock	$88.64
Premium	10%
Acquisition price	$97.51
Market price per share of Random stock	$10.55
Shares of Random to equal one share of Target	9.24
Number of Target shares outstanding	10 million
Number of Random shares to be issued	92.4 million
Implicit price paid to acquire Target	$975 million

natural gas prices, operating synergies, tax law changes, and the like. One could also measure the impact the acquisition would have on Random's risk profile, along the lines described in Table 107.

Not uncommonly, acquisitions provide a return on the capital deployed but not a high enough return to cover the cost of the capital, thus diminishing the value to the acquiror. And beware, companies that make bad acquisitions often themselves become acquisition candidates.

In some cases the target's cost of capital is different from the acquiror's. When that occurs, the acquiror ought to use the target's cost of capital, because that will better reflect the risk profile of the target. If the target has unutilized debt capacity that the acquiror intends to use, then the target's weighted average cost of capital ought to reflect the potential use of such debt. This financial synergy, when it exists, may be part of the value creation of a successful acquisition. A variation on this is for the acquiror to recalibrate its own cost of capital on a post-deal basis and measure the impact accordingly. The cost of capital of the combined entity will reflect the blended risk/return profile. Whether the acquisition is financed with stock, debt, or internally generated cash, the weighted average cost of capital, and not only the cost of debt or of equity, should be used in measuring the cost of capital.

If the returns are likely to be high, and if the model accurately and convincingly reflects and quantifies such, then the prospect of an enhanced return ought to drive up the price of the acquiror's stock. To illustrate, suppose Random were to agree to buy Target for $975 million, payable in cash, and that to finance the purchase Random plans to sell stock. Suppose also that there was good reason to believe that operating synergies and other factors would cause the value of Target in Random's hands to be $1.5 billion. If Random were dealing with underwriters in an initial public offering or with the private equity market, an accurate and reliable model ought to enhance its bargaining position, drive the price of its stock up toward $13.28, and diminish the dilution of its existing shareholders.

A good valuation of the target offers the buyer one further benefit. If the buyer is successful, the model can give management a clear road map for what it must do to create value after the acquisition. For example, suppose the market value per share of Target is $88.64 and Random pays a 10% premium to buy Target, believing that it can cut the overhead by 20%. Random had better do so, or it will have paid too much and will diminish its own value, to the detriment of its owners (unless it can compensate for such failure by better margins or being lucky with another variable).

This brings up an important point. Suppose Random's management is right in believing that in its hands, overhead can be cut by 20% and that, accordingly, the value of Target to Random really is $97.51 per share. If Random pays this amount, who comes out ahead? Clearly Target's shareholders. When the buyer pays for all the synergies, it wins only if it manages the acquired company so well that it exceeds its own most reliable estimates.

At times a buyer and seller seem to have reached an impasse. When this occurs, effective counsel can sometimes invent solutions that get the proposed transaction back on track. After all, lawyers often have more experience than clients in structuring deals. For instance, if Target were a private company and its owners believed the value per share was $97.51, based on their estimate of future natural gas prices, and if Random had a lower estimate and believed $88.64 was more realistic, then rather than walk away from each other, they might make a deal providing that Random would pay $88.64 in cash (thus giving the sellers liquidity), and Target would issue a new class of stock to its selling shareholders. The latter stock might have rights, for example, providing that for each year in which Target were to generate NOPAT above a threshold amount, Target would pay such excess as follows: (1) half to Random and half to the holders of the new class of stock until the sellers received total consideration of $97.51 (such threshold to be increased or compounded at Target's cost of equity) and (2) above that level, one-quarter to the holders of the new class of stock and the balance to Random. The new stock would expire or be mandatorily redeemed by the issuer for a nominal amount after a specified number of years.

Whether that structure or some other, counsel can use variables such as classes of stock, percentages, and durations to allocate returns and risks in a way that accommodates the respective rights and risks of the parties. Having a clear sense of financial techniques and methodology, coupled with a distinguished legal tool kit, empowers the lawyers to have a high value added.

Similarly, the company that can accurately project its own financial performance, as well as that of any acquisition candidate, is in the best position to take steps that enhance its value. In doing so it will be captain of its fate and the most likely to make decisions and negotiate its acquisitions, financings, and other major transactions successfully.

Creating Value
by Acquisition—
Jousting with the
Acquisition
Windmill

Chapter

12

Unfortunately there are numerous ways in which value can slip away. Many companies deploy capital for ill-advised new projects in the company's core business. Some do so by spending too much to buy other companies. The stated rationales usually have a ring of plausibility and often are very seductive. As noted earlier, a frequently flawed reason to do an acquisition is that it will increase earnings. Another song of the siren is to increase earnings per share, but in the process ignore increases in risk that drive down the price/earnings multiple.

Yet another dangerous reason given for acquisitions is to diversify in the belief that by reducing earnings volatility by buying a company, the earnings of which tend to move counter to those of the acquiror, the buyer will have more stable earnings, which will reduce its risk and hence its cost of capital, with corresponding increase to corporate value. When this rationale is carefully thought out and implemented, as described on pages 224–226, it can have merit. However, more often than not, the rationale of achieving diversification is superficial. Further, most investors would rather do the diversifying themselves; they would prefer to have the company pay a dividend or buy back stock, which puts in the owners' hands cash that can be used to diversify or serve such other purpose as the shareholder may wish.

Management, however, usually does not like to pay out more cash to shareholders than it must, for two reasons. First, most investors must pay federal—and in many cases, state and even local—taxes on the cash they receive from the company; hence, for every dollar they receive from the company, they may have only about $.60 left to reinvest. Investors would need to achieve approximately a 67% return on that just to be back where they started had the company been able to reinvest the dollar profitably. Managements find it embarrassing to admit to their company's owners that they cannot find good projects and earn a return on the full dollar that will outperform the return the owners could get on their after tax $.60.

Second, regardless of the words management often uses to express commitment to serving shareholder interests, the empirical evidence shows that management compensation is far more closely linked to (1) the size of the company (measured by sales) and (2) the number of employees reporting to them (directly or indirectly) than to creation of shareholder value.[1] Consequently, there is

---

1. *See, e.g.,* Judith H. Dobrzynski, *Getting What They Deserve?*, N.Y. TIMES, Feb. 22, 1996, at D-1.

considerable impetus to grow. If the internal growth opportunities are lacking, growth by acquisition becomes the obvious means.

This occurs notwithstanding the overwhelming evidence that, on average, acquisitions destroy shareholder value for the acquiror. In an exhaustive study of hundreds of acquisitions in the first half of this decade, Business Week and Mercer Management Consulting, Inc., found that the performance of acquisitions had fallen far short of their promise.[2] Of 150 deals worth more than $500 million from January 1990 through July 1995, only 17% created substantial returns for the acquirors, as contrasted with 30% that substantially eroded shareholder value. (The other 53% had only a minor impact on the acquiror's value.) Further, as noted in chapter 6, acquisitions made during the 1970s and 1980s for stock substantially underperformed those made for cash.

Novell, Inc., the networking company, illustrates the point. Seeking to become a major rival to Microsoft Corporation, Novell embarked on a series of acquisitions. The most notable was the 1994 purchase of WordPerfect Corporation, for which Novell paid $1.4 billion in a stock swap. Yet rather than build up Novell, the acquisition drained resources and diverted Novell's focus from its core networking business, allowing Microsoft to make inroads into Novell's market leadership in the traditional network operating systems market. Novell sold the WordPerfect product line in 1996 for consideration worth approximately $200 million, retaining the smaller Group Wise product line, and its stock slid from $36 per share (adjusted for splits) in 1992 to $11 per share in August 1996.[3]

The successes have tended to be buildups in fragmented industries, such as funeral homes, ambulance services, and health clubs, and those in which the acquiror uses the seller to strengthen its product line. Yet there is hazard even in these contexts, as Quaker Oats Company learned by paying $1.7 billion for Snapple, a blunder that has cost more than a few Quaker Oats employees, including its chief executive officer, their jobs.[4]

Diversification of business or product lines works best when management has thought through exactly which risks it is trying to hedge the company against. Even when management has thought carefully about those risks, there is rarely a good reason why investors cannot take such hedge positions on their own if they want, by buying shares in companies that provide the desired hedge. Just as product extensions are risky, geographic diversification by acquisition is also fraught with hazards, as Ford Motor Company learned when in 1989 it paid $2.6 billion for Jaguar[5] and then had to pump in approximately $6 billion more, investments on which returns have been negative.[6] One can understand why Peter Lynch, the legendary former manager of Fidelity's Magellan Fund, termed diversification by companies as "diworsification."[7]

---

2. Phillip L. Zweig, *Special Report: The Case Against Mergers*, Bus. Wk., Oct. 30, 1995, at 122–30.

3. Lee Gomes, *Novell's Frankenberg to Quit as Chief: Announcement Is to Be Made Today*, Wall St. J., Aug. 29, 1996, at B-14.

4. Richard Gibson, *Quaker Oats Feeling the Pressure for Big Changes in the Wake of the Fizzled Snapple Acquisition*, Wall St. J., July 25, 1996, at C-2; Richard Gibson, *Quaker CEO, Led by Snapple Shakeup, Tells Outlets Time's Ripe for Fresh Start*, Wall St. J., July 22, 1996, at B-5.

5. *See* G. Bennett Stewart, III, The Quest for Value 486 (1991).

6. Heidi Dowley & Keith Naughton, *Jaguar Starts to Claw Its Way Back*, Bus. Wk., Feb. 2, 1998, at 56.

7. Peter Lynch, Once Upon Wall Street 146 (1989).

A further reason frequently given by management to support an acquisition is that they are buying a bargain. To be sure, Warren Buffett was very astute when Berkshire Hathaway, Inc., bought shares of Coca-Cola Company in the late 1980s for an average price per share of $6.50[8] (adjusted for stock splits), which had by 1997 appreciated elevenfold to $72 per share. However, for corporate management to go into the market once or twice a year (if that) and buy another company on the basis that the latter is underpriced means beating the market. By contrast, the market has thousands of people at work every day scanning and analyzing data, and talking to management, trying to find undervalued securities. The odds of management beating that, when its expertise lies not in finding undervalued companies but rather in running what they have, are slim indeed.

Yet another stated rationale in support of an acquisition is that there are synergies. In counting the synergies, it is appropriate to count not only the operating synergies that may occur between the two companies, but also any financial synergies. If there are tax advantages, their value can appropriately be counted as a financial synergy. Also, if the target has a less levered capital structure than it might more wisely have, then the value of the incremental tax shield can also appropriately be measured as a financial synergy. (If the buyer plans to use its own debt rather than equity to buy the target, the value of the buyer's incremental tax shield is not appropriately counted as a synergy because that value could have been enjoyed by the buyer without buying the target.)

Unfortunately the expected synergies often fail to materialize. In the case of operating synergies, usually the reason is that the management of the buyer did not think through how the two companies (or divisions of the companies) could be combined in a way that either increases revenues or reduces costs. Synergies usually happen, if at all, at the molecular level, whereas too often the thinking about synergies is general.

For instance, in 1987 Borden, Inc. paid $100 million for Laura Scudder, a western potato chip company, the centerpiece of which was the number two market share in California. Thinking it would enjoy synergies and save on overhead, Borden closed all Laura Scudder's California plants and served the California market out of its more efficient plant in Utah, at which Borden had excess capacity. That sounded great on paper, and Borden proceeded as planned. However, when Borden's trucks carried the potato chips over the Sierra Nevada Mountains to California and the other western markets, the jostling caused the potato chips to break. By the time the bags of potato chips arrived on the shelves, customers left them there because the contents had crumbled.[9] The company could have tested for this and other potential pitfalls before making the purchase, but it had not examined the acquisition in that level of detail. Borden pumped another $65 million into Laura Scudder but finally threw in the towel in 1992 and sold it to another regional company for $15 million, a loss of $150 million, or 90% of its investment.[10]

---

8. *See, e.g.*, BERKSHIRE HATHAWAY, INC., 1995 ANNUAL REPORT.

9. Kathleen Deveney & Seuin L. Hwang, *A Defective Strategy of Heated Acquisitions Spoils Borden Name*, WALL ST. J., Jan. 18, 1994, at 1.

10. *Id.*

This was but one of 91 acquisitions, most of them fiascoes such as wall coverings and Krazy Glue, made by Borden's management from 1986 through 1992.[11] Borden's stock, which had hit a high of $32.75 per share in 1991, was finally sold to KKR, Inc., in 1994 in an exchange worth approximately $12.50 per share, amounting to a destruction of market value of $3.3 billion in 3 years as the acquisition chickens came home to roost.

Even when there are real synergies, buyers—more often than not—pay too much to acquire them. Through most of 1995, the average premium paid on acquisitions over $500 million was 37%, down from 41% in 1994 but up from 26% in 1993.[12] If the equity value of the target is $1 billion and the synergies have a value of $400 million, then the combined value of the target's equity in the hands of the buyer is $1.4 billion. However, if the buyer pays $1.4 billion to make the acquisition, then the only winner is the seller. As noted earlier, only if the premium paid in excess of the seller's market value is exceeded by the value of the synergies does the buyer come out ahead.

---

11. *Id.*
12. Zweig, *supra* note 2, at 128.

A Map for Value Creation

Value Creation and Growth

To this point we have considered two kinds of companies, both of which are growing: those that earn a return in excess of their cost of capital (Wal-Mart Stores, Inc., for example) and those that earn a return less than their cost of capital (Borden, Inc., for example). The former type of company creates value, and the latter destroys it.

The same two categories of companies exist among those that are not growing. Each poses a special set of challenges, and we will consider each in turn.

One can think in terms of a quadrant (see Sidebar 31) consisting of two variables, the first being whether the company is earning more or less than its cost of capital and the second being whether the company is growing in the sense of deploying new capital in its business. We previously examined what happens to growing companies that do or do not earn their cost of capital, such as Wal-Mart and Borden, respectively. But how can companies that are not growing create new value for their owners?

_____ **Sidebar 31** _____

A Framework for Assessing Alternative Ways to Create Value

Companies may be growing or not growing, and they may be earning a return (r) in excess of, or less than, their cost of capital (c^*). These four major possibilities are depicted in Table 109.

Companies in quadrant I should cease deploying new capital that will not earn its cost. Thereafter, they should follow the prescriptions for quadrant III companies. Quadrant II companies should keep doing what they are doing for as long as possible. Quadrant III companies are in trouble and ought to give particularly serious consideration to spin-offs, leveraged recapitalizations, and changes to their compensation systems to align executive and shareholder interests, as discussed later in the chapter. Quadrant IV companies are in the best position to consider stock repurchases or leveraged recapitalizations.

	c* exceeds r	r exceeds c*
	Table 109	
	Indexing Growth and the Cost of Capital	
Growth	I	II
No growth	III	IV

Quadrant IV Companies: Earning a Positive Spread but Not Growing

These companies are like Wal-Mart (at least through its fiscal 1997), except they do not enjoy the opportunity to make new investments in the industries with which they are familiar, because such industries are mature and slow growing.[1] The companies may be sound and well run, but their businesses simply do not lend themselves to enough new investment to absorb all the companies' cash flow. They are building their existing businesses as rapidly as they can, but are still generating more cash than they can deploy in their existing businesses and earn a return in excess of their capital costs. They should at least be congratulated for not having made new investments that have destroyed value, but how, if at all, can such companies create new value for shareholders?

Investment bankers will besiege these companies with acquisition proposals, and the temptation to make an acquisition will be intense. Internal proposals from divisions or other units must also be screened carefully, for some may be wise uses of capital, but many will not.

_____ **Sidebar 32** _____

Spotting Cash Cows and Cash Absorbers

A quick way to identify whether a company is a cash generator or a cash absorber is to determine whether, on average over time, its growth rate exceeds its return on equity times 1 minus the payout rate. If it does, then the company is not, over time, generating enough cash to finance its growth. The formula is as follows.

$$g = \text{return on equity} \left(1 - \frac{\text{dividend}}{\text{profit after tax}} \right)$$

g = maximum rate of growth the company can sustain over time without raising new equity

1. In this context, the relevant growth is in revenues.

The concept is fairly simple. The return on equity (net of the dividend payout rate, which is why the formula includes an adjustment for the dividend payout) determines how rapidly the equity account grows. As the equity account grows, the asset base can grow, and as the asset base grows, the sales level ought to rise. This all assumes that the asset to equity ratio and the revenue to asset ratio of the company will remain about the same over time (please recall the discussion of the DuPont Formula in chapter 4). If there is good reason to believe they will not, then the maximum sustainable growth rate must be adjusted. A well-prepared set of projections is the best way to do this when one is looking forward. Whether one is looking forward or looking at historic numbers, any time one sees the return on equity significantly exceeding the growth rate over time, it usually indicates that the company is generating more cash than it can effectively reinvest in the business. The converse is also true. If a company is growing at a rate that exceeds the return on equity, adjusted for the dividend payout rate, the company will, sooner or later, need to go back to the equity markets.

Gillette's Creation of Value

Gillette Company faced this situation in 1988. In 1986 it had completed some significant capital spending projects, and in 1987 its cash flow from operations had been $322 million, more than ever before in the company's history. However, it needed barely half that sum, $147 million, for new plant and equipment (P&E) and $25 million for additional working capital. In mid-1988, the company cut back capital expenditures slightly, and it was evident that once again Gillette would generate more cash than it would need for new investment in P&E and working capital. Gillette's debt to equity ratio on December 31, 1987, was 1.8 (and its asset to equity ratio a rather high 4.6), in large measure because of the debt it had assumed in warding off Revlon's 1986 hostile takeover attempt, as described in chapter 2.[2] Yet the company was in a position to carry more debt without undue risk because its razor and blade business was large and stable, generating steady cash earnings even during recessions.

All this invited a new hostile takeover attempt in 1988. To ward off that attempt, Gillette borrowed another $800 million in long-term debt (the financial highlights of this are shown in Sidebar 16, chapter 4) and used it to purchase 19 million shares, amounting to approximately 17% of its outstanding stock.[3] On a book basis, the company's financial leverage became infinite. Specifically, as of December 31, 1988, Gillette's asset to equity ratio and its debt to equity ratio were both infinite because its book equity was a negative $85 million.[4] However, because its brand name had considerable value—though not on its generally accepted accounting principles (GAAP) books—the company's equity had a positive net worth on a fair market

2. Gillette Company, 1986–1988 Annual Reports.
3. Gillette Company, 1988 Annual Report.
4. *Id.*

value basis. Even more important, Gillette's earning power remained strong, as reflected in the company's December 31, 1988, market capitalization of $4.8 billion. Investors who bought in before the 1988 recapitalization for $7 per share (adjusted for stock splits) by 1997 held shares worth $98 per share and had received nearly $4 in dividends. By virtue of its strong cash earnings, Gillette has had no difficulty servicing this debt and has since used its cash flow to reduce its debt levels gradually.

FMC's Leveraged Recapitalization

FMC Corporation, a Chicago-based conglomerate, provides another example of how a leveraged recapitalization can create value for shareholders, especially those earning a return in excess of their capital costs but not able to find attractive growth opportunities.[5] The company did a major leveraged recapitalization in 1986, but not until after it had exhausted several other important methods of increasing shareholder value.

By the late 1970s the company's performance had for some years been respectable but undistinguished, and the new CEO, Bob Mallott, wanted to make some improvements. Mallott's first step, taken in the late 1970s and early 1980s, was to introduce a system for measuring division performance based on cash return on assets. Because the company had substantial assets that it believed were on the books at well below market values, management began to measure assets based on their fair market values. As explained in chapter 4, that not only reinforced division managements' incentive not to ask for more capital than they could effectively use, but also strengthened their incentive to divest unused property, plant, and equipment (PP&E), cut working capital, and return cash to headquarters when feasible.

A related change, adopted in 1982, was to develop a current cost accounting system for internal use—thus, for example, charging divisions with depreciation based on market values rather than historic costs. Particularly in the high inflation period of the late 1970s and early 1980s, this made a substantial difference, for reasons explained in chapter 6, Sidebar 23 (which describes Bethlehem Steel's predicament in 1981).

Two further changes were made, as described in chapter 4. Briefly, having been among the early companies to evaluate line management based on earnings before interest and taxes (EBIT) to capital employed, which amounts to a focus on operating profit and assets utilized, FMC began to assess each unit with a cost of capital, determined on an after tax basis, which made line managers more alert to tax considerations.

Mid-1980s

The above changes tightened conditions substantially and improved performance (see Table 110) to the point that by 1984, the company bought in approximately one-third of its own stock. However, in 1985 the company continued to generate more cash than it could effectively redeploy in its existing businesses, and it began to examine carefully some acquisition targets. It conducted thorough due diligence of

---

5. The material for this discussion of FMC Corporation is based on discussions at FMC headquarters on December 7, 1994, and documents provided by the company at that time.

	1979	1980	1981	1982	1983	1984	1985
Table 110							
FMC 1979–1985 Performance							
Sales growth	9%	12%	10%	12%	2%	3%	(2%)
Return on equity*	12%	13%	15%	14%	13%	19%	19%

*Income from continuing operations as a percentage of equity

several acquisition candidates and nearly bought one or two. However, in the final analysis, it found the terms too rich for its diet.

Rather than pursue what it considered to be pricey acquisitions, the company focused on doing a leveraged buyout (LBO). Fearing a shareholder accusation that management was "stealing" the company, management explored the idea (passed on to Mallott by Warren Buffett) of doing a leveraged recapitalization.

Issues for FMC to Consider

FMC became intrigued by the idea of leveraged recapitalization, but some issues were difficult. How much to borrow? How many shares to buy? What percentage of the company should it buy? Its cash flow from operations had been running $350 million to $400 million per year, some $200 million above what was, on average, needed for capital expenditures. Because FMC's marginal borrowing cost at the time was 9% and because the effective tax rate on domestic earnings was expected to run at least 33%, the result was an after tax cost of debt of approximately 6%. Therefore the $200 million in excess cash flow would support $3.3 billion in new debt. If the company were to borrow even half that sum and buy in stock at $70 per share, it could buy in 24 million shares, 69% of the outstanding stock. However, the board was reluctant to take the company private.

The Deal

Several considerations were key in the company's development of its recapitalization plan. First, a stock redemption was more advantageous to shareholders than a dividend because under tax law in effect in 1986, the existing shareholders would get capital gains treatment if they reduced their holdings by more than 20%. Second, by reducing the public float, management would have a larger stake in the business, which would more tightly align the interests of management and investors. Third, although most banks wanted tight loan covenants, Morgan Guaranty Trust Company, the banking subsidiary of J. P. Morgan & Company, Inc., did not. By using Morgan the company retained a high degree of autonomy. Furthermore, FMC's pension plan had excess assets that could be reached to service the debt if necessary. (This would happen indirectly. By virtue of the overfunding, future cash contributions to the pension fund would, to the extent of the overfunding, be unnecessary. This would free up cash.) In addition, FMC had assets it could sell if it needed cash, which happened later when FMC Gold Company did an initial public offering. Table 111 shows that cash generation before the recapitalization indicated a strong and steady ability to service debt.

Table 111
FMC Cash Generation

	1980	1981	1982	1983	1984	1985	Cumulative
				($ million)			
Cash generated* before working capital reduction	56.3	109.0	98.8	203.9	204.0	119.4**	791.4
Working capital reduction	(17.3)	(4.8)	129.2	107.6	46.4	(13.9)	247.2
Total cash generation*	39.0	104.2	228.0	311.5	250.4	105.5	1038.6

*Net of capital expenditures
**Ignoring Lithco acquisition

Thus, when it came to a decision, there were compelling reasons for leveraged recapitalization:

1. The company's businesses were mature and slow growing. There was no place to put cash to earn a favorable return.
2. FMC had just completed a major capital spending cycle and saw no big investments pending.
3. Acquisitions looked pricey. There were three on the table but management, to its credit, subjected all the proposed acquisitions to the test of whether they were in the shareholders' best interests and concluded that they all failed this key test.
4. FMC was overcapitalized. Cash gave shareholders a poor return and made the company vulnerable to a hostile takeover.
5. Because FMC's businesses all had strong market positions, market share, and international strength, the company was already well balanced.
6. There was no reason to believe that diversification would add value.

Thus, new leverage would provide the best financial structure for the company given the low growth, but cash generating, nature of the businesses. The reduction in the float would (1) provide an incentive to management by giving it a bigger piece of the company and (2) structure the buyback in such a way that shareholders could participate.

The Details

On February 20, 1986, with the stock trading at $70 per share, the company proposed to pay the following for each share:

> Public shareholders: $70 plus 1 share
> Thrift plan: $25 plus 4 shares
> Management: 5⅔ shares

This implied a post-deal value per share of $15, and each category's share had a pre-deal value of $85.

Ivan Boesky got news of the deal two days before it was announced, bought shares, argued that management was stealing the company, and demanded that the company pay more to outside shareholders. It was soon revealed that someone at Goldman Sachs & Company, the company's advisor on the deal, had tipped off Boesky. FMC later sued Goldman Sachs, which made an interesting argument in its defense. It admitted having tipped off Boesky, but argued that it had no duty *not* to do so, and that the company— the shareholders—had not been injured. The case was settled. In any event, to get the deal done, the company sweetened it. For each share, consideration was paid as follows:

Public shareholders: $80 plus 1 share
Thrift plan: $25 plus 4.209 shares
Management: 5⅔ shares
Implicit value per share: $17.14 post-deal, $97.14 pre-deal

One of the strengths of the recapitalization was that if the company did well, management would do the best. Its stake in the company rose from 18% to 35% and later to 41%, of which top management held 3%–4%. The rest was held widely, right down to the shop floor, and all participants in the 401(k) plan participated in the deal. Ownership in FMC before and after had changed as follows.

Table 112
FMC Ownership Before and After Recapitalization

	Number of Shares Before		Number of Shares After	
Thrift plan	3,221	(9.0%)	12,912	(28.5%)
Paysop/Trasop	394	(1.1%)	2,220	(4.9%)
Pension plans	2,684	(7.5%)	—	
Management	143	(0.4%)	816	(1.8%)
Total internal	6,442	(18.0%)	15,948	(35.2%)
Public	29,358	(82.0%)	29,358	(64.8%)*
	35,790	(100.0%)	45,306	(100.0%)

*Needed to dilute ownership of original shareholders to less than 80% of what it was previously, under then existing tax laws to assure capital gain treatment (64.8% / 82.0% = 79%).

FMC borrowed $1.64 billion to finance the dividend.

If any shareholder did not like the deal, he or she could use the $80 to buy stock. After the dividend, the value per share dropped to $15, with the result that any shareholder could have bought 5⅓ shares for the $80 dividend received. At that point any shareholder would have had 6⅓ shares (the 1 share received in the deal plus the 5⅓ shares thus purchased) less any capital gains tax, which depended on the shareholder's tax status and tax basis.

If the company were to do better and the stock price were to rise, management would gain the most. For example, if the price per share were to rise to $25, then management's 5⅔ shares would be worth $141.67 (a 46% appreciation), whereas the public's holdings ($80 plus 1 share) would be worth only $105 (an 8% appreciation).

Table 113
Capital Profile

	Before ($ million)		After ($ million)	
Debt	371	Existing debt		275
Equity (market value)	2,506	Bank debt		1,240
Total	2,877	Subordinated debt		400
		Total debt		1,915
		Equity (market value)		503*
		Total		2,418

*This was the equity's market value. The book equity became negative $591 million.

However, if the stock value were to fall, management stood to lose the most. For example, if the stock price were to fall to $10 per share, then management's 5⅔ shares would be worth only $56.67 (a 42% drop), whereas the public's combination of $80 plus 1 share would be worth $90 (a 7% drop). In that sense, management held a leveraged equity stake and a double-edged sword—an amplified reward for success and a greater penalty than the public shareholders for failure.

Table 114
FMC: Value of Recap Package to Different Parties

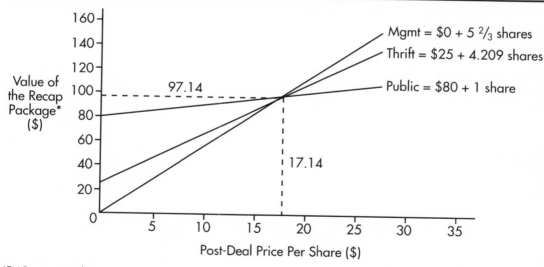

*FMC corporate documents.

Although shareholder approval was required, it was easy to get, and FMC did its own proxy solicitation. There was one nuisance suit, but no predator came out of the woodwork. Nor did the recapitalization siphon off so much cash to service debt that FMC had to starve its businesses. FMC's cash flow rose after the recapitalization and remained healthy.

Table 115
FMC's Post-Recapitalization Cash Flow*

Fiscal Year	($ million)
1986	$41
1987	92
1988	200
1989	277
	$610

*FMC corporate documents

And its debt service still allowed for adequate and increasing use of cash for investment.

Table 116
FMC's Use of Cash

Percent of Cash Used for*	1986**	1987	1988	1989	1990
Debt service	33	78	59	42	29
New investment	67	22	41	58	71

*FMC corporate documents
**Post-recapitalization only

The company's operating performance improved after the recapitalization, perhaps reflecting the greater management incentive.

Table 117
FMC Operating Performance after Recapitalization*

	Before Recapitalization Five-Year Average	After Recapitalization		
		1986	1987	1988
Revenue growth	(1.3)%	(7.9)%	4.5%	4.7%
EBIT/beginning capital	12.9%	17.8%	18.9%	21.4%
EBIT/sales	7.1%	10.1%	9.6%	9.8%
Total debt/total capital	19%	145%	84%	78%
EBIT/interest	6.6x	1.2x	1.5x	1.8x

*FMC corporate documents

The market caught on to the value creation. From February to May 1986 (three months), the stock value went from $65 to $97 (the $80 per share received in cash plus the $17 market price per share), a 49% increase, amounting to over $1 billion (35,790 shares times $32 per share value rise).

It is instructive to see what drove the value creation. Most important was the value of the tax shield, as taxable dividends were converted into tax deductible interest payments. As you may recall from chapter 10, the value of the tax shield is equal to the debt (in this case $1.64 billion) times the tax rate (in this case 40%), or a tax shield value of $656 million.

Second, note what happened to the existing (that is, pre-recapitalization) $371 million debt holders. Remember, the risks inherent in the business do not change. What can change is the allocation of risk among the classes of capital. By forcing the pre-recapitalization debt holders to tolerate an incremental $1.64 billion in debt, management gave equity holders further leverage, from which only the equity holders could benefit. The pre-recapitalization debt holders, like the equity holders, were exposed to added risk on the downside, with no corresponding upside potential. By creating that nonreciprocal risk/reward relationship to the benefit of the equity holders, the recapitalization created (or more precisely, transferred) value to them. Though that is difficult to quantify, FMC management estimated that value to be $50 million. This is measured by the change in the market value of the debt on the date of the announcement. Unfortunately, other events, such as changes in interest rates, may also impact such change, which muddies the water. If the debt is privately owned, measuring the impact is almost impossible, although it might be estimated by comparing the impact of comparable changes on publicly traded debt securities.

In addition, the company estimated the present value of the after tax benefit of the cost savings due to the overfunding of the pension plan to be $150 million. Moreover, although also difficult to quantify, the market clearly liked the strong signal that the company would not make uneconomical investments. The reduction or elimination of that risk surely was reflected in the post-recapitalization stock price and had value.

Finally, the deal was understood by the market to give management a major incentive to maximize cash earnings. By aligning these forces, FMC created considerable value not only in the transaction itself but in the ensuing years. The investing public benefited from this action, as underscored by FMC's stock performance, set forth in Table 118.

Lesson for Slow Growth Companies Earning Their Cost of Capital

Thus Gillette and FMC illustrate very well what companies can do to create new value even if they do not have growth opportunities. A crucial first step is to avoid making investments in, or buying, businesses that will not earn the cost of capital.

For companies not wanting to confine themselves to avoiding that sin of commission, there is another arrow in management's quiver, as exemplified by Gillette and FMC. A simple way to conceptualize this is to consider a company that has a good business and can earn a return of 25% for several years until its returns drop sharply to 10% although still above its weighted average cost of capital of 7.5%, as shown in Table 119.

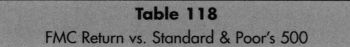

Table 118
FMC Return vs. Standard & Poor's 500

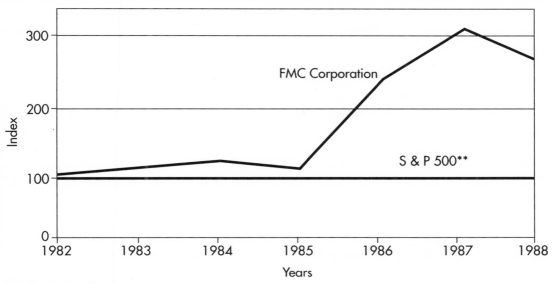

* FMC corporate documents
** The S & P index is pegged at 100 and FMC's stock price is charted against that index.

This performance alone is commendable. To do better, a company fitting that profile can create additional value by driving down its weighted average cost of capital through leveraging.

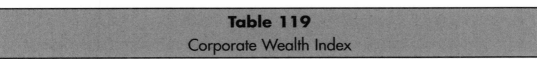

Table 119
Corporate Wealth Index

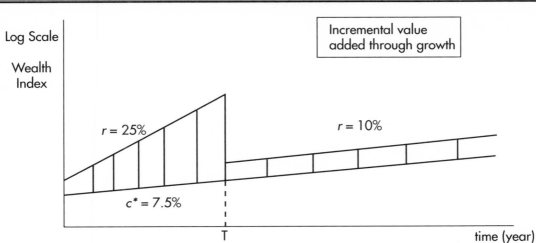

G. Bennett Stewart, III, *The Quest for Value* (1991), at 287.

Merely by reducing its weighted average cost of capital, a company can increase its wealth creation. Subtly, but interestingly and potentially powerfully, the incremental leverage can also indirectly increase the return on capital. That is because the leverage creates a risk that can be a powerful motivator. With the leverage, management will be more likely not only to work evenings and weekends, but also be more alert for opportunities to improve the company's performance. In fairness to management (and to keep the better managers from leaving), the company needs to link the management compensation system to the cash earnings and/or value creation of the company. Doing so both (1) gears management's own wealth index to the augmented risk to them, and (2) aligns owner-and management interests.

This model, as illustrated by FMC and Gillette, is a road map for companies wanting to create value even when growth is not really a value-enhancing possibility. But to use this model, companies should have the advantage of earning returns above their cost of capital. What can be done by those hapless companies that not only cannot (and should not) grow, but cannot even earn their cost of capital?

Quadrant III Companies: Destroying Value without Even Growing

Virtually all companies in this quadrant were winners at one time. The problem is that they cruised past the point where they were creating value. That is, perhaps mesmerized by their own success and believing their own pronouncements of accomplishment, they continue to deploy capital into the same or new businesses (or acquisitions) even though the returns on such capital are insufficient to cover the cost of capital. They have invested below the c^* line.

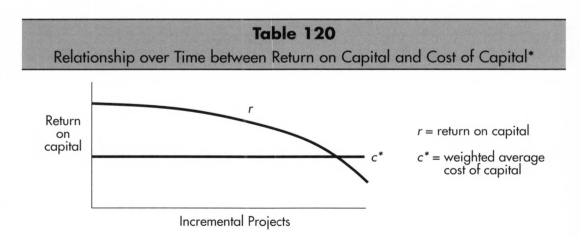

Table 120

Relationship over Time between Return on Capital and Cost of Capital*

r = return on capital

c^* = weighted average cost of capital

*This table also appears as Table 103, and is reproduced here for the reader's convenience.

The company may still have projects that are by themselves earning attractive returns. Unfortunately, enough of the company's projects are earning sub-par returns to pull the company down. What can be done? Lest it be thought that companies in this quadrant are the exception, they are not. The average company, almost by definition, creates an economic value added of approximately zero, although investors get what they expect or require. This is because the company's return on capital approximates its cost of capital. This in turn is because the cost of capital reflects opportunity cost, which reflects average expected returns. Moreover, in a market-based, competitive economy, above normal returns are difficult to sustain. Because earning a return in excess of the cost of capital is difficult, a great many companies fail to do so. In 1995, for example, many of the companies in the auto, steel, and trucking industries, among others, failed to earn their cost of capital.[6] Moreover, growing more rapidly than the inflation rate plus the population growth rate is, on average, difficult, especially for companies in mature industries. Hence there are a great many quadrant III companies, and they constitute a significant part of the economy.

The first step in improving is to recognize what is happening. Simple and pedestrian as that may sound, the disease often goes undiagnosed not only at publicly held, but also at privately held, companies. If management and the board are not alert to the problem, there is no substitute for vigilant and expressive shareholders. The California Public Employees' Retirement System (CalPERS), TIAA, and other institutional investors became more proactive during the early 1990s, which no doubt has done a great deal to keep many companies from continuing on a path that was ruinous of shareholder value.[7] Witness the institutional investors finally putting the wood to the board at Kmart Corporation, which had been destroying value for years. Although the CEO was replaced in 1994, Kmart earned less than its cost of capital in 1996;[8] as of mid-1997, it was too soon to know whether the board's actions were too little and too late to save Kmart.

Once the problem has been identified, though, what can management do to lead a company from quadrant III to quadrant II (growing and earning its cost of capital) or, more likely, quadrant IV (not growing but earning returns that exceed the cost of capital)? There are several techniques. None of the possible courses of constructive conduct are available exclusively to quadrant III companies, and none are panaceas. However, each is especially worthy of serious consideration by quadrant III companies and, if conceived and implemented correctly, each can be a valuable step in the right direction.

More on the Leveraged Recapitalization

Since the early 1980s, literally thousands of companies have been restructured, whether voluntarily or involuntarily. During the 1980s the market for corporate control forced change on many inefficient organizations. More recently, the principal

---

6. Irwin Ross, *The Stern Stewart Performance 1000*, 9 Bank Am. J. Applied Corp. Fin. 115–28 (Winter 1997).

7. Stephen L. Nesbitt, *Long-Term Rewards from Shareholder Activism: A Study of the CalPERS Effect*, 6 Continental Bank J. Applied Corp. Fin. 75–80 (Winter 1994).

8. *See* Kmart Corporation, 1996 Annual Report (analysis in text based on this report); *see also* Ross, *supra* note 6.

drivers of the corporate control market—hostile takeovers and LBOs—have been less active, although some institutional investors have become more active in pushing for change at underperforming companies.

Perhaps the most notable of these is CalPERS, which, over a span of 6 years beginning in 1987, targeted 42 companies for attention. On average the return to shareholders at 38 of these 42 companies had underperformed the Standard & Poor's 500 by 66.4% over the five years before CalPERS's initial letter to management. Essentially, CalPERS's focus for 18 of the companies selected for attention during the 1987–1990 period was on technical issues of anti-takeover devices, and the focus for the other 24 companies selected during the 1991–1992 period was on operating performance.[9]

The CalPERS initiative has been successful for both groups of companies. Underperformance has been arrested, and returns have been achieved averaging 7.2% per year above Standard & Poor's index. The initiative has been especially successful for the 24 companies where the focus was on operating matters. These companies, having on average underperformed the market by 85.6% before CalPERS contacted them, outperformed the market by 100% over the four years after CalPERS contacted them.

Yet the vast majority of quadrant III companies face no explicit pressure from the capital markets to improve their efficiency (although eventually they will). Consequently the major impetus for improving the performance of quadrant III companies must come from within, led by executives and directors. Assuming that such impetus occurs, how can companies force timely, effective change upon themselves? One avenue is the leveraged recapitalization. FMC's case, as previously described, illustrates the financial aspects of a leveraged recapitalization. There are more micro-level aspects of a leveraged recapitalization, which, although not exclusively or even primarily financial in nature, can be crucial in making the recapitalization successful for the underperforming company.

The successful leveraged recapitalizations tend to have three factors in common—high financial leverage, significant managerial and board equity ownership, and intense monitoring. Safeway Stores, Inc., which operates some 2,300 grocery stores, primarily in western, southwestern, and mid-Atlantic regions, combined these factors to improve its performance dramatically.

Safeway Stores

From 1976 through 1985, Safeway's operating profit as a percent of assets was consistently and significantly below the median for the grocery industry, in part because of the increasing presence of smaller, nonunionized chains in its markets. Safeway estimated that its employment costs ran 33% above the industry norm, which had a significant impact on operating margins because labor costs constituted approximately 70% of nonfood expenses.[10]

---

9. Nesbitt, *supra* note 7.

10. *See* David J. Denis, *The Benefits of High Leverage: Lessons from Kroger's Leveraged Recap and Safeway's LBO*, 7 BANK AM. J. APPLIED CORP. FIN. 38, 42 (Winter 1995).

In part to defend itself from a hostile takeover attempt by the Dart Group, controlled by the Haft family, Safeway agreed in 1986 to be acquired by KKR, Inc., at a price that reflected a 58% premium above Safeway's pre-takeover contest price. The transaction was financed primarily with debt, which accounted for 97% of the post-transaction capital. KKR contributed 96% of the post-transaction equity, and management contributed the balance. Soon thereafter management exercised some options to purchase shares at $2 per share, well below the acquisition price of $69 per share.

Before the transaction, Safeway directors and officers had owned 0.7% of the firm's equity, having a value of $24.6 million, and after the transaction they owned 10.3%, having a value of $19.3 million. Although this represented a cashing out of about 20% of their dollar investment, directors and officers increased their percentage ownership by a factor of 15.

Board Composition and Ownership Stake

A more important change occurred in the composition of the board. Before the restructuring, Safeway's board consisted of 18 members, 14 of whom were outsiders, with a median tenure of seven years and collective ownership of 0.03% of Safeway's stock. The predominance of outside directors indicates that this factor alone is not sufficient for effective board leadership. The difference between a 0.03% stake and a 10.3% stake in the company was significant. Peter McGowan, Safeway's CEO, commented, "I think we had a good board when Safeway was a public company before the LBO. But the level of scrutiny and questioning is just not comparable. In our board meetings with KKR, anything can be brought up, and management has to really work to defend itself. It is just utterly different. . . ."[11]

Executive Compensation

Before the LBO, Safeway was similar to a great many other companies in that the correlation between the cash compensation of the executives and the performance of the company was very low. Among publicly held companies, the link between pay and performance may be most tenuous at the smallest companies. A recent study of 1,934 companies by Graef Crystal, a compensation expert, using 1994 data, found zero correlation between the CEO's pay and the company's performance at the 484 smallest companies, which ranged in market cap from $1.4 million to $132 million.[12] It was not much better at the 484 largest companies, where Crystal's statistical analysis found that on average, only 6.4% of the CEO's pay could be justified by performance. Apparently the institutional investors have had some, albeit modest, impact on the largest companies, but have not had time to turn their attention to the small companies.

To break from this pattern and its own history, Safeway made major changes after the buyout. Whereas before the transaction the maximum bonus that could be earned by a top executive was 40% of base salary, after the transaction it was 110%

---

11. *Id.* at 42.
12. Judith Dobrzynski, *Getting What They Deserve?*, N.Y. TIMES, Feb. 22, 1996, at D-1.

(and many observers question why there ought to be any limit). More important, there was a much greater attempt to link the bonus to corporate performance. Further, to guard against only short-term perspective, only half the bonus was paid in the year earned. The other half was banked and then paid two years later, but only if the corporate goals for the subsequent two years were met.

It is worth noting that the prospect of a bonus is by no means the only executive motivator in this context. Recent theory and evidence indicates that financial leverage, especially in slow growing and underperforming firms, affects management performance by making default and bankruptcy the consequence of a failure to improve. When companies default on their debt and file for bankruptcy protection, managers usually lose their jobs and face serious career challenges. They certainly are likely to earn less than before, even if they do not lose their jobs. The mere threat of this outcome provides a major incentive to improve performance. To analogize to Samuel Johnson's observation that nothing so focuses a man's attention as the knowledge that he is about to be hanged, little so focuses an executive's attention as the prospect of bankruptcy. The empirical evidence shows that by raising that specter, high leverage focuses executives' attention on generating earnings and cash, and meeting loan covenants and debt repayment schedules. It might be possible to achieve the same results without recapitalization, and doing so may well be worth the effort. But when such efforts fail, the leveraged buyout might be the best tonic, especially when compensation is linked to performance on the upside as well as on the downside.

Effects of High Leverage at Safeway

If Safeway had not improved its operating performance, it would have defaulted on its loans, even if it had eliminated all new capital expenditures. There was a risk that to improve cash flow, management would cut back on discretionary expenses, such as advertising and maintenance, which would enhance current cash flow at the expense of future business strength. Indeed, some such cuts were made, but one cannot determine to a certainty in this case whether they were excessive except by assessing the subsequent results.

Even with the reduction in some operating expenses, Safeway had to sell some assets to service the debt, choosing from among the poorest performing 60% of the stores, which had been subsidized by the top performing 40%. The sales were made to unionized buyers. Before making the sales, management recognized that the price for the stores would be higher if labor concessions could first be obtained. The unions did not want the stores to be sold to nonunion buyers, so to protect jobs they acceded to wage concessions of 20%–30%. By selling these stores, Safeway was able to service the debt and maintain the same level of capital expenditure as before the leveraged transaction.

Outcome

From November 1986 when it went private until April 1990 when it went public (approximately 3½ years), Safeway's shareholders earned a return of approximately 250%.

Sealed Air Corporation

A similar experience occurred at Sealed Air Corporation, a New Jersey-headquartered manufacturer of protective packaging materials and systems.[13] Founded in 1960, by 1988 it had grown its revenue base to $345 million, and it prided itself on a strong set of patents. However, its stock price was languishing, and its once excellent manufacturing operations had become lackluster. To compound the problem, some of its key patents were about to expire, and an attempt to energize and improve the manufacturing program had proven disappointing. Although it knew that recapitalization would not alone suffice to revitalize the company, the board in 1989 engineered a leveraged recapitalization.

Over the 5½ years after the recapitalization, Sealed Air's total shareholder return was 442%, as contrasted with a 42.3% return to the Standard & Poor's 500 Index over the same period. The reason for the high return was that operating performance improved significantly. Revenues rose 31% and operating profits rose 70%, even though assets rose by only 9%. Over the short term, new capital expenditures were reduced, but research and development (R&D) spending over the five years after the recapitalization was 31% above prior levels.

The keys were inside the organization. Mindful that leverage alone would not be adequate, the first step management took was to define success and to communicate the objectives to employees. Immediately after the transaction closed, the CEO issued a newsletter to employees speaking not in terms of "maximizing shareholder value" or "earnings per share," but rather, in terms the employees would find much more helpful as a guide to their actions, such as "putting the customer first" and "generating cash flow."

To monitor the company's performance against its objectives, each plant reported to headquarters monthly—and in very specific terms—about areas such as customer service (including percentage of on-time deliveries), product quality (including percentage of shipping errors), inventory levels (including data on actual versus objective), changeover times for manufacturing lines, and material yields.

To hold the employees' attention to these measures, the company adopted a new bonus plan that linked payments to both income statement measures (primarily earnings before interest, taxes, depreciation, and amortization, or EBITDA) and balance sheet measures (designed to encourage employees down to the plant level to minimize working capital needs). The allocation of fixed assets was managed more tightly by headquarters, which became more selective in prioritizing its capital expenditures. By choosing the measures that drove value creation, communicating the criteria for success clearly, linking compensation to meeting those goals, and adding the sense of urgency created by leverage, Sealed Air created the recipe for transforming a moribund manufacturing company that dramatically outperformed the Standard & Poor's 500.[14]

---

13. Karen Hopper Wruck, *Financial Policy as a Catalyst for Organizational Change: Sealed Air's Leveraged Special Dividend*, 7 Bank Am. J. Applied Corp. Fin. 20–37 (Winter 1995).
    14. *Id.*

Cain Chemical

The octane that can be created when there is a strong link between compensation and performance is further illustrated by Cain Chemical, Inc. (CCI), founded in 1987 by Gordon Cain, who had spent 30 years as an executive in the chemical and petrochemical industries.[15] Cain cobbled CCI together from 6 unrelated and lackluster polyethylene, ethylene, and ethylene glycol facilities along the Texas Gulf Coast. The strategy was to acquire capacity in the ethylene industry and to take advantage of what Cain believed would be an excess of demand over capacity in the industry. CCI was financed nearly 90% with debt. Of the equity, 15% was held by an employee stock ownership plan (ESOP) in which all employees participated. This was supplemented by a profit sharing plan, also made available to all employees, in which 10% of the earnings in excess of a threshold linked to EBDIT went into a profit sharing pool. Quarterly, the pool was divided pro rata in accordance with the employees' salaries.

Every time the company distributed the profit sharing checks, a senior executive met with the employees at each plant as a group and reviewed the plant's performance on safety and the plant's performance in terms of EBDIT. The executive explained how the plant had done during the quarter relative to its budget, the factors that were critical in determining EBDIT, and how the plant had done relative to those factors, including pricing, volume, and costs. The executive always took questions from the employees and always gave straight answers, in the belief that a knowledgeable employee would be in a better position than an uninformed employee to do the right thing. Management was assiduous about holding these meetings promptly, within a week after close of the quarter, so that employees would receive swift, clear feedback about their performance and quickly see the impact of their performance upon their compensation. Not all the employees understood all the financial details of EBDIT, but they understood the key drivers of success, and they signed on—including wearing T-shirts that said "EBDIT" on the front and "Every Body Doing It Together" on the back. It did not take many quarters before employees were asking about how even the smallest decision they might make would affect EBDIT.

The impact on performance on the plant floor was dramatic. Employees wanted to know how many pounds of ethylene they produced per hour because they knew that higher productivity translated, through EBDIT, into cash in their pockets at the end of the quarter. In one situation, rather than send out a broken motor and wait two days for a repair, thus slowing down the plant, a mechanic—on his own initiative—stayed all night to repair the motor so that the plant would not miss a day of operation at full pace. In another instance, employees traveled at their own expense on their days off to help employees at other locations with plant turnarounds. During the entire first year of operation, down time was cut dramatically. As a result, gross margins increased over 50%, from 18% to 30%. To be sure, the ethylene price increases that Cain predicted had materialized, but productivity increases also were significant.

On May 18, 1988, Cain and the other equity holders received an offer from Occidental Petroleum Corporation to buy CCI's equity for $1.1 billion, a 25 to 1 return on their $44 million investment. Because so many managers had built significant net

---

15. Analysis in text is based on interviews with company investors. *See also* M. C. JENSEN & B. BARRY, GORDON CAIN AND THE STERLING GROUP (1992).

worths over the year yet lacked liquidity, the shareholders accepted the offer. Each—yes, each—employee gained, through the ESOP, over $100,000, and the buyer offered each employee his or her job on an ongoing basis. The May 5, 1988, *Wall Street Journal* carried a full-page ad paid for, and signed by, all the 1,337 employees.[16] The ad said, "To Gordon Cain for his vision of a company where each employee is part owner and for the privilege of sharing the creation and success of our company." Cain had taken a collection of no growth, underperforming, minimalist facilities and through a combination of careful financial structuring and insightful human resource policy converted them into a blockbuster.

Although not strictly speaking a spin-off, Cain's methods are well suited for the spin-off. To be sure, there are cases in which new leadership is needed, and those in which the business is so bad that nothing will save it. In many situations, though, when the incentive packages are well conceived and implemented, the energy that Cain tapped can be an effective way to convert a value destroying company into a value creator.

Summation Concerning Leveraged Recapitalizations

To summarize, a leveraged recapitalization can create an urgency that motivates management to improve performance. It may well be that a company can achieve the same result without this spur to action, but if such efforts fail the leveraged recapitalization might well merit consideration.

If the leveraged recapitalization is undertaken, several other actions ought to accompany it. First, whatever the composition of the board, its members ought to have a meaningful financial stake in the company. Second, the compensation system ought to be adjusted to align management interests with shareholder interests and to give management an upside potential to go along with the downside risk associated with the recapitalization (if for no other reason than that otherwise the more able people might leave). Third, corporate objectives ought to be clearly established and communicated, and the performance of those objectives carefully and closely monitored.

The Spin-Off

There is another approach that can be useful for quadrant III companies to consider, especially if they have simply become too diversified. American companies have decentralized very effectively since the 1920s when Alfred Sloan began the process at DuPont and General Motors Corporation, and especially since World War II. In the process, profit responsibility (usually measured by return on assets, EBIT to capital employed, or a comparable measure) has been pushed down to the division level, giving headquarters' management the opportunity to grow by diversification. A few companies, most notably General Electric Company, have been successful in managing a highly diverse set of businesses. More commonly, companies find there is a core they can manage effectively. Eastman Kodak Company, for example, has done better since it spun off Eastman Chemical Company in 1993, later divested Sterling Drug, Inc., and focused on its photographic and imaging businesses.

---

16. WALL ST. J., May 5, 1988, at 17. Some editions included the word "Thanks" repeated hundreds of times rather than the signatures.

General Mills, Inc., has been strengthened by divesting its furniture, luggage, and apparel business to focus on its traditional core of packaged foods and food-related services. Companies that find they have strayed too far from their core and distinctive competencies have at times found they are wise to divest the other businesses, whether by selling them or spinning them off.

When done correctly, a spin-off can be a significant creator of shareholder value. This can be due to better management of the spun-off company, greater ability of investors to assess value, or a combination of these factors. A spin-off is a corporation's distribution of all the shares of one of its subsidiaries to its shareholders. If a business, such as a division, is not held in subsidiary form, its assets and liabilities can be transferred to a subsidiary created for this purpose and then the shares of the subsidiary can be spun off. After the spin-off, the company's shareholders own shares in two companies—the corporation itself and the former subsidiary. Through the spin-off, the latter has become an independent corporation with exactly the same shareholders as the company that did the spin-off. The spin-off itself involves no transfers of cash and no taxes.[17]

Although spin-offs have historically been comparatively rare, in recent years more companies have been doing them. AT&T, Quaker Oats Company, Cooper Industries, Inc., Sears, Roebuck & Company, Marriott International, Inc., ITT, and Dial Corporation are but a few of the companies that have spun off units in recent years. The value creation has been virtually uniform, unmistakable, and considerable.

Consider Quaker Oats's decision to spin off its wholly owned subsidiary, the toy maker Fisher Price, based in Buffalo, New York. When the spin-off was announced on April 24, 1990, Quaker Oats's stock was trading at $48 per share. Indeed, news of the spin-off had leaked, and the stock price rose in the two weeks before the announcement. From the date of the announcement until trading in Fisher Price began on July 1, 1991, slightly more than 14 months later, Quaker Oats's stock price had risen to $64, an increase of 33% during a period in which the New York Stock Exchange Composite Index rose 10%. Interestingly, in the two weeks after the spin-off, Quaker Oats's stock price did not decline, although over the next two years it traded in the range of $53 to $77. However, during that period, Quaker Oats shareholders held two pieces of paper, one representing their shares in Quaker Oats and one representing their shares in Fisher Price. The Fisher Price shares opened at $20 per share on July 1, 1991, and by September 1993 the market price had reached $67 per share (adjusting for the 2 for 1 stock split). The result was that from April 10, 1990 (two weeks before the announcement) until September 30, 1993 a shareholder who began with one share of Quaker Oats stock, acquired the additional share of Fisher Price stock, and held both through September 30, 1993, saw the per share value of his or her holdings rise from $44 to some $140, a threefold appreciation in slightly less than 3½ years. During the same period, the New York Stock Exchange Composite Index appreciated by 34%.

By and large, senior executives are not inclined to do spin-offs because they like to keep their best performing units. If they do spin-offs at all, they would rather get rid of their losers. Unfortunately, that is poor planning from a tax and cash flow

---

17. Section 355 of the Internal Revenue Code provides that spin-offs may be done on a tax exempt basis if all the criteria of that section are met.

standpoint. Suppose Parent Corporation has two subsidiaries, one of which has been a winner, and the other of which has been a loser. The subsidiaries' balance sheets are summarized as follows.

Table 121
Balance Sheets for Subsidiaries of Parent Corporation

Rocket Corporation			**Dog Corporation**		
Assets	**Liabilities**		**Assets**	**Liabilities**	
1000	Liabilities	500	500	Liabilities	1000
	Equity	500		Equity	(500)
1000		1000	500		500

Parent Corporation is considering whether to sell or spin off these subsidiaries. If it does a spin-off, Parent is deemed to have divested the unit, and it removes the assets, liabilities, and net worth of the subsidiary from its own books and simply transfers them to the books of the spun-off company. Hence, were Parent to spin off Rocket, Rocket's balance sheet would be as set forth above, and Parent's equity would be reduced by $500. This would be advantageous to Parent because it would have diminished the amount of capital with which it is working. Further, it would have divested the assets without needing to recognize a gain for tax purposes. By contrast, had Parent sold Rocket for its value (probably well in excess of its book value), there would have been a taxable gain, and the cash implications would have been less favorable than with a spin-off. Thus, from the standpoint of preserving cash and building a foundation for superior future performance, Rocket should be the unit that is spun off.

As for Dog, parents do not like to sell losers because they have to recognize the loss, which has adverse implications for their GAAP earnings. However, the sale at a loss shelters some taxes and thus, from a cash standpoint, is preferable to a spin-off. In the above example, if Parent spins off Dog, then Dog becomes an independent company, having inherited the above balance sheet. Parent's balance sheet sheds the assets and liabilities although its equity account rises, having divested the negative equity. However, because the spin-off is not a taxable transaction, the parent has lost the opportunity to recognize the loss. Had Parent sold Dog, it could have used the loss to shelter other income and thereby reduce its payable tax and increase its cash flow. Thus, although managements tend to spin off the losers, they ought to sell them to get the benefit of the tax deduction for the loss.

Even when the right unit is selected, a spin-off will not turn lead into gold. However, when it works well, a critical variable is almost always at work. Ordinarily, before the spin-off occurs, the management of the unit consists of middle managers in a substantially larger corporation. They may be extremely talented, and they may have stock options, but by and large, they do not feel or think like owners. Rather, they tend to be treated as, and think and feel like, mere cogs in a larger system over which they have scant control or influence and the value of which they

Table 122
Returns to Shareholders*

	IPO Date	Split-Adjusted IPO Price	Closing Prices 10/31/97	Compound Annual Return from IPO to 10/31/1997
Thermedics	8/1983	$2.53	$17.00	14%
Thermo Instrument	8/1986	1.90	36.06	30%
Thermo TerraTech	8/1986	2.78	9.25	11%
Thermo Power	6/1987	8.50	8.38	0%
Thermo Cardiosystems	1/1989	1.51	21.63	35%
Thermo Voltek**	3/1990	0.75	7.19	34%
ThermoTrex	7/1991	8.00	23.00	18%
Thermo Fibertek	11/1992	3.56	10.75	25%
Thermo Remediation	12/1993	8.33	7.63	(2%)
ThermoLase	7/1994	3.00	15.56	65%
Thermo Ecotek	1/1995	8.50	14.19	20%
ThermoSpectra	8/1995	14.00	10.38	(13%)
ThermoQuest	3/1996	15.00	17.88	11%
Thermo Sentron	3/1996	16.00	12.00	(17%)
Thermo Optek	6/1996	13.50	16.94	18%
Trex Medical	6/1996	14.00	12.88	(6%)
Thermo Fibergen***	9/1996	12.75	12.56	(1%)
Thermo BioAnalysis	9/1996	14.00	17.38	21%
Thermedics Detection	3/1997	11.50	10.50	N.M.
Metrika Systems	6/1997	15.50	16.38	N.M.
Weighted average return on spun-out companies (equal dollar investments)				22%

*Thermo-Electron internal company document
**Price at time of acquisition
***Includes price of one share of common stock and one right

impact little. Often, although not always, their compensation is almost entirely a fixed amount, and any link between their compensation and the performance of their employer is slight. Many of them have long since been "nine-to-fivers," not particularly tempted to take much initiative, and even a bit jaded, with the thought that even if they did try to do something extraordinary for their company, it would either not be noticed or would bring them as many headaches as benefits.

After a spin-off, however, such individuals have a real incentive to work hard and often become extraordinary, especially if they have a compensation system that gives them a realistic sense of ownership. One of the positive features of the spin-off is that although there are the same number of shares outstanding, the company is a much purer play than previously, when it was only part of a substantially larger enterprise. Whereas stock options granted by the parent previously went to headquarters executives and senior management of multiple divisions, now 100% of the stock options are for the management and other employees of the unit that was spun off. All of a sudden their equity stake has become multiplied, and they begin to feel like owners, having been transformed into individuals who see a much stronger link between their performance and their net worth. The alchemy of the spin-off lies not merely in the financial structuring but in its ability, if it is done right, to tap into the desire of previously ordinary folks to become extraordinary.

Thermo Electron, based in Massachusetts, puts a slightly different spin on this.[18] Founded in 1956, Thermo encourages entrepreneurs inside the company to experiment with new ideas, and Thermo supports and incubates those ventures. When they are ready, Thermo goes to the market to finance them.

Since 1983, Thermo has developed 13 businesses to the point where it has spun them out to the public. Thermo executives term them *spin-outs* rather than *spin-offs* because Thermo always retains majority control, and the stock is sold to the public rather than distributed to existing shareholders. The proceeds of the offering go to the new company. After the spin-out, Thermo—for a fee of 1% of revenues—provides administrative support, such as legal services and investor relations. In this way there are administrative economies of scale, but entrepreneurship is encouraged. Each spun-out company continues to get support from Thermo, but executives of the spun-out companies have their own companies to run, and their equity stake and stock options in the spun-out company give them a significant personal upside potential.

It has worked well. Since Thermo began spinning out companies in 1983, it has produced a compound annual return of 26% through September 1997, as compared with 18% for the Standard & Poor's 500. As Table 122 shows, the shareholders have fared very well. For instance, investors who bought shares of Thermo Cardiosystems when it went public in January 1989 at $1.51 per share would enjoy better than a 14 to 1 return in nine years. After witnessing Thermo's performance, it is difficult not to accept the view that a tight link between compensation and incentive packages on the one hand, and financial performance on the other, is in the shareholders' best interests.

Concluding Comment

There are numerous ways to create value and numerous ways to destroy it. Effective corporate leadership is familiar with the former and alert to the latter.

Skillful interpretation of financial statements can help one assess the company's circumstances and indicate what management has done, can do, and—in some cases—must do. Good financial projections can be a useful map for the future and help corporate leaders know the likely financial consequences of different operating and financial courses of conduct.

---

18. Steve Bailey & Steven Syre, *And Thermo Begat* . . . , Boston Globe, Mar. 19, 1996, at 41.

Summary of Key Financial Terms and Ratios

This summary of key financial ratios, terms, and formulas is intended for easy reference. As a summary, there is a risk that the terms are oversimplified, and users are encouraged to look to the text for more definitive explanations.

B
Beta; a means of calculating the cost of equity

b
Borrowing rate

Break Even
Break even occurs when $0 = N(P - VC) - FC$; i.e., when the number of units sold times the contribution per unit (price less variable cost/unit) less total fixed costs equals zero.

c
Unlevered cost of capital

c*
Weighted average cost of capital
$c^* = c[1 - t(D/TC)]$

Cash Flow
This term is ambiguous. Be careful. It is often construed to mean "net income plus depreciation plus any other non-cash deductions (most notably deferred taxes, amortization) for the period." Often new investment in working capital and plant and equipment are deducted from the foregoing in calculating cash flow.

D
Total Debt

Days Accounts Receivable

(Accounts Receivable/Sales) $\times$ 365 = Days Accounts Receivable
Days Sales Outstanding (DSO) is the same.

Days Accounts Payable

(Accounts Payable/Cost of Goods Sold) $\times$ 365 = Days Accounts Payable

DuPont Formula

Profit/Sales $\times$ Sales/Assets $\times$ Assets/Equity = Return on Equity

E

Total Equity

EBIT

Earnings before Interest and Tax

Economic Value Added

$(r - c^*)TC$ or $(TC \times r) - (TC \times c^*)$ = Economic Value Added

FRP

Financial Risk Premium; i.e., cost of equity in excess of c; pertains to a particular stock

Financial Leverage

Debt/Equity; or Debt/(Debt + Equity); or Assets/Equity
Distinguish operating leverage, which is high when fixed costs are a high percentage of total costs.

Intensities

Capital intensity: plant, equipment, and other fixed assets as a percentage of total assets
Labor intensity: sales per employee
(*note:* watch trends; compare with the industry)

Liquidity Measures

Working Capital = Current Assets – Current Liabilities
Current Ratio = Current Assets/Current Liabilities
Quick Ratio = (Current Assets – Inventory)/Current Liabilities

Margins

Gross Profit/Sales = Gross Margin
Operating Profits/Sales = Operating Margin
Net Income/Sales = Net Margin = Return on Sales

MRP
Market Risk Premium (approximately 6%); historic return on equities in excess of risk-free yields ($Rm - Rf$)

Maximum Growth Rate
The maximum sustainable growth rate over the long run without outside financing: $G = ROE (1 - \text{payout rate})$. Payout rate is the percentage of profit after tax, paid out as dividends or in stock repurchases.

NOPAT
Net Operating Profit after Tax ("net" means net of depreciation; calculated on an unlevered basis; grossed up by adding back non-cash expenses)

PAT
Profit after Tax

PBT
Profit before Tax

r
Rate of return; equal to NOPAT/TC

Return on Assets
Profit after Tax/Total Assets

Rf
Risk-free rate of return (i.e., T-bills)

Rm
Return on the S&P 500 on average over time (can use other indexes of well-diversified equities as surrogates for the market)

ROE
Return on Equity; Profit after Tax/Equity

ROA
Return on Assets

ROAE
Return on Average Equity (i.e., the PAT divided by the average of beginning and ending equity)

t
Tax rate

TC

Total Capital (including debt, deferred tax, and equity, grossed up by adding back any write-offs, capitalized R&D, LIFO reserves, previously amortized goodwill)

Turnover

Sales/Inventory = Inventory Turnover at Retail (*note:* one could use average inventory)

Cost of Goods Sold/Inventory = Inventory Turnover at Wholesale (*note:* one could use average inventory)

Sales/Assets (or average assets) = Asset Turnover

y

Cost of equity

$y = c + \text{FRP}$

$y = \text{Rf} + \text{B} (\text{Rm} - \text{Rf})$

Index

About the Author

Robert B. Dickie is the founder of The Dickie Group, which provides comprehensive training in finance and accounting to most of the country's leading law firms and the in–house legal departments of numerous Fortune 100 companies. In addition, The Dickie Group provides financial services including corporate valuations, damages assessment, and expert witness services.

Mr. Dickie is a graduate of Yale University and the School of Law at the University of California, Berkeley (Boalt Hall). He was a corporate specialist at Shearman & Sterling in New York, and is a member of the state bars of California, Massachusetts, and New York. He is a former professor of management, with tenure, at Boston University's School of Management and has served on the board of directors of several privately owned corporations.

Sidebar 18 in chapter 5 was written by Philip Saunders, Jr., who provides litigation support and business valuation services at the Weston, Massachusetts, economic consulting firm of Philip Saunders Associates and as a member of The Dickie Group. He has over 30 years of investment and finance experience, holds a B.A. from Yale University and a doctorate in economics from the London School of Economics, and has authored articles on the application of economic and financial analysis to various legal issues.

The Dickie Group
26 October Lane
Weston, MA 02493
781–894–0009